DOCTOR WHO™

REGENERATION

Philip Segal
with Gary Russell

HarperCollins*Entertainment*
An Imprint of HarperCollinsPublishers

Gary's dedication
To David Bailey, who was there at the start of this
particular journey, and suffered accordingly.

Phil's dedication
To my wife, Stephanie, for all her love, support and, most of all, her patience.
To my son Noah, lots of love.
Peter Wagg for recognising poison when he saw it.
And to Gary, because it's rare to find a friend like you.

HarperCollins*Entertainment*
An imprint of HarperCollins*Publishers*
77-85 Fulham Palace Road
Hammersmith, London W6 8JB
www.**fire**and**water**.com

First published 2000
1 3 5 7 9 8 6 4 2

Copyright © Philip Segal and
Gary Russell 2000

Doctor Who™ BBC used under licence

Philip Segal and Gary Russell assert
the moral right to be identified as
the authors of this work

A catalogue record for this book
is available from the British Library

ISBN 0 00 710591 6

Designed by Gary Gillatt

Printed and bound in Great Britain by
Scotprint, East Lothian, Scotland

Gary would like to thank the following. Why? Because, if they had not been who they are, this book would not exist:

Rebecca Levene and Peter Darvill-Evans, ex-of Virgin Publishing who got the stone rolling. To Justin Richards and Ben Dunn at BBC Books who made sure it gathered no moss. And above all to David Brawn at HarperCollins who gave it a most satisfactory final home.

Andrew Pixley, Marcus Hearn, David J Howe and Stephen James Walker for encouragement, information and, frankly, the inspiration to do this!

Gary Gillatt for help, advice, sanity and friendship.

Clayton Hickman, whose technical expertise brought a cover idea to life.

Shaun Lyon, whose *Outpost Gallifrey* web page (www.gallifreyone.com) has been invaluable (as always); and Chad Jones, who, along with everyone too numerous at Gallifrey One conventions, have been nothing short of marvellous over the last few years, making me feel very welcome in LA and providing many helpful opportunities that would otherwise have proved impossible.

Corey Klemow, whose determination to help source 'that song' knew no bounds. Well done!

Rona Selby and Nuala Buffini, who got me into this little minefield in the first place.

Paul Condon, Jim Sangster, Steve Lyons and everyone else ManoptiCon-wise. You all know why!

John B, John A, Jac R, Kathy S, Simon S, Mike T, Nick B and especially Jase for understanding my concept of deadlines and how I deal with them.

The lovely Ben and Andy of Galaxy 4.

Daphne Ashbrook, Yee Jee Tso, Sylvester McCoy, Geoff Sax and Jo Wright for being so terribly nice about all this a few years on. And Phil Segal, for having more faith in me than I deserved.

But the biggest thank you is for Steve Cole, without whom this book could never have actually happened.

CONTENTS

• Prologue •

A CHANGE OF IDENTITY

Paul McGann and Daphne Ashbrook – a new Doctor and companion for the 1990s.

ay 2000. Paul McGann, the Eighth actor to portray the Doctor on television since 1963 has recently returned, albeit briefly and minus the wig and costume, to the role. He has been recording some audio drama plays in a studio in Bristol – an opportunity for him to give the character another go, and for his vast number of fans to hear him face the monsters, thwart the villains and save the world a few more times.

But why? Why, if *Doctor Who* is not on the television screens anymore, do all these actors, writers, directors and above all the fans care so much that they need to hear McGann again? Why have BBC Books published more than 40 novels featuring this particular incarnation of the Doctor if, as television moguls of the last few years are to be believed, *Doctor Who* is a dead property? Why has *Doctor Who Magazine*, a four-weekly publication that focuses on just this one show, printed more than 400 pages of comic strip adventures of this Doctor? And why did BBC2 dedicate an entire evening's output in November 1999 to the show, culminating in a second screening of McGann's solitary television outing, this time in a previously untransmitted, unedited, version? What is the appeal of this extraordinary television phenomenon?

No one has ever accurately answered that – indeed, were they to be able to, no doubt the

formula would have been bottled, shaken up a bit and poured out every September by the BBC as they launch series after series which they hope will capture the hearts and minds of their audience as *Doctor Who* did. *Jonathan Creek, Crime Traveller, Randall and Hopkirk (Deceased), The Magician's House* – even their lavish, if over-wrought, adaptation of *Gormenghast* – all had a small touch of *Doctor Who* about them. The situations, the grotesque or off-the-wall characters. The whimsical, slightly self-mocking humour. But none of them, no matter how successful (or not) they were in their own rights, can hold a candle to *Doctor Who* in terms of the affection the British public (and indeed, the show's legion of followers around the rest of the world) have for this one, very peculiar, programme.

Since the 1996 *Doctor Who* television movie was first broadcast during the second May Bank Holiday weekend, a great deal has happened to the show.

The BBC's commercial arm, BBC Worldwide, launched their aforementioned book range, alongside a vast number of other, licensed-out *Who* merchandise. *Radio Times*, the Corporation's listings magazine offered its readers a weekly comic strip, whilst BBC Audio came up with some cassettes and CDs of *Doctor Who* stars, including McGann, reading new short stories.

Rumours about a new series, of course, continued to fly. One Atlanta-based company

Above: 1999 Comic Relief Doctor and assistant – **Rowan Atkinson and Julia Sawalha. Right: Filming the sketch at Pinewood studios.**

said they were searching for a deal with a British independent to make a new series. The BBC denied any knowledge. An American animation company also stated an interest in doing a cartoon version, and claimed they had taken high-level meetings with BBC Worldwide to secure a licence. The BBC denied any knowledge. Newspaper reports announced that the Sci-Fi Channel, the American cable network with a smaller European subsidiary based in London, were entering negotiations to make a new series. The BBC denied any knowledge. So, as it happens, did the Sci-Fi Channel.

By far the most noteworthy event happened in early 1998. The option held by Universal since the 1996 TV Movie had passed, and with it the studio's interest, having got nowhere in the eighteen months since it was aired. At the Cannes Film Festival on 18 May, in answer to a question about BBC Films, of which he was the head, David Thompson said that he was looking into a new £6 million version of *Doctor Who* and that it was in the early stages of development. To some extent, this was true – the BBC had entered into a dialogue with Miramax and their UK partner, HAL Films. But that was all it was at that stage – a discussion. Instantly, the BBC denied that any such film

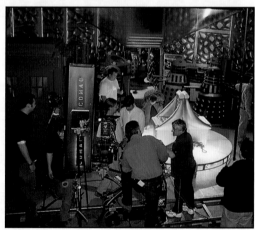

was taking place, saying that Thompson was quoted out of context and that any rumours were 'wild speculation' and that they had 'no plans for a *Doctor Who* movie – no such project is in development'.

By November 1998 it was the 35th anniversary of the show. In contrast to five years before, when all the world wanted a slice of the *Doctor Who* cake, the celebrations went by quietly, with only BBC Worldwide Publishing putting any effort into repromoting the series via its growing range of books, videos and audios.

1999 started very favourably – a new series of audio-only brand-new adventures for the past Doctors began to be released on CD and cassette, whilst on television, as part of the BBC's annual charity telethon *Comic Relief*, *Blackadder* star Rowan Atkinson assumed, albeit it both briefly and with tongue firmly in cheek, the mantle of McGann's successor, the Ninth Doctor, followed over the next fifteen or so minutes by Richard E Grant, Jim Broadbent, Hugh Grant and latterly Joanna Lumley, using up the Doctor's remaining regenerations in very quick, and witty, succession. A cleverly observed and affectionately made satire, it never insulted the programme which it sought to spoof, but gently mocked some of its clichés. Alongside starring turns from the Daleks, Jonathan Pryce as the Master and Julia Sawalha as the Doctor's faithful companion Emma, *The Curse of Fatal Death*, as it was named, was the closest anyone had got to 'new' *Doctor Who* since the TV movie went out.

The Miramax film, if there truly was such a thing, apparently died during 1999 and despite a number of rumours to the contrary, it seemed that any hopes of a new TV series died along with it. Everyone loved *Doctor Who*. Everyone believed it was a viable commodity with a potential future, yet no one was actually willing to put their money where their mouth was and finance one. As the year closed, one final gasp of fun came in the form of another satirical look at the show – as part of the November BBC-2 *Doctor Who* theme night a trio of the BBC's top young comedians, Mark Gatiss, David Walliams and Paul Punter produced a sketch showing Gatiss, as the Doctor, faced with two aliens (Walliams and Punter) trying to frighten him. Again, it was a gentle pastiche of the best and worst excesses of the show, but reinforced the fact that this was a television series that had not only seeped into the subconscious of an entire generation, but was now firmly established as a part of British culture.

As the new century began, no matter how many magazines, books, audios, DVDs or videos were sold, the future for the show still looked somewhat bleak. Even Paul McGann, standing in that recording studio, creating new *Doctor Who* for the ears, was disappointed that it wasn't what everyone else wanted – a new TV series.

If all these books, videos, rumoured films and TV series, spoofs and tributes were prevalent ten years after BBC Television actually stopped making the series, then one particular incident must be partially responsible for the show's continued presence.

In 1996, seven years after the BBC closed the lid on the show, a brand new television movie version, written and produced in America and starring Paul McGann as the Doctor, was shown. We've seen part of the impact it had; what follows now is a look at how that one special episode was created, and the driving force behind it – a man called Philip Segal…

Above left: Joanna Lumley, the Doctor's final incarnation? According to Comic Relief she is!

Above right: Anthony Ainley was called upon to play the Master one more time for the BBC's *Destiny of the Doctors* CD-ROM adventure.

**Daphne Ashbrook
and Paul McGann**.

• Briefing •

THE PRINCIPAL PLAYERS

Daphne Ashbrook
American actress cast as Grace Holloway. Daphne comes from a very talented family of actors. Previous genre roles included the title role in the *Melora* episode of *Star Trek: Deep Space Nine* and a show-stealing performance in the second, and last, transmitted episode of the astonishingly excellent US TV series *Sleepwalkers* – which, like *Doctor Who*, was doomed through network executives' lack of foresight and guts. For *Doctor Who*, Universal insisted she become a blonde, but, thank goodness, that was vetoed by Fox.

Alex Beaton
Was assigned to *Doctor Who* as a way of ensuring that it did not go over budget. He has worked on Universal projects for many years, most notably as a line producer, doing stints on *Kung Fu*, *Wiseguy*, *Harry O* and *Knight Rider*. He currently handles the production concerns for *Universal's Action Pack*, which included *Hercules: The Legendary Journeys* and *Xena: Warrior Princess*.

Peter Cregeen
BBC head of serials at the time *Doctor Who* went into hibernation at the BBC. The target of many scathing attacks by *Who* fans, the poor chap was only doing his job, although the promises he made about the show's destined return did tend to sound more hollow as time went on. He resigned from the BBC and remained an independent producer for many years. He had no direct involvement in the version of *Doctor Who* that finally made it to the screen.

Robert DeLaurentis
After some years in films, which included writing a sequel to *The Sting* and working on the Dudley Moore movie *Unfaithfully Yours*, Robert found himself at Universal. After producing shows such as *Alfred Hitchcock Presents* and *St Elsewhere*, he moved over to Fox, before co-creating the NBC television series *Mann and Machine*. Robert is currently a writer for hire who works at the upper levels of Hollywood television series.

Tony Greenwood
As Director of Consumer Products International, Tony was *Doctor Who*'s greatest help and supporter within BBC Enterprises/Worldwide. Shortly after *Doctor Who*'s completion, he left the BBC to work for Granada Television, heading up their video and product-placement divisions.

Matthew Jacobs
Joined the project after a successful early career as a director (*Hallelujah Anyhow*) and writer (*Paperhouse*), and has just finished writing and directing a film for the BBC entitled *Mothertime*. Matthew also wrote a draft of a big-budget Francis Ford Coppola feature entitled *Mirror*. Matthew still lives outside San Francisco with his wife and two sons.

John Leekley
Continues to write and produce television for the networks.

Sylvester McCoy
Scots actor who played the seventh Doctor

between 1987 and 1989, having previously been in productions as diverse as *Tiswas* and *Vision On*. More recently, he played the kidnapper Michael Samms to critical acclaim in the Channel 5 drama *Beyond Fear*. He always maintained that, despite any inconvenience, he would do his utmost to return to *Doctor Who*, even if it was just for a five-minute regeneration scene, if asked. He upheld that promise and was rewarded with a twenty-minute dignified finale.

Paul McGann

Liverpudlian actor who rose to prominence with the controversial BBC drama *The Monocled Mutineer*. Subsequent TV and film roles made him hot property. His most prominent genre role, in *Alien*[3], ended up being drastically curtailed in the final edit. His large legion of female fans found him at his most adorable in *Withnail And I*. And who are we to argue?

Eric Roberts

Brother of the equally famous movie star Julia, Eric won an Oscar nomination for his role in *Runaway Train*. He joined *Doctor Who* to play the latest incarnation of the Master shortly after winning rave reviews for his portrayal of a dying AIDS sufferer in *It's My Party*. His movie *La Cucharacha* won Best Picture at the 1998 Austin Film Festival.

Geoffrey Sax

Geoff's earliest association with *Doctor Who* was directing a famous parody called *Dr Eyes* for seventies sketch series *End of Part One*, which was nominated for an Emmy. He later won a BAFTA award for his work on *The New Statesman*. In Hollywood he has directed the pilot for a television series entitled *The Van Helsing Chronicles*. His most recent triumphs are his daughter and the one on the way.

Philip Segal

After years overseeing productions such as *seaQuest DSV*, *Twin Peaks*, *thirtysomething*, *The Young Indiana Jones Chronicles* and *Earth 2*, Philip now has his own production company called Polestar Group. He spent two years on an overall deal at Paramount Studios, where he developed the ABC miniseries *Encounter With Tiber*, which is about humanity's first successful attempt to land on Mars. He is currently working on several film projects, including a retelling of the infamous Jack the Ripper story, as well as producing a live-action Japanese project entitled *G-Saviour*.

Steven Spielberg

Needs little introduction. The BBC obviously thought so too! *ET*, *Jaws*, *Close Encounters*, *Raiders of the Lost Ark*, *Schindler's List*, *Saving Private Ryan* … oh, and *1941*, but no one's perfect. His Dreamworks Studio continues to grow.

Yee Jee Tso

Young Canadian actor who played Chang Lee.

Previous genre appearances in early episodes of *Sliders* and in *Highlander* still failed to prepare him for the phenomenon that is *Doctor Who*, but when he realised what he had become a part of, he grasped it wholeheartedly.

Peter Wagg

The driving force behind *Max Headroom*, Peter was working at Yertez Productions when he found employment as line producer for the two aborted *Doctor Who* projects detailed in this book. Although he did not actually work on the final version, his spirit permeated it throughout. Now he is head of the world-famous *Cirque Du Soleil*'s TV and film production unit and lives in Montreal. As a thank-you, the character of Professor Wagg in the movie was named after him.

Trevor Walton

Another Brit living in LA who adored *Doctor Who* and was instrumental in its finally getting off the ground at Fox, where he was senior vice president. While still at home, he was a producer for WitzEnd, masterminding series such as *Girls on Top*. Then he went Stateside, to CBS, where he was instrumental in bringing back popular series such as *Lonesome Dove* and *Cagney and Lacey*. Trevor left the Fox network about eight months after *Doctor Who* aired. He took some time off and now has his own production entity in Los Angeles.

Michael Wearing

After a long and distinguished career producing hard-hitting and frequently controversial drama for the BBC, he resigned his post in the spring of 1997. He is currently developing and producing films for the Scottish Film Board.

Jo Wright

Jo's exemplary work at Thames TV, Channel 4 and then the BBC made her ideally suited to work on a project as complex as this. Apart from her success with the Minette Walters drama *The Sculptress*, she was also producer on series as diverse as *Out of the Blue*, *Lovejoy* and BBC2's 'yoof' travelogues, *The Rough Guide To …* Jo moved over to a spell on *EastEnders* after finishing work on *Doctor Who* and then she left the BBC, in the summer of 1997, and now heads up London Weekend Television's drama department.

Alan Yentob

BBC1 Controller during the mid-90s and undoubtedly the show's biggest champion within BBC Television. At the end of the 1993 TV documentary *30 Years in the TARDIS*, he made an on-air promise that we would see *Doctor Who* on our screens once more. It was pretty much due to his constant support that we did. What a guy! By the way, he's the only executive from this era left at the Beeb. Everyone else associated with the show moved on to other jobs. Coincidence or curse? Who knows …

Philip Segal and Geoffrey Sax.

Our stars!

• Introduction •

WHAT IT'S ALL ABOUT

O ver the last 35 or so years, a great deal of words have been written about the BBC television serial *Doctor Who*. Books, fanzines, CD-ROMs, magazines and newspapers have been bursting full of every scrap of information that may be deemed highly useful and informative. Probably an equal amount has been written that is neither. You may therefore think, What else is there to say on the subject?

And that's a pretty good question – although one that you're expecting this book to answer, otherwise why are you reading it?

So what does *Doctor Who – Regeneration* offer that hasn't been provided before? Well, two things really. First, it's a journey through the making of what is officially known as *Doctor Who*, but more commonly known as 'the McGann TV movie' or 'the 1996 TV film' or 'that American thing starring Paul McGann and using the Pertwee logo'. As a production, owing to its contemporaneous nature, it is the least well-documented era of *Doctor Who*. That alone is why I am excited enough to sit here and put it together.

Far more importantly though, it's the first book to go properly behind the scenes of a segment of the show, from its inception to completion and beyond; and to be co-written by someone who was actually there. Philip Segal was the driving force behind the resurrection of *Doctor Who* in the 90s. As the executive producer, he ultimately had responsibility for everything, good and bad, to do with the project – a responsibility he has never shirked.

Some people loved the TV movie. Some people loathed it. Nearly everyone has something constructive to say about it and, with hindsight, as with any piece of art, there are things that, with more time/money/cooperation/ freedom/restrictions/etc., could have been different. Better maybe.

One thing you will see during the course of this book is that Philip isn't one to shy away from noting the bad alongside the good. He'll take the blame when it's his to take. He'll also apportion it elsewhere when it isn't. Unlike with most television, where speaking the litany approved by the publicists and marketing people is the only truth, the requisite passage of time has gone by and Philip is able to speak his mind and tell it as it was. Or as he saw it, which is the most one can ask for. Say hello, Phil.

Hello, everyone.

There, now you can see that, whenever Philip is writing, it's in that nice emboldened, dark typeface, as opposed to this rather insipid, wimpish one that signifies my input. This rather characterises us. Philip is a bold, powerful kind of guy. Me, I'm the … well, plain traditional one, to use a typographical analogy.

Occasionally I've quoted some of the other folk associated with the production, but only sparingly. After all, this is Philip's book – I'm merely a guide, filling in the blanks where necessary and once in while, behind-the-scenes-where-you-can't-see-it, I'll give him a pointer in the right direction, a helpful push forward or, now and then, suggest putting something more tactfully and so avoid litigation. (Boy, you should see what he said about [NAME DELETED] and how they [FACT DELETED] while busy [ACTION DELETED]. Sadly, you can't!)

So, what exactly is this then? A reference book? Yes, of sorts. Sure, it's packed with some facts 'n' figures, but we're trying not to take the rather dry and cram-it-all-in approach that it's so easy to do with this kind of

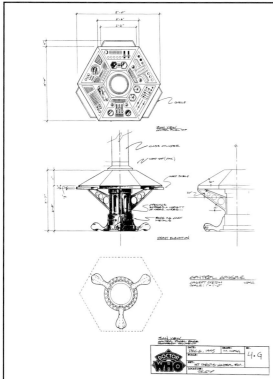

thing. No, it's more a biography of a production than a traditional *The Making of …* book. Hopefully you'll enjoy the behind-the-scenes artwork and production photos, but the text is rather more personal than you'd normally get.

Over to you, Phil.

A small red semi-detached house at 133 Audely Road in the suburb of Hendon in London, England, is the most unlikely place to start this story, but that's precisely where it begins. This was the home of my grandparents for most of their adult lives and it's

also where I first came face to face with a certain mysterious time traveller known only as 'The Doctor'.

As I sat upon my grandfather's lap, I watched with amazement and wonder. What was this strange yet alluring show? The opening episode, 'An Unearthly Child', unspooled before my wonderment-filled eyes. It's a love affair that has lasted over thirty years.

My inspiration for wanting to bring *Doctor Who* back to the big screen came from the alluring power of a character that has stood the test of time. My travels with the Doctor are chronicled in this book. Producing *Doctor Who* was not only a dream come true for me but an adventure in time and space I will cherish for ever. I was the kind of child who had only a small circle of friends. Because both my parents worked long hours, they relied on my big sister and the television to babysit. In today's society this practice would be frowned upon. For me, it's the key to my success as a producer.

I was brought up on television from the glorious 60s. Irwin Allen was, and still is, a god in my eyes. This book details the whole story of how the television movie was produced as well as my seven-year struggle to persuade the BBC, BBC Worldwide, Universal Pictures Television and the Fox Network to let me make a new *Doctor Who* here in America, a version that would play around the world and, if successful, hopefully regenerate into a new television series. My journey ended on 14 May 1996, when the film made its premiere here in America. This then is the story of that odyssey …

Behind the scenes in the TARDIS cloister, and a design drawing for the TARDIS console.

‘A decision was taken to rest the programme for an extended period, so that when it returns it will be seen as a fresh, inventive and vibrant addition to the schedules – rather than a battle-weary Time Lord languishing in the backwaters of audience popularity. ’

Standard BBC Viewers' and Listeners' Correspondence Section reply circa 1991

• 1989 - 1992 •
THE DIMENSIONS OF TIME

Sylvester McCoy and Sophie Aldred – the last *Doctor Who* 'team' of the 1980s.

Dates have always been important in *Doctor Who*'s history. Most fans can quote 23.11.63 (some have been known to use parts of it as PIN numbers for ATMs!) and even 06.12.89. For those scratching their heads, these are the first and last UK transmission dates for *Doctor Who*, as made and broadcast terrestrially by BBC Television – I add 'terrestrially' to pre-empt objections by all those who point to subsequent cable and satellite transmissions. I like to get things straight from the word go.

Many of us also know that 27.05.96 is equally important as the day that the Beeb showed the *Doctor Who* television movie (henceforth referred to as the DWTVM to distinguish it from the *Doctor Who* series as a whole).

However, possibly the most important date since that one in 1963 is 13.07.89. But why? What was going on around then in the world of *Doctor Who*? Well, strictly speaking, nothing unusual. Sylvester McCoy and Sophie Aldred were in a rehearsal room at the BBC's Acton rehearsal building, going through various scenes with the director, Alan Waring, and guest stars including Sylvia Syms, Frank Windsor, John Hallam and Ian Hogg. The story they were preparing was Marc Platt's three-part *Ghost Light*, the final story to go into production during the show's 26th consecutive year. One of *Doctor Who*'s more erudite and complex scripts, it was destined to

actually go out second in the run of four stories later in the year and, although some have commented that the story was complex and occasionally difficult to follow, it was undoubtedly one of the best-made, best-acted and most novel *Doctor Who* adventures in many years.

Like so much of television in the late 80s, *Ghost Light* was clearly 75 minutes of drama created for the video age, destined to be watched again and again rather than viewed and forgotten, as was so much television made ten years earlier. When McCoy and Aldred went into rehearsals that morning, one doubts they had even the slightest inkling of what was going on elsewhere in the BBC that would have such a major impact on their careers, let alone the show as a whole.

At this time, the BBC was perceived by many to be suffering at the hands of the Conservative government, now in their tenth year of domination over the British political world. Margaret Thatcher was leading her cabinet forward, creating a division within politics quite possibly unique in history. People either loved or loathed her leadership – very few were ever heard to say, 'Maggie? Yeah, I s'pose she's OK really, but then again …' One of the groups targeted most often by the government was the BBC.

It saw the Beeb as lazy, left-wing, self-congratulatory and sedentary – a dinosaur organisation that was weighted down under

TO: MR. ROGER LAUGHTON
        Director/Co-Producer BBC

FROM: PHILIP SEGAL
        Columbia Pictures Television

DATE: 7/12/89

RE: DR. WHO

Dear Roger:

It was a great pleasure speaking with you today. I am delighted that
there is initial interest in developing "Dr. Who" for an American
audience. Following is a very rough outline of the way I see this project
proceeding creatively. There are also a number of questions that
you could perhaps furnish some answers to with regard to your involvement
financially and I will address those issues as well.

We could approach a co-production/co-venture possibility with the BBC,
or we could produce the show for the BBC and license it back to you
while supplying an American network. Obviously, there are a great deal
of questions that have to be answered. Specifically:

1. What is your current budget for "Dr. Who"
2. What are your licensing agreements
3. Is the series produced with a deficit
4. Have the format rights been given to any other producers
5. How would you feel if an American actor portrayed the role

Columbia Pictures Television would probably want to own this show in the
U.S. markets. We would be talking about a series budget of
about $850.000 to $950.000 per episode in a one-hour format. We would
probably want to produce a pilot which would cost probably within the
realm of $1.9 million dollars to $2.5 million dollars. Please bear in
mind that my numbers are all geared towards a one-hour format
which we have found to be the most successful selling tool. If we
were to enter a co-production participation based on these figures,
what would your participation be?

Obviously, if such a show were to be produced and had a successful run
over more than three years, the profit made from syndication could be
very lucrative for you. I look forward to hearing your thoughts and
comments.

Best regards,

Philip Segal

the real and international marketplace. BBC Enterprises had frequently quoted *Doctor Who* as one of its greatest success stories. By the early 1980s, it was citing sales to more than a hundred countries around the world, with overzealous PR bods suggesting that the money Enterprises made from *Doctor Who* sales and licences was enough to finance the show itself.

The truth was, of course, that BBC Enterprises rarely worked in such a manner – most money that came into Enterprises went into a vast pool, and, once overheads had been met, the majority of its profits went back into the general programme-making parts of the BBC in general, rather than one particular programme. Whether *Doctor Who* really did make enough to finance the show itself is unknown, but the claim does seem to have a ring of good PR and rhetoric rather than substantiated truth.

During the 1980s, however, BBC Enterprises gained a new department, BBC TV Co-Productions. This area would, as the name suggests, find partners to co-finance programmes (usually prestigious drama or big-league documentaries presented by David Attenborough or Desmond Morris), giving the backers first-run rights in their home country and a share of the profits. *Doctor Who* had

Above: Producer John Nathan-Turner had steered *Doctor Who* through its last ten years at the BBC and, after some turbulent times, things had begun to settle down by the time he was joined by script editor Andrew Cartmel (right) in 1987.

bureaucracy and a belief that, under the charter that provided it with the licence fee and therefore little in the way of commercial revenue, it did not have to be competitive. Nevertheless, the BBC had had a few enlightened mavericks high up, the most recent being Michael Grade.

However, by the latter days of the 1980s, it seemed to many industry observers that the government wanted the Beeb to be run by accountants and faceless grey suits rather than programme makers. One of the decisions made at the time was that the corporation could no longer be as cosy and secure as it was – a percentage of its output needed to be supplied by outside independent contractors. This of course resulted in a large influx of administrators and an exodus of talented programme makers – and drama in particular fell victim to this.

The BBC had a subsidiary called BBC Enterprises, usually referred to as the commercial wing of the corporation. Enterprises was there to sell programmes abroad, oversee or license out merchandise and generally represent the BBC in

already benefited from this in 1983, when the ABC Network in Australia helped finance the show's twentieth-anniversary special, *The Five Doctors*. In 1989, Roger Laughton was Director, Co-Productions, BBC Enterprises (or D. CP. BBC Ents, as the abbreviation-friendly Beeb would have it), and on the morning of Thursday 17 July, while *Ghost Light* was being prepared, he took a call from a young television programme executive (drama) called Philip Segal at

Columbia Television in Los Angeles. Philip takes up the story…

In 1989, I was working at Columbia Pictures in the television department as a director of development. It is here that I first decided to go after the rights to *Doctor Who*. I remember watching several of the shows from the Sylvester McCoy era and thinking how run-down and tired the show felt. I must admit there were a few stories during that time period that sparked my interest, but that was it.

I felt bad for Sophie Aldred and Sylvester. All that hard work and very little care for its handlers. One morning I got into work very early – it must of been around 6 a.m. here in America – and started dialling some numbers my assistant had gotten for me. I ran my finger down the list of characters that held various jobs at the Beeb. Here's one, I thought: Roger Laughton.

I called his office. I told him who I was, and what I wanted, and the first thing he did was laugh. He laughed at me. I didn't think I was being funny. Once he realised that I meant business and that I knew my *Who*, he was a little more forthcoming. He gave me the name of someone else I needed to talk to over at BBC1.

Now I want to introduce you to the second victim in my quest to breathe new life into the Doctor: Mark Shivas. His title was Head of Serials at the time, so I thought I would start with him.

The phone rang several times, before the matronly sounding voice of his PA answered the phone. I waited and finally Mark came on the line.

I introduced myself and made several pleas about why I thought the show should have a second chance, but here in the States. I remember Mark showing very little interest in what I had to say. He was friendly enough and he certainly did not hang up on me, so I took that as at least a small sign of encouragement. He told me that, since the show had just gone out of production and had really lost its fans at the Beeb, it would be a difficult discussion to have right away. I thanked Mark for his candour.

On 3 August 1989, *Ghost Light* episode three was recorded in Studio 3 at BBC Television Centre. It was be the last time the *Doctor Who* series would be before the cameras there in the twentieth century.

But, before we said our goodbyes, Shivas gave me the name of his colleague at the time who, if anything were to happen, would be the point person. His name was Peter Cregeen. Peter worked for and with Mark and, as near as I could tell, was supposed to be some kind of in-house producer who had, according to Mark, 'a more focused interest in the show and would be more help to you than I would'. I made a note of the name and Mark and I said our goodbyes. I began to explore my options.

It was at this point that Shivas and Cregeen announced they would be visiting the States. It wasn't until after that visit that I was told of changes that would be made to the executive team at BBC Enterprises. These changes also included a change in managing directors – the new one was James Arnold Baker.

James was a very nice man and did make some effort to give me hints as to how to move negotiations forward. It would be some time, however, before I could actually act on his suggestions.

Before going any further, it is prudent to look at the state *Doctor Who* was in when Philip first began these talks. Both Sylvester McCoy and Sophie Aldred were contracted to do another season after production ended on *Ghost Light* – Sylvester for an entire fourteen episodes, Sophie for just eight of those. Both the producer, John Nathan-Turner, and script editor, Andrew Cartmel, wanted to move on. Nathan-Turner was the last of the BBC's in-house drama producers: in other words, he was on the staff payroll rather than being a freelancer brought in to do a particular job, as Cartmel was. For him, leaving *Doctor Who* would have meant leaving the BBC, but, after ten years producing one particular show, he was exhausted.

He had tried to move on from the series at least three times before. Ever since 1985, when the former controller of BBC1, Michael Grade, had pressed a metaphorical pause button on production to free up funds for the then-new Daytime TV schedules, the series had been on shaky ground. Experiments in changing transmission days (weekdays, back to Saturdays, then weekdays again) and episode lengths (the 22nd season had gone out as thirteen 45-minute episodes rather than the two dozen 25-minute episodes of the previous few years) had failed. Viewers were giving up.

Grade's successor at BBC1, Jonathan Powell, was publicly somewhat less than enthralled by the show and, Nathan-Turner has intimated many times, Powell all but stated that, if Nathan-Turner went, the show would

go too. Meanwhile the show's fans, some of them at least, were quite scathing in their disparagement of Nathan-Turner's management of their favourite series, and seemed willing to sacrifice it if only to get him moved off. The displeasure of a very vocal minority had reached the likes of Powell and other 'suits', and the feeling seemed to be that, if even the so-called die-hards didn't like it, then what was the point in carrying on?

Nevertheless, both Nathan-Turner and Cartmel began preparations for the 27th season. Although Cartmel was planning to move on to the BBC's flagship hospital drama *Casualty*, it would seem he had prepared the way for a new script editor (possibly the writer Ben Aaronovitch, who had wowed fans the year before with *Remembrance of the Daleks*). Scripts were talked about, plans made, even a new companion to replace Sophie Aldred's popular Ace was created, and notes were prepared. As far as Nathan-Turner was concerned, as with Aldred and McCoy, this was going to be the last time he wanted to be involved with a new season of *Doctor Who*.

One cannot help but wonder whether Philip Segal's original letter, reproduced at the start of this chapter, was the final nail which those at the BBC who disliked the show used to hammer down the lid of *Doctor Who*'s coffin. The corporation was under government

Opposite: Sylvester McCoy during the recording of *Ghost Light*.

Although not the final show to be made, the third episode of *Survival* (shown being recorded on location, below) went out on BBC1 on 6 December 1989 – the last episode of Doctor Who to be solely created by BBC television.

pressure to farm out more shows to independents, and was probably anxious to rid itself of a series originally created by people long since gone – people, it has to be said, of a whole different BBC ethos. So Auntie must have seen all this as a godsend.

However, while all this was going on at BBC Enterprises, the *Doctor Who* production office in Shepherd's Bush was shutting up shop after the end of the recording sessions for *Ghost Light*. There would be a few audio-only pick-ups going on right up until just before broadcast, but effectively that was it. Unusually, there was nothing forthcoming from the head of drama series, Peter Cregeen, confirming budgets or anything else for Season 27.

As Cartmel prepared to make his move over to *Casualty*, John Nathan-Turner started winding down the *Doctor Who* production

office, preparing to close its doors for the first time since 1963. Now free of *Doctor Who*, he went off, having optioned a book that he and the director Alan Wareing hoped to turn into a TV show.

At this point, it was still hoped that, after a short break, a new producer and script editor would be assigned the old office in the BBC's Union House. Nathan-Turner himself left the BBC at the end of August, although he did resume responsibility for the final season during its transmission.

Philip Segal, meanwhile, was busy back at Columbia. Enthused by Roger Laughton's responses, if not those of Mark Shivas, he was contacting some of his peers at the company, including Steve Berman and Jimmy Veres. He told them that his contact with Laughton had been encouraging and that the whole deal was the result of a conversation he had had with the ABC network the week before. On the same day as Philip contacted Laughton, Veres and Berman, he sent ABC's Dramatic Series Development team details of his conversations. Right from the beginning, it was important to have one of the four US networks behind the idea.

Not a lot happened after that in Philip's terms. On 1 August he wrote to Laughton, pointing out that he would be in England later that month during his European honeymoon (he got married on 6 August) and asking for a meeting with both Laughton and Cregeen. Laughton arranged this and, on returning to the States, Philip received a fax from Laughton on 28 August. This contained two major points. The first was an assurance that any deal with Columbia would ensure that 'a relaunched *Doctor Who* can have the maximum impact while retaining its *Doctor Who*-ness'; secondly – and more importantly – reaffirming something that had come up in the meeting that had occurred: The fact that, while the BBC were seeking a co-production deal to relaunch *Doctor Who* on TV, 'we have a company interested in developing a *Doctor Who* movie'. (The company concerned was Green Light, which became Coast to Coast and ultimately Daltenrays – for the purposes of simplicity, it'll be referred to as Daltenrays for the remainder of this book.)

Laughton ended his fax by noting that 'the immediate objective must be to reach some kind of consensus about who does what next and with whom', possibly implying that a new TV show and the proposed movie must co-exist and dialogue must take place to ensure all parties were happy. Daltenrays had been preparing their *Doctor Who* film since 30 June 1987 and said they would enter production in March 1990. One of the Daltenrays' producers, Peter Litten, said at

During 1991, a number of bids to make a new series of *Doctor Who* were presented to the BBC, including one from former script editor Gerry Davis (below) and Dalek-creator Terry Nation (right), both respected writers of fantasy television.

this time, 'Nobody would have spent the money we have on a film that isn't going to happen.' Interestingly enough, they did.

This proposal to keep all parties sweet was to prove to be a marvellous ideal but, eventually, an impossibility.

Philip's reply to all this on 28 August was conciliatory. He said he had no intention of doing anything other than retaining the spirit of the show, but pointed out that he was 'very concerned about reintroducing story content as the spine of the series', an understandable sideswipe at what Philip perceived as one of the contributing factors to the series' current lack of interest – it had become too culty and not mainstream enough, relying too much on its own history instead of broadening its outlook. He also made it clear that Columbia would retain creative control, but with everything overseen by the BBC.

Once again, marvellous ideals but not something that would be that practical. Unfortunately, whereas the eventual TV movie and Daltenrays' proposed theatrical film were miles apart thematically and creatively, this concept of cooperation all down the line between the BBC and the US producers would prove to be something of an albatross around everyone's neck. Oh, and succumbing to a wave of personal nostalgia, Philip also requested a copy of the 1979 story *City of Death*. His excuse? 'I believe this particular story is as close to a US-type-produced episode as I've ever seen.' Yeah, we believe you.

Meanwhile, one of John Nathan-Turner's last tasks was to contact Sylvester McCoy and Sophie Aldred on Monday 11 September, and tell them, officially, that the BBC had cancelled their ongoing contracts for *Doctor Who*. If there was to be a 27th season of *Doctor Who* made by the BBC, it would not automatically star the seventh Doctor and Ace. While nothing could stop a new company negotiating with either actor in the future (and both hoped that such a company would), the BBC was effectively terminating their continuation with the series, bar the odd press launch and other duties to promote the current season.

At a *Doctor Who* convention McCoy stated forlornly that 'the BBC don't want to make *Doctor Who*. They aren't interested in a series that's lasted twenty-six years.' While this is not strictly true, it's easy to see why people unaware of what was happening at BBC Enterprises and in Los Angeles could think that.

The first problem reared itself the very next day after Philip requested his free copy of *City*

of Death. Essentially Roger Laughton replied that, no, the BBC would not be willing 'at this stage' to let Columbia oversee the story development. Effectively what Columbia were wanting to do was license the show rather than enter into a co-production deal, much as Daltenrays had a licence to make the film version.

Another thing that needed sorting out was the potential clash between that theatrical movie and Columbia's project. On 27 September, Philip put into writing for the first time an outline of Columbia's intentions: '... we have the ability to produce either a two-hour or a one-hour pilot and series.' He went on to say that the problem arose in sharing world TV rights with the BBC. He then suggested dismissing the concerns of the theatrical movie – the two were separate and not mutually dependent. Each could exist without needing to fear the other. One wonders how much pressure Laughton and the BBC were under from Daltenrays to squash Columbia's plans. It is not unreasonable to expect a UK film company to be somewhat alarmed at learning that a possible TV movie was in preparation, to be made by one of the world's largest entertainment corporations, based upon a property they had optioned some years before.

Philip also wanted the BBC to get a move on: 'I have now received interest from a network.' This was not, however, ABC. It was the then relatively newborn fourth US network, Fox. As a result of this, BBC Enterprises received an

Philip Segal felt that the 1979 story *City of Death* had the approach and style he felt was right for a new series of *Doctor Who.*

official offer and proposal from Jan Abrams's office at Columbia Pictures Television Inc. It was an interesting deal, offering the BBC up to $15,000 every six months to a maximum of eighteen months for the rights. On top of that were sums of money payable on completion of a pilot, commencement of a series, the rights to remake stories from 'the London series' and, perhaps foolishly bearing in mind the earlier conversations – but at the same time probably standard for a deal such as this – first refusal on the theatrical movie rights to *Doctor Who*. A bit of a bummer, this, since the BBC had already given those to Daltenrays, whose licence would not expire before this deal was due to go through.

The following day, the BBC held a midseason press launch, to keep interest in the season going and to offer Peter Cregeen the chance to go on record about the show's future. '*Doctor Who* has lasted twenty-six years and I can't see any reason why it shouldn't continue,' he said. 'We are committed to more *Doctor Who* in the future'.

A few weeks later, he added, '*Doctor Who* is one of the BBC's most important programmes. There is no reason why it should not run for another twenty-six years.

The best possible way to take *Doctor Who* through the 90s may involve having it made outside.' Indeed, another BBC spokesman added that a new season was unlikely to go into production until January 1991 at the earliest.

The BBC of course had other offers on the table. Exactly which other companies expressed an interest – and when – is unclear. Much sound and fury has been printed as to who actually approached the BBC, who said they had approached the BBC, who said they might like to approach the BBC if it wasn't raining too hard that day and the cat wasn't sick and who thought it would make good publicity if they said they were making a bid. But there's little paperwork around to substantiate many of these claims and a lot probably got no further than Columbia did here.

When Roger Laughton wrote back to Columbia on 27 October, it was with a polite thanks, but no, thanks. 'We are continuing to discuss the future of *Doctor Who*,' Laughton explained, adding, 'As you know, there will be a *Doctor Who* movie.' He also said that the BBC wanted to wait until the following year 'before making any further moves on a series', and added that the corporation would prefer to go the full co-production route rather than license out the programme lock, stock and barrel.

So that, it seemed, was that. On the week of the show's 26th anniversary, *Radio Times*, the BBC's listings magazine, received a number of 'Oi, wot's goin' on?' letters, to which Cregeen offered another variation on his now standard reply. 'I would like to reassure *Doctor Who* devotees that there are no plans to axe *Doctor Who*. There may be a little longer between this series and the next than usual, but I very much hope that it will continue to be as successful in the 90s as it has been for the last 26 years.'

As if to commemorate his promotion to Manager, Drama Development, at Columbia, Philip received a communiqué from Felice Arden, one of the Daltenrays producers, on 4 December. (Prior to this Philip had contacted them and commented that he hoped they at least would get to make some new *Doctor Who*.) They sent him a copy of the script, then entitled *Doctor Who: The Timelord*, by Johnny Byrne. He read it but was disappointed, as he felt that it lacked 'the direction and human characteristics needed to propel this character into the 21st century'. He also told them, 'I wish you the best of luck in your endeavours. This clearly is the end of the road for me.'

However, that wasn't entirely true. He stayed in touch with Arden, along with Peter Litten and Harold Cellan. He suggested that he become involved, via Columbia, with their movie. His idea was that, in America, the movie would be transmitted on TV and act as a pilot for a new show, while remaining a theatrical release in Britain and the rest of the world.

In the middle of December, he wrote to Roger Laughton again, asking for confirmation of the BBC's commitment to the Daltenrays project. Laughton replied that the BBC had no objections to Columbia's going in with Daltenrays – they had seen the latest script and approved it – but the potential series rights were not available.

'We still aspire to bring *Doctor Who* back as a major UK television series ... This deal might well involve a UK-based independent production company and would certainly involve BBC Enterprises.' So the short answer was yes to going in on the movie, no to a spin-off series.

After requesting more tapes to be shown to the CBS executives, Philip informed the Columbia people that the deal was looking positive, at the same time checking that the

company were in a position to secure the deal should it go through. All things being equal, it was looking very positive that, less than three months after the BBC pulled the plug on Season 27, it may well be kick-started again via the Daltenrays project.

Columbia's President, Scott Sieglar, was enthusiastic but CBS still weren't entirely convinced. After all, if what Philip was telling them about the series' popularity, success and income-creating potential was true, then why, they wondered, had the BBC actually stopped making it? A not entirely unreasonable question and one going through everybody's mind at the time. The BBC's response was an interesting one.

Much was made at the time of the various companies reportedly interested in the series. One of those most referred to was Cinema Verity Ltd, an independent and highly successful production house set up by Verity Lambert, who, ironically, had been the very first producer of *Doctor Who* in 1963. Many fans of the show were overjoyed to discover her interest and yet, curiously, Cinema Verity themselves always denied any such intentions. For Lambert, the programme was an important part of her past, but where was the value in simply retreading old ground?

So how did the stories get out that Cinema Verity were even involved? Well, these things do leak out but, as in this case, fans frequently miss the truth in their desire to hear what they want to hear. On 29 January 1990, Roger Laughton wrote to Philip Segal, with two important points to impart. The first of these was that at this time 'there are no other active *Doctor Who* proposals around, except yours and the [Daltenrays] movie script'. This is significant because, apart from scotching the rumours that the BBC were fending off bids right, left and centre, it also once again separates the potential Columbia/CBS deal from the Daltenrays project. The second point is that this marks the entry of Verity Lambert's presence into the drama. The BBC appear to have asked her to 'represent the BBC's interest in reviving *Doctor Who*'. Effectively, it seems that Cinema Verity were employed by the BBC to be a go-between. Perhaps the Beeb did not believe they were as experienced in dealing with US companies as large as CBS or Columbia, whereas Verity Lambert's people certainly seemed to be.

Laughton's letter gave Philip official authorisation to enter into formal discussions with CBS regarding the BBC-Columbia co-production. It also suggested that Philip meet up with Verity as soon as possible to discuss script development, and went on to state that the BBC wanted a series (not a movie any more, note) to air in the autumn of 1991.

Doctor Who's very first producer, Verity Lambert, was asked by the BBC to help set up a new production deal with CBS/Columbia.

(One other thing Laughton's letter seemed to query was the intention to make each episode 46 minutes rather than 23, which Laughton suggested may be a problem. This was an odd thing to mention bearing in mind that most TV drama in Britain – bar soap operas – had long since made the progression to nearly 50 minutes per episode years before. Indeed, *Doctor Who* was the last half-hour drama on British television.)

Before meeting up with Verity Lambert, Philip was visited on 26 February by Mark Shivas and Peter Cregeen in Los Angeles. In anticipation of this, Philip talked to Lambert by telephone, concluding that '[Verity and I] are creatively in the same game.' He hoped that, when she visited LA at the end of February, they could both go to CBS to make their pitch, but Lambert was unable to make the US trip in the end. And so Philip prepared to meet with Cregeen and Shivas, both of whom were still restless about the co-production deal, understandably concerned about how much control the BBC was going to retain over what was, after all, potentially a major property and franchise for them.

And then events took a turn for the worse. On the day Philip was due to meet the two executives, he resigned from Columbia. 'I have been offered and accepted the position of Director of Current Programming for ABC Television,' he told Roger Laughton. 'However, the seeds that I have planted here have germinated and I hope the dialogue between you and Columbia continues.' It didn't.

In early 1990, after spending several years at Columbia, I joined ABC (American Broadcasting Corporation) to become a programming director. This move was very exciting for me personally, but it meant that I had to put my plans on reviving *Doctor Who* on the back burner. My position at ABC required me to work only on shows that had been ordered into production. My brief at this time was not to develop new products for the network.

However, after two very successful seasons at ABC my chance to quietly work on *Doctor Who* again came in the guise of an offer to work for Steven Spielberg, which I quickly accepted. I was now engaged in the development and production of television programmes – and guess which one was on the very top of my list. Even though *Doctor Who* continued to haunt me, I was simultaneously developing shows such as *seaQuest DSV* and *Earth 2*.

The next important step forward for *Doctor Who* came for me while I was developing *seaQuest*. I received a memo from James Arnold Baker, managing director at BBC Enterprises, informing me that he would be leaving his position soon but suggesting I speak to an executive there by the name of Tony Greenwood. Never one to miss a beat, I quickly placed a phone call to Tony followed by a fax asking him to call me regarding *Doctor Who*. I explained that I was an executive at Amblin Entertainment (Spielberg's production company) and that we were interested in *Doctor Who*. Yes, I admit it, I used Steven's name and powerful influence to hook the BBC – and obviously it worked.

In May of '92 we were previewing television shows for non-US companies interested in obtaining a licence to show *seaQuest* in their territories. I was busy escorting very high-powered executives around the sets. Marcus Plantin, who at the time scheduled the ITV networks, was being shown around the sets along with Alan Yentob, who was then Controller, BBC2.

Johnny Byrne was the writer most closely associated with the Daltenrays version of *Doctor Who*. He had scripted both the 1980 serial *The Keeper of Traken* (right) and 1984's *Warriors of the Deep* (below).

As we all walked along, I was turning my head to the left to talk to Alan and right to talk to Marcus. Alan would ask me a question about *seaQuest* and I would answer any question with, 'You know, I'm very passionate about *Doctor Who*.' He just looked at me as if thinking, What psycho have they left me with? It was Marcus who got all his questions about *seaQuest* answered and, needless to say, it was ITV who ended up with *seaQuest*. Quite possibly something I think they would later regret, but then, that's something for another book.

My relationship with BBC Enterprises began to get stronger. Tony Greenwood and I quickly became fast friends. I liked his approach and his honesty. Every time I contacted Tony about the show he was quick to respond. You see, I knew that, if I was ever really going to have a shot at getting my hands on *Doctor Who*, the Beeb would have to think that it made sense for them to give it to me. The combination of my passion and knowledge and Steven's name really shook the tree.

Philip's first contact with the BBC itself came almost as soon as he arrived at Amblin. In June 1991 he contacted Mark Shivas again. The projected deal with Columbia TV had gone nowhere without Philip to drive it forward. CBS had lost interest as well, and the BBC was back to examining bids from other interested parties, including one from Terry Nation and Gerry Davis, creators of the Daleks and Cybermen respectively – ironically with the backing of Columbia Pictures.

They had made their bid known at the time - almost to the day – that Philip had left Columbia. Similarly, Daltenrays continued their plans to make their movie. Over the period before Philip joined Amblin, they had scrapped scripts, announced potential commencement dates for filming and even discussed the newspaper rumours about potential stars (all sorts of people, including Donald Sutherland, Rutgar Hauer and Sylvester McCoy, seemed to be 'top of the list').

The latest draft, by the former *Doctor Who* scriptwriter Johnny Byrne, was called *The Last of the Time Lords*, and the producers went on television with preproduction drawings and plans as well as preparing a colourful promotional poster for the movie.

The fans were doing their best as well, although a rather misguided 'Day of Protest' plan to jam the BBC switchboards backfired as the BBC denied that many calls had been made, and Peter Cregeen offered only a new variation on his traditional stance, this time dismissing the fans with, 'We hope to be able to make a new series of *Doctor Who* but we want to get the formula absolutely right and it doesn't mean we are closing the doors on the TARDIS yet.'

James Arnold Baker of BBC Enterprises went a step further and said that '... the property is an old one, it's had its day and is no longer commercially viable.' A blunt, if somewhat short-sighted, dismissal from the Chief Executive of the Beeb's commercial wing when, at the time, home video sales of old *Doctor Who* stories were raking it in for them and Virgin Books were preparing a whole new range of original novels, the *New Adventures*, to continue the story.

And so Philip's letter to Mark Shivas started the ball rolling all over again. A great deal of talking went on over the next few months, and, while the official BBC stance remained not to confirm anything, things moved apace once Philip had made a friend in the BBC Enterprises' Home Entertainment Executive Tony Greenwood. Even the previously cynical

James Arnold Baker was enthused by the possibilities. But, to the general public, it was business as usual.

'*Doctor Who* will be back but not in the near future. When it returns, the programme will be vibrant, vital and improved – not a tired old Time Lord who comes back too soon.' This was the latest BBC statement and, despite a few more contenders to the rights outing themselves to the press (including the former *Doctor Who* producer Derrick Sherwin and a company called Naked Eye, who claimed to have Tom Baker's involvement guaranteed), nothing much happened.

When Gerry Davis died of cancer in the autumn of 1991, his and Terry Nation's plans faded and the only other thing of any real interest was a claim by an actor called David Burton that he had already made a pilot starring him as the Doctor. No one ever actually admitted to making such a thing and, although Mr Burton spent a great deal of time driving around in a car adorned with the slogan THE NEW DOCTOR WHO, he and his new series eventually sank without trace.

'There is no question of *Doctor Who* being abandoned. It is still an important programme, and when the time is right it shall return. *Doctor Who* is too valuable a property for us to relaunch until we are absolutely confident of it as a major success once again,' said the BBC towards the end of the year as it transmitted a thirty-minute tongue-in-cheek documentary about the series called *Resistance Is Useless*.

BBC Enterprises, meanwhile, were going great guns once again with Philip Segal. As Philip says, it is no surprise that the names of Amblin and Spielberg probably had much the same effect as if he'd walked up with a cheque for ten million dollars and presented to them *ex gratia*.

One of the first things Enterprises did was sort out exactly who owned which copyrights on the series. Effectively, this meant that, while individual monsters and characters were usually created by freelancers who retained the ownership, the BBC owned their appearance, because costumes and other things visual tended to be done by in-house production staff. Indeed, the BBC could lay claim to only a handful of items, including the sonic screwdriver, the Whomobile, the TARDIS, the Time Lords, the Master, Gallifrey, UNIT and the Key to Time. Oh, and of course 'the format of the series', a rather all-encompassing description at best. Enterprises were very quick to point out that they were not prepared to buy out the rights to everything else – although presumably they would not stop Amblin doing so.

They also began to investigate the minefield that is the copyright situation on the Daleks – noting that, although they were 'essential to the series', the rights could be tricky to sort out 'particularly now that news of our discussions with you has leaked'. That last comment is rather amusing in the light of the fact that, at the time it was written (January 1992), the Amblin interest had not actually leaked outside the BBC itself at all.

Over the next couple of months, talks went on between Philip and both the BBC and BBC Enterprises. As they did so, the Daltenrays project was floundering to a small extent. 'Those people seem incapable of getting anything together for so long,' said their script writer Johnny Byrne of his employers. But the company had not given up, with Felice Arden busy in America trying to get funds together. But BBC Enterprises seemed very uninterested in what would have ended up as a small British picture. The word 'Amblin' reflected in their eyes like neon hoardings and they were doing everything they could to keep Spielberg's company interested. The irony was that Spielberg had little interest himself – *Doctor Who* was Philip Segal's pet project as far as he was concerned and he was more than happy to leave it in Philip's hands.

In March, Philip contacted Peter Cregeen and instigated 'the appropriate negotiations'. But nothing happened, and in April Cregeen replied that, after many months of discussions, 'I think a new series is premature. When the time is right – and I think it needs a while off the air – we may yet make another series in-house.' This was both unexpected and bizarre, but there was nothing that could be done at this stage.

Some time in June of 1992, I received a call from the producer Peter Wagg. Some of you may remember him from *Max Headroom*. He had contacted me about a project. I told him that I would love to meet him and say hello. I did not mention what, but I did tell him on the phone that I had a project I wanted to discuss with him.

Ironically, the project both Philip and Wagg, a British expat, wanted to discuss was the same thing. Wagg was working for a company called Yertez in Los Angeles when Felice Arden of Daltenrays got in touch, wanting to contact one of their directors, the British director Alan Parker. Wagg, who knew Philip from some earlier dealings and was aware that he had an interest in *Who*, contacted Amblin. Philip and Wagg met and discussed the project and Peter was immediately enthralled with the idea of doing the series, one he'd loved over the years.

Wagg had recently produced a project called *The Masked Marvel*, another remake of an existing property, so he was well geared up for the pitfalls that *Doctor Who* might present. Segal was back in touch with Mark Shivas and Peter Cregeen by October 1992 and Peter Wagg met with them soon afterwards, along with James Arnold Baker. No one knows exactly who said what to whom, but something clicked at that point. With Wagg aboard, the deal was, while not exactly going full steam ahead, removed from the back burner a little singed but otherwise undamaged.

By early November Arnold Baker was enthusiastic about a project that, just a year before, he'd declared 'no longer commercially viable'. He sent a set of bullet points to Philip outlining various issues and queries. Among these were questions about the extent of Steven Spielberg's involvement and how the money would be split (particularly as both BBC and BBC Enterprises were involved financially), and there was also a comment about the Daltenrays film. Arnold Baker pointed out that 'if principal photography hasn't started by 3rd January 1994' their option expired. More importantly, had that option been exercised, they had the rights to two sequels. Understandably, Arnold Baker thought this was a point best kept between them so as not to scare Amblin and whichever US network was going to become interested.

The bullet points ended with a hitherto unmentioned fact: '… we came close to doing an animated series of *Doctor Who* last year' (1991). No one had mentioned it before then and only now were the BBC asking if that might prove a problem in the future. The project had faltered quite early on however, after discussions between Anna Home of BBC Children's Programmes and Jonathan Powell had not reached any firm conclusions. With Peter Wagg at his side, and Tony Greenwood waving the flag at BBC Enterprises, everyone prepared to go into 1993, the 30th anniversary of *Doctor Who*, with great enthusiasm, anticipation and expectation of what was to come. Shame, really …

Very few aspects of the *Doctor Who* mythology actually come as part and parcel of the series' rights. They include the Time Lords (left, top), the 'Whomobile' (left, bottom) and the Master (above).

Above: Peter Davison, Pudsey, Sophie Aldred and Colin Baker pose for *Dimensions in Time*, the BBC *Doctor Who* drama actually made for the series' 30th anniversary. Despite the appearance of past Doctors, companions, monsters and the cast of soap opera *EastEnders*, an interesting curio is all it could ever be – a new series it was not.

Opposite: Kate O'Mara and Sam West humiliate the Doctor for Children In Need.

• 1993 •
THE WHEEL OF FORTUNE

As 1993 began, letters were flying back and forth between lawyers and a lot of wrangling was taking place on a number of thorny questions. Much of this had begun towards the end of 1992, which had been rather exciting for everyone. Letters had gone from Amblin's attorneys to BBC Enterprises' legal team, setting out their ideas, concepts and a general 'wants list'. Among those were BBC Enterprises' insistence that Philip Segal be named as a 'key man' in a special clause – in other words, if Philip was taken off the project, the Beeb would pull out.

Very flattering, but also dangerous. To expect Amblin to devote a lot of time and money to a project that could be effectively wiped out if Philip resigned from the company or got hit by a bus was something Amblin could not buy. There were other wranglings, too: the rights to what could be bought and sold, and by whom, and in which territories, for instance, and how far the BBC would be involved creatively. (It was established very early on that the BBC wanted an executive producer of their own in on it from the very start.) And the corporation also wanted a 'services fee', a 'quite substantial' amount to be paid to allow Amblin access to old scripts, episodes and previous production personnel.

'I indicated I thought the idea was preposterous,' said Amblin's attorney, 'but they seemed serious about it and I let it go. For the time being.'

Another thing that was essential to both parties was the creation of a series 'bible', basically a guide for writers, directors and others so they could see what this 'new *Doctor Who* property' was about, where it was intended to go episodically and how it was envisaged illustratively. Peter Wagg and Tony Greenwood were both very keen to be in production before the 30th anniversary in November 1993.

The lawyers continued to battle it out on a number of questions:
• Amblin wanted exclusive North American rights to distribute not just the new series but the existing one to offset their costs;
• the BBC wanted Amblin to pay entirely for the bible, and to have the unilateral right to disapprove of all casting, the bible and other 'creative elements';
• they were still insistent that Philip Segal, now along with both Wagg and Spielberg, be contractually obliged to the show (if any of them left, the deal was off);
• the BBC didn't want Amblin to have merchandising rights, and wanted the deal to be nonexclusive (i.e. the Beeb could sell *Doctor Who* as a concept to someone else and thus Amblin could have a competing TV programme elsewhere in the world).

And so it went on...

THE 30th ANNIVERSARY

From the middle of 1992 it became very clear that the BBC, and BBC Enterprises in particular, wanted to capitalise on *Doctor Who*'s forthcoming 30th anniversary. Despite the show not having been on the air since 1989, Enterprises were all too aware of its popularity: their regular video releases were selling very well indeed, there were a large number of regular *Doctor Who* conventions around the country and all the other *Doctor Who* licence holders were reporting brisk business. All that was needed to keep the buoyancy was a new *Doctor Who* programme itself.

Thus it was in late 1992 that two BBC Video producers, David Jackson and Penny Mills, convened a meeting with one of their freelance writing staff, Adrian Rigelsford, himself an author of a couple of factual books about the series. Jackson and Mills wanted to make a direct-to-video *Doctor Who* special – nothing too expensive but, at the same time, it had to be of transmission quality. A budget was put

together (rumours of £30,000 floated around at the time) and, over the next few months, the script was created. Rigelsford was joined in his task by Joanna McCaul, with whom he had worked on previous screenplays. Together they concocted *Lost in the Dark Dimension*, which, rather than drawing the Doctors together as previous specials had done, used an alternate timeline created by the evil Professor Hawkspur, in which the fourth Doctor (Tom Baker) never regenerated. It became the task of Ace (under her real name Dorothy McShane) and the Brigadier to put time back on the right track and ensure that all the Doctor's lives are saved.

During May 1993, BBC Enterprises had held a news conference at the Ark in Hammersmith to launch their range of 30th anniversary merchandise and announce that they were getting together with Marvel Comics and DSL (the company that regularly organised *Doctor Who* conventions) to hold a large convention later that year, which would be open to the general public,

with talks, displays and, of course, lots of merchandise. At this launch Tony Greenwood, as Director, Consumer Products, announced that Alan Yentob's sentiment that 'it doesn't mean we are closing the doors on the TARDIS yet' was coming true and that, before long, there would be new *Doctor Who*.

Much speculation followed and it appeared that what Greenwood was talking about was *Lost in the Dark Dimension*, especially when, after some leaks to the media, BBC Enterprises were forced to make an official announcement in early June. However, not everything was as well received as the BBC might have thought. Certainly a number of past Doctors were none too pleased at doing what were, essentially, one- or two-scene cameos, while Tom Baker (already under contract) had the lion's share of the production. Nevertheless, scripts were sent out to actors via their agents and availability was checked.

Some aspects of the scripts were rewritten to accommodate the understandably aggrieved Doctors, one of whom commented that the script was more a re-promotion of the fourth Doctor than a celebration of 30 years of the show itself.

Some time previously, the show's last producer John Nathan-Turner had suggested to BBC Enterprises that he produce a direct-to-video project, but it had been scrapped by an uninterested BBC Video as unworkable. No one was more surprised than Nathan-Turner when, with an alarming degree of tactlessness, he was invited to come aboard as a project consultant. Unsurprisingly, he opted not to, feeling that neither the script's potential nor the likelihood of its actually coming in on budget was particularly high.

Meanwhile, many different departments in the BBC's craft sections were busy preparing preproduction drawings and suchlike, while Graeme Harper was on board as director, Chris Fitzgerald as the creature-effects designer and Nic Jagels as the production manager. Nigel Jones of BBC Design, Dave Chapman of BBC Video Effects and Tony Harding of the BBC Visual Effects Unit were asked to contribute, and Harding asked one of his designer assistants, Alan 'Rocky' Marshall, to come up with a new

Two Daleks prowl the South Bank for *30 Years in the TARDIS*.

Kate O'Mara and Peter Davison pose in Albert Square with a horde of their *Dimensions in Time* co-stars.

version of the Special Weapons Dalek. Fitzgerald produced numerous sketches of new Cybermen and Ice Warriors (for the sixth-Doctor sequences).

A lot of work went into *Lost in the Dark Dimension* – ultimately all for nothing because, on 9 July, Tony Greenwood confirmed to the press that the special was cancelled. Although the reasons for this were many, it was no coincidence that, at Peter Cregeen's insistence (he was to be the producer for BBC TV of *Lost in the Dark Dimension*), Tony Greenwood sent Philip Segal a brief summary of the plot plus a list of crew and actors already 'confirmed' for the production. According to the memo from Greenwood, among the actors were Brian Blessed as Hawkspur and Ian Hogg as Reverend Merrick – although the memo also noted that David Bowie had expressed an interest in playing Hawkspur.

Philip had then asked to see the script, aware that, while new *Doctor Who* was a common aim for everyone, if they had a flop on their hands, it could set everything back, possibly for ever. He let Tony know his opinions on the script and, from the point of view of the hoped-for co-production deal with

Amblin, just how badly he thought this might affect things. Although not single-handedly responsible for stopping *Lost in the Dark Dimension*, Philip's input was valued enough by both Cregeen and Greenwood to help influence their joint decision to drop it.

Almost immediately, two other 30th-anniversary opportunities presented themselves. First, there was *30 Years in the TARDIS*, a documentary, produced by Kevin Davies for *The Late Show*, under the guidance of John Whiston. A series of connected clips, reconstructions of famous moments and interviews with just about everyone who could be interviewed (although Peter Davison was notable by his absence), the documentary went out close to the show's anniversary and an extended version was released by BBC Video a few months later, called *More Than 30 Years in the TARDIS*!

BBC Radio got in on the act: Radio 4 commissioned a five-part drama called *The Paradise of Death* from the former producer Barry Letts, reuniting Jon Pertwee with Elisabeth Sladen (as Sarah Jane Smith) and Nicholas Courtney, while that story's producer, Phil Clarke,

also made a Radio 2 documentary, *Doctor Who – 30 Years*.

Finally, it was decided to give the fans something new in November and the BBC's annual Children In Need telethon was responsible for a thirteen-minute mini-epic entitled *Dimensions in Time*, by John Nathan-Turner and David Roden. This saw the various Doctors and companions in and around both Greenwich and later Albert Square (of *EastEnders* fame), battling various enemies led by the Rani. Members of the *EastEnders* cast also appeared, spread across various time zones, and, although more than slightly tongue-in-cheek, it raised a lot of money for charity and, for the first time in ten years, saw *Doctor Who* return to the cover of *Radio Times*.

By the end of 1993, it was not only the fans who knew it was the Doctor's 30th anniversary. From that first press call, via the *Lost in the Dark Dimension* débâcle, the new radio serial, the big convention, the documentaries, some repeats and finally *Dimensions in Time*, the BBC realised that there was proven interest from other viewers, too, to warrant having *Doctor Who* back on their screens.

(Above) Tom Baker returned to the role of the Doctor in *Dimensions in Time*, wishing his dear friends good luck. Good luck sadly evaded writer Adrian Rigelsford and director Graeme Harper (right), who did their best to get *Lost in the Dark Dimension* off the drawing board.

other, leaving the creative people unable to make any constructive moves in any direction.

By June, the Daltenrays project had gained a new partner, Lumiere Pictures. They were immediately alarmed to learn that Amblin were also interested in *Doctor Who*, and contacted Charles Denton, Mark Shivas's replacement at BBC Drama. One of the things Lumiere implied was that there existed a possibility that Lumiere, Daltenrays, the BBC, BBC Enterprises and Amblin would combine forces. Philip quickly contacted Charles Denton, assuring him that no such idea had been mooted from Amblin's side and they would be quite strongly against such a thing, having come as far as they had.

Another obstacle that greeted Philip in June 1993 was project that Enterprises were considering funding, *Lost in the Dark Dimension*. This was to be a direct-to-video drama production to celebrate the series' 30th anniversary. Philip told Charles Denton, Alan Yentob (now having succeeded Jonathan Powell as Controller, BBC1), Peter Wagg and Tony Greenwood that he thought the project was doomed, suggesting the script and the proposed £80,000 budget were not mutually productive. He felt that if Enterprises wanted to spend £80,000 on promoting

Philip and Tony Greenwood also got embroiled in all this, Greenwood pointing out that Amblin's deal financially was unfair and, as the biggest co-producer of programming in the world, the BBC had a great deal of experience in this sort of thing. While probably very true, bearing in mind this is the company who wanted to bring Verity Lambert in as a go-between, this sudden aggressive stance about the whys and wherefores of co-production is odd. Nevertheless, Philip and Tony were determined to keep trying.

By March, it appeared that a deadlock had occurred between the respective lawyers, and Philip realised that it was going pear-shaped. 'Tony, I really feel that we have taken five giant steps backward. I find myself in the same position I was three years ago when I tried to make a deal with Roger Laughton.' And so things began to take on an almost *Dallas*-like twist as the lawyers tried to out-jargonise each

Doctor Who, then why not spend it in promoting their proposed deal with Amblin rather than undercutting the potential prestige of that with an in-house video drama?

By the end of July, nothing much was happening, and Philip could see that the window of opportunity necessary to sell *Doctor Who*, via the all-important bible, to a network was disappearing. If this chance was missed, it would be a whole year before a new pitch could be made. But on 2 August, Tony Greenwood – now in his new role as Director of Consumer Products International for BBC Enterprises – sent the confirmation Philip had been waiting for. Trouble was, the lawyers didn't agree – as they saw it, the BBC was still avoiding acknowledging any of Amblin's requirements. While they battled it out, Philip and Tony got down to the nitty-gritty of getting things moving in anticipation of a successful agreement being reached. Philip even tried to get a sonic screwdriver sent over, but could the BBC find one? Nope. Mike Tucker of BBC Visual Effects, a long-time champion of the show, even offered to make him one! Meanwhile, at the bottom of one memo from Philip to Tony was a tiny P.S.: 'Michael Crawford is in Los Angeles. He is very, very keen …'

By the summer of 1993 my dialogue with the BBC had become fast and furious. Tony Greenwood and I were actually beginning to talk about how a deal would be structured. My biggest hurdle at this point was the simple fact that Amblin was funded by and supported by Universal Pictures. The history of this fact was tied to Spielberg's success with *ET* and *Jaws*.

Universal had a 50 per cent interest in everything Amblin Television was involved in and making a deal that cut the pie up so much that neither party had a chance to really make any money was a problem. For me, just another hurdle.

At this point I was riding high, because I really believed that I would be able to convince Universal and the BBC that a marriage made all the sense in the world. Little did I know that, by pressuring Universal into a deal, I would be stuck with writers I did not care for and production personnel I did not wish to work with.

Nevertheless, by summer's end, champagne was flowing in my office at Amblin. Tony Greenwood and I were celebrating the deal and I had a smile on my face bigger than a Cheshire Cat's. It didn't last very long, but, for milliseconds, I felt victorious!

Due to Amblin's continued involvement, *Lost in the Dark Dimension*, or *The Dark Dimension* as it had transmuted into, was history. Instead, BBC1 had concentrated on a thirteen-minute romp around the set of the popular soap *EastEnders* – made featuring the casts of both series and shot using a new 3-D technique – as a special for the annual Children in Need telethon. BBC2 commissioned a brand-new documentary, *30 Years in the TARDIS*, which ended with an enigmatic Alan Yentob promising the director Kevin Davies that talks were going on and, before too long, *Doctor Who*

Josh Maguire, the young host of *30 Years in the TARDIS*.

fans around the world might just possibly, perhaps, see a new Doctor before too long.

By now, the British press had latched on to the Amblin connection. Apart from Michael Crawford's name, everyone else in the entertainment industry seemed to be 'confirmed' as a star. Or a director. Or both. Eric Idle. David Hasselhoff. Leonard Nimoy. Michael Palin … As time went on, some of them did become briefly involved with the project. Others were more directly attached to the Daltenrays project. Many however were just names on lists that were as expansive as the tabloid imaginations that created them.

Oh, and Philip finally got his sonic screwdriver, one droplet of joy amid a sea of turmoil.

Universal, meanwhile, were chucking more obstacles at the BBC than anyone could have imagined. They required a stake, they required consultation, they required a third of everything. As they saw it, it was now a three-way split between the BBC (i.e. BBC Television and BBC Enterprises), Universal TV and Amblin. And this was before a US network (which would also want a share of profits, creative control, input and goodness knows what else) even got near it.

Will Wyatt, managing director of BBC Television, made a visit to LA and met up with Philip, adding his very worthwhile support to the project. On so many sides, the indications were looking good. On so many others, they looked less so. It might not have been approaching the adage, 'too many cooks …' just yet, but the kitchen staff were getting very nervous.

• 1994 •

FLIGHT THROUGH ETERNITY

In the middle of January 1994, Tony Greenwood and some colleagues from BBC Enterprises met at Amblin with Philip Segal and Ed Masket, from MCA Television (i.e. Universal). On Thursday, 13 January, the BBC, Universal and Amblin were in agreement, a deal had been made and, exactly 55 months from the day of his first call to Roger Laughton, Philip Segal was the producer of a brand-new version of *Doctor Who*.

Then his troubles really started.

There were two misfires before the film that starred Paul McGann actually got made. There was also an actor that I secretly wanted to play the Doctor long before I had found and fallen in love with Paul. I'll talk about that later on.

Back to the misfires. We'll start with the production that I now call the Leekley one. Although this production came and went very fast, I will go into a few of the details on what that really was. Some readers may recall a book written by Jean-Marc Lofficier entitled *The Nth Doctor*. This contained interviews with John Leekley, Robert DeLaurentis and a few others who had contributed to the stack of ideas and scripts that were being developed as film and television projects in the late 1980s and early 1990s. I am also a part of *The Nth Doctor* story and was friendly

with Jean-Marc during the period in which we developed the John Leekley script.

Although it's quite detailed in what went on with the script, the book doesn't explain what really compelled and drove the creative strategy behind *Doctor Who*'s regeneration.

I met John Leekley on the Universal lot. He was under contract to the studio's television division and early in 1993 had come to Amblin to pitch me a project of his own. While he was in my office he noticed some *Doctor Who* memorabilia and we had a nice conversation about it. I remember liking his passion and his writing. Passion and liking someone's writing do not always add up to a successful marriage, however – if there's one thing I have learnt about the development process over the years, it's 'go with your gut feelings'. My gut feeling was not to speak to a studio writer about *Doctor Who*. I wanted to go into the marketplace and see who else was out there. I had even begun to enquire about British writers.

In fact, on one of several visits to London, I had met with Terrance Dicks and we discussed his thoughts about taking a crack at a script idea he seemed very keen on, and I think he would have done a good job. However, that was not to be, and my forward progress was dampened by a call from the studio, asking me why I had not contacted any of their writers about the project. As usual, I

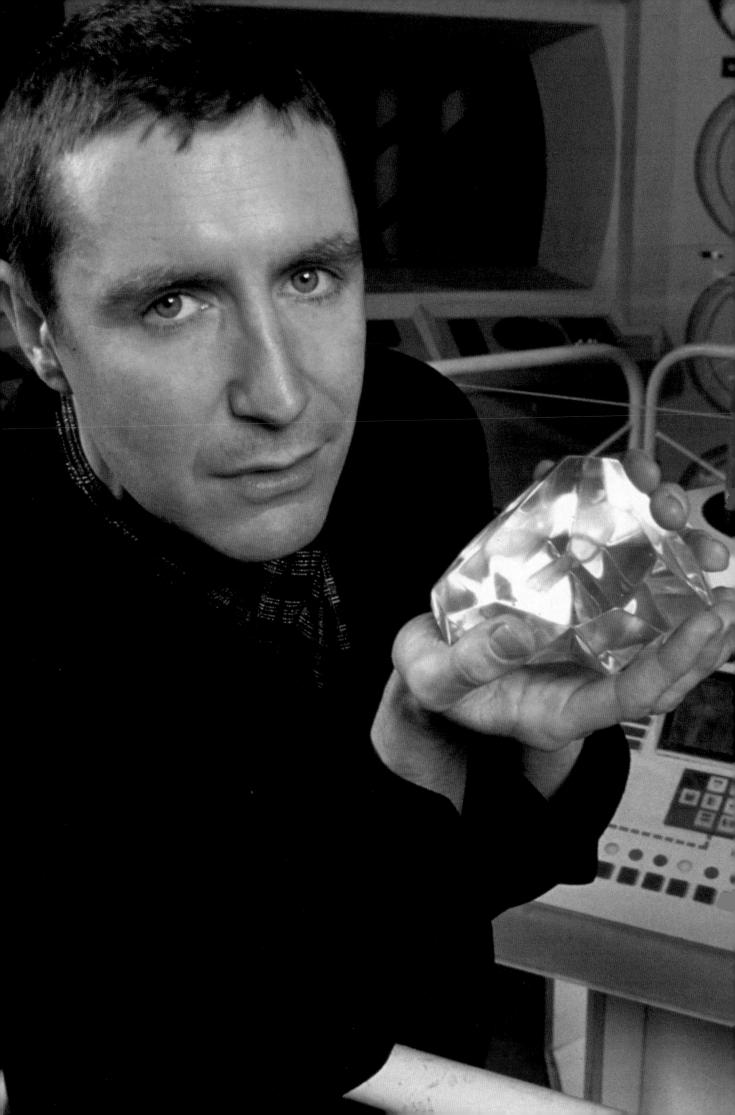

other younger British companies who were emerging as broadcasting powerhouses and thus threatening the BBC's domination in certain areas of the world.

As laborious and uninteresting as this last statement may seem, it is the very essence of why *Doctor Who* was allowed to regenerate in the '90s. Soon after the deal had closed, Universal insisted I work with John Leekley on the project. I thought about fighting the decision, but time was not on my side and, if I was to have any hope of having Doctor Who ready to pitch to the networks in time for the following season, I had to act.

So I called John Leekley, invited him to lunch and offered him the job. He was very pleased; I was very nervous. By this time, I had also contracted Peter Wagg to come on board as my co-executive producer. Under the original plan, I was going to act as an executive on the project only because of my contract with Amblin. Peter was going to be my eyes and ears.

At this point, I also hired a production designer by the name of Richard Lewis. Richard had worked with me on a series called *The Young Riders* while I had been working at ABC Television. We soon became friends and he then worked for me on a pilot I made for ABC while at Amblin called *The Class of 61*, and after that Richard did *seaQuest DSV* with me. His brief was to help me create a 'bible' in pictures with Leekley's words to help sell the concept of *Doctor Who* to an American network. We went to work.

As work on the bible progressed, I felt like I was having to walk on eggshells around John. Having said that, I did like some of John's ideas, and that made our short-lived relationship even harder to bear. John saw the core of the story as a deep unwinding of the lost relationship between the Doctor and his father. He saw everything as ugliness verses beauty. This went from a crystalline Gallifrey (which I did not like, because I felt it touched on the world created for the original *Superman* movie, which the Salkinds had produced in the '80s) to the Kane-and-Abel legend, revealing that the Doctor and the Master were actually brothers (which I did like).

The prolific Terrance Dicks (above left, with former producer Barry Letts) has written scripts for *Doctor Who*, script-edited the series through the early 1970s, and penned countless novels and novelisations. He was also one of the first people Philip Segal wanted to discuss his new project with. 'Philip came over to England,' Dicks recalls, 'and said, "I'd like you to do it as I think you're the best person for the job." He later phoned up and told me that Fox wanted a writer with a US work record. I said, "Well, thank you for thinking of me!"'

was diplomatic but I continued my search without talking to anyone from the studio.

I got a call from Ed Masket, Universal Television's business affairs man, telling me that the BBC deal was close to being finalised. This was the first time I truly believed in my own heart that *Doctor Who* would become a reality. By this time, Tony Greenwood and I had become good friends. We no longer looked at the project as 'them against us'. Both he and I carefully constructed each move we made. The BBC had certain needs, and I relied on Tony to tell me what those needs were.

Without Tony, *Doctor Who* would not have seen the light of day. Tony was very precise about his agenda with me. If the BBC could create the right deal, they would in fact be distributing an 'Amblin' product; that would have been a huge feather in anyone's cap, especially the Beeb's. I recognised the BBC's desire at that brief moment to break into the international marketplace and become a major contender in the US.

As my deal with the BBC was being consummated, big changes were being made on the broadcast scene in the UK. A new channel, Channel 5, was being envisioned, satellite TV was going strong, and some areas were cabling up. For a moment, the BBC had a brief opportunity that would hopefully enable them to break into the US market. This would allow them to compete with these

I think at this point all the negative energy I was sending out into the universe finally imploded the project. Several things began to happen all at once, but, so as not to leave anything out, I'll pause to explain what happened before this incarnation of the project stalled.

After a leather-bound version of the bible was completed, Peter Wagg, John Leekley and I boarded a plane for London. This was a required visit to get the BBC's feedback on the bible. Even though Amblin had creative control, it was very important to me that Alan Yentob was happy with what I was doing – besides his having been very loyal to me, I valued his opinion. The fact is, Alan Yentob is *Doctor Who*'s most loyal supporter at the BBC.

While John, Peter and I waited at Los Angeles airport, in the first-class lounge no less, John noticed David Puttnam sitting in the lounge. Inspired by his work, John insisted we all say hello to Puttnam and tell him what we were doing. I was reluctant and slightly embarrassed at this.

This brief encounter with Puttnam did prove to be interesting for me, however, from one perspective – he suggested we look at a film he had just produced called *War of the Buttons*. He wanted us to look at an Irish actor he had cast as the schoolteacher in the movie. The actor's name was Liam Cunningham. Puttnam thought he would make a great Doctor.

Upon arriving in London, Peter Wagg contacted our London casting agents, John and Ros Hubbard. John and Ros had agreed to introduce us to some possible Doctor candidates while we were in London. In fact, we had several days of meetings with actors and I even remember watching a slew of videotaped auditions and showreels of actors.

While we were in London, Tony Greenwood became our official liaison with the BBC. One morning we were slated to meet with the executive whom Alan Yentob had assigned to the project. His name was Michael Wearing. I had heard the name and had been told by several friends in London that he was very well respected. The morning we met with Wearing, I remember he brought another exec with him to the meeting – a woman by the name of Jo Wright. She was introduced to me as the Drama Serials Producer of *Doctor Who* for the BBC.

I tried very hard to process this introduction clearly and professionally, but for some reason I didn't. I was angry that someone else might be trying to push the project in a direction I did not want to take it. I now realise that, had I been in a better frame of mind, I would have gotten to know Jo sooner and taken her advice. I later came to respect her and appreciate her involvement in the project. Our battles were few and far between, but Jo always held her ground and always gave me great ideas. I'd now like to publicly thank her for her encouragement and support.

The offices at the BBC buildings never struck me as being very conducive to creative thought – everywhere you looked there were massive monoliths of concrete and metal, all tastefully decorated in bland and drab colours. It all felt like a sterile institution with no heart or soul. I was very worried that Wearing was going to pass the project off on to Jo, and so, at the time, I had a lot of hostility building up inside me. I was not thinking very clearly: all the years of trying to set the project up and all the rejection and promises that never came to be had made this trip to London very hard for me. Outside, I wore the label of producer. Inside, I was very confused and tired. At the end of the meeting with Wearing and Wright we left behind the leather-bound bible for them to read. They promised to give us their notes before we returned to America.

That evening, we were taken by cab to Alan Yentob's home to meet with him and discuss his thoughts about the project. We were ushered into a basement office, nicely

A fortuitous encounter with Sir David Puttnam on a plane to London led Philip to take a serious interest in actor Liam Cunningham as a possible new Doctor.

Liam Cunningham was one of a number of actors who did videotaped auditions on 9 March 1994, reading a script extract adapted from the series' bible by John Leekley. The Doctor converses with Napoleon on the subject of military history (see page 45).

Opposite: Paul McGann's first *Doctor Who* photo-call at the Longleat exhibition (see also page 27).

appointed. I remember his explaining that they were remodelling and he apologised for not meeting us at his office, but he had to be home to meet with builders. Tony Greenwood, John Leekley, Peter Wagg and I attended this meeting. Alan was basically pleased with the direction we were taking the show in, and, after a good hour of discussing the project, we shook hands and left. But not before I had fallen through and broken the wicker chair I had been sitting on in his house. My only reason for committing this memory to paper is that it produced a very much needed laugh for everyone. Humour had been slowly leaking out of the trip and my chance, albeit disastrous, meeting with the poor wicker chair broke the ice.

Back at our hotel, John and Ros prepared a batch of actors for our auditions. Another embarrassing moment happened between the Hubbards and John Leekley when Ros had mistakenly left John's name off the audition sheets as producer. He was listed only as the writer and this really pushed his buttons. You see, John was one of the executive producers and, in the US television market, that credit is more important than the producer credit. So, obviously, seeing his name on a document as just the 'writer' was insulting.

The casting sessions themselves were quite gruelling. We must have met fifteen to twenty actors a day, but none of the very talented individuals we saw really had what I thought the Doctor needed. So in some ways the whole process was rather disappointing.

However, one thing did come out of the process: this trip marked a very important moment in the history of this incarnation of the project. It was actually the beginning of the end for John Leekley's involvement in *Doctor Who*. I knew that once we had committed to John Leekley creatively he would for ever be tied to this particular project in one way or another. Any writing that he had done for me would automatically be arbitrated by the US Writers' Guild, an incredibly powerful force in US television. If they felt his contribution was significant enough, then he would always have some kind of credit on the project, whatever form it took.

And indeed it came to pass that John did seek credit on the project that came to be known as the *Doctor Who* movie for the Fox network starring Paul McGann. Obviously he was not successful in getting that credit. We made the Guild understand that, because the body of existing work over the previous thirty-odd years was so significant, he was simply upstaged, as it were, by the very programme he aimed to conquer.

That's the funny thing about the *Doctor Who* mythology: in some ways it has outgrown us in every aspect. Any producer, including me, could never presume to overthrow the project creatively. The force is too large. No one can ever really claim to have completely created anything by themselves for it.

Doctor Who also has a funny way of consuming you. Once bitten, you are compelled to come back for more. Is it the character itself? Or the fans and the power of a world that we seek to be a part of?

Before heading back to the United States, Peter Wagg, John Leekley and I took a much-needed break from the grind of getting things started and went out to the old Ealing Studios. The BBC had arranged a field trip for us where we were shown the very stage upon which so many William Hartnell and Patrick Troughton episodes were recorded.

Actor and comedian Tony Slattery entertained Segal, Peter Wagg and the Hubbards before, during and after his audition.

One of the stages was being used as a warehouse for re-created and original props from the last ten or fifteen years of *Doctor Who*. BBC Enterprises had been actively involved in travelling exhibitions of *Doctor Who* for the sole purpose of promoting the video line.

We were shown a wooden TARDIS, Sea Devils, a Yeti, several Daleks and other props that had been laid out specifically for us to see. Clearly we were expected, because as we entered the stage, dry ice filled the air and the *Doctor Who* theme tune echoed throughout the sound stage. I must admit that for one brief moment I got very nostalgic. I do remember thinking that all these dusty props were probably all that remained of the original series. It was almost too much to actually contemplate being in production on a new version of *Doctor Who* at that point.

After seeing the display of props, we were taken to a small room off the main offices of the studio to have lunch. Gathered at the lunch where several executives from the various factions of the BBC, including Michael Wearing and Tony Greenwood. As I looked around the table, I remember thinking that this moment truly represented the first time I felt a full and complete endorsement from the BBC.

The following day, we were on our way back to Los Angeles, armed with some minor character and story notes. It was at this point that we began pitching the show to the various networks. NBC was first, followed by ABC, CBS and Fox. It was CBS and Fox who ultimately began a dialogue about the project. The other two networks were simply overcommitted to other projects and saw no place for *Doctor Who* on their respective schedules. Eventually, CBS offered us a six-episode commitment, but the then head of the network, Howard Stringer (one of the few Brits in LA who didn't have a nostalgic soft spot for the Doctor), rejected the idea and wanted no part of the show.

We were then left with Fox. The head of series at that time, Robert Greenblatt, was a friend and was keen to try to develop a script. Greenblatt was also a fan of John Leekley, so we appeared to be in pretty good shape. Although I did not see a future for this incarnation of the project, nevertheless we were moving forward.

We had started writing the storylines for the series version in August 1993. This version of the pilot script was being developed by the series television division of the Fox network, not the studio. The movie version that finally aired on Fox was ultimately produced through their Movie of the Week department (Movies for Television).

Peter Wagg, John Leekley and I went through meeting after meeting to put the story together. This is always the hardest part of developing any television project. Until the network approves a story, you can't write the script. At this point in the proceedings, we were still attached to Amblin. This meant that there were several approvals that would have to be gotten before we could proceed. Those approvals would include Universal, Amblin, Fox, the BBC and BBC Enterprises. My head was spinning.

We kept working with John and John kept rewriting. In late September we had a story, which did finally get approved. John then began the official writing process, even though Peter and I knew that he had already been working on scenes long before everyone had given their agreements to the story. This was the one and only time in the entire process of working with John and Peter on the project that the three of us actually agreed. We all knew that, if we delayed getting the script written any later than September, we would miss our window of opportunity to get the pilot ready for May.

Remember, at this point in the proceedings we all thought we were trying to get a series made, not just a film. John's draft of the script was finally ready for everyone to read in October. I remember thinking how long the summer had felt.

I now recognise some mistakes that were made in the development process of that version of the script. First of all, we scouted and budgeted too early on in the process. John had given us an early draft of the script sometime in July/August, and it was based on that and the existing detailed story that I pushed the button on scouting locations and hiring a line producer to work with us on budgets and the scout. At this point, I was also financially responsible for our production designer, Richard Lewis, and a staff of artists. It was all too much work too soon. The truth is, the first draft presented for approval on the Amblin side as well as for the network got two radically different reactions. Robert Greenblatt of Fox liked the script very much. Steven did not. He felt it was too close to the *Indiana Jones* concept and did not want to continue supporting this project.

I was devastated. All I could think of was the reaction the BBC would have to this news. It took me several days to build up enough courage to call. I had to play it very carefully. My goal now was to keep the project alive no matter what. Tony Greenwood at

In an ironic twist, Mark McGann read for the role his brother eventually won.

BBC Enterprises took my call. I considered him a friend so I was careful not to overplay my hand. Tony had been remarkable in keeping the flow of information and enthusiasm alive, and this would be a major blow to his personal interests inside the Beeb. Tony was, after all, the architect of the whole deal.

Tony called me several days later to inform me that the BBC was still excited about the project and had gone too far to stop the process or shut it down.

It was at this point in the proceedings that I had the unenviable task of letting John Leekley know he would not be the writer on this project any longer. Admittedly, John had spent a lot of time on *Doctor Who* and, I suppose, felt a certain disgust at being let go. But John's personality was such that he made it all seem like water off a duck's back.

CASTING

Chris Bowen, with Sylvester McCoy in the 1989 story *Battlefield*.

A memo written in January 1994 listed several possible actors to play the Doctor. Names put forward were Joss Ackland, Alan Bennett, Jeremy Brett, Simon Callow, Robbie Coltrane, Tom Conti, Peter Cook, Tom Courtney, Brian Cox, Jim Dale, Charles Dance, James Fox, John Neville, Paul Freeman, Michael Gambon, Robert Hardy, Nigel Havers, Ian Holm, Nigel Hawthorne, Barry Humphries, John Hurt, Derek Jacobi, Richard Johnson, Freddie Jones, Ben Kingsley, Robert Lindsay, Herbert Lom, Alec McGowan, Ian McKellen, Leo McKern, Ian MacShane, Edward Woodward, John Mills, Alfred Molina, Ron Moody, Sam Neill, Bob Peck, Donald Pleasance, Jonathan Pryce, Patrick Stewart, David Threlfall, Antony Sher, Peter Ustinov and John Wood, while on the back of the memo are a number of lines of scribbled additional notes adding Rob Lowe, Peter O'Toole, Tim Curry and Eric Idle. While a majority of these actors were far older than Peter and Phil had in mind, it was a good grounding from which to begin their thoughts.

Peter Wagg dropped a memo to Alan Yentob on 4 February about casting ideas – pointing out that they had appointed the Hubbards as their London casting agents, commissioned to find a Doctor. Among their initial thoughts were Michael Crawford, Tim Curry, Eric Idle, Roger Rees, Billy Connolly, Trevor Eve, Michael Palin, Robert Lindsay and Jonathan Pryce. Of these, Palin had immediately said he wasn't interested.

Peter Wagg also wanted to trawl the London stage and television productions to find someone with the right potential and said they planned casting sessions during his and Phil's visit in March. Wagg also brings up the subject of the Doctor's Time Lord grandfather – 'a very strong on-going story arc … and [I] believe the perfect casting would be Peter O'Toole … Peter has responded favourably …' Due to some complications in his personal life, he would be free and was potentially very interested in the project.

On 18 February, Wagg informed Yentob that, with filming not that far away, they needed to have found the Doctor by Wednesday, 9 March.

They had by now followed David Puttnam's advice and viewed his film to keep an eye on Liam Cunningham – and were very impressed. Wagg also said that the Hubbards had added some more potentials to the list, keeping the part in a younger age bracket. The additional names were Peter Capaldi, Rupert Graves, Hugh Grant, Rufus Sewell, Rik Mayall, Hugh Laurie, Griff Rhys-Jones, Rowan Atkinson and, of course, Liam Cunningham.

By 28 February, the Hubbards had sorted out a final list to contact and maybe arrange interviews for the March visit by Phill and Peter Wagg. In addition to many of the names above, they added Rob Heyland, Bill Armstrong, Philip Franks, Paul Bown, Neil Duncan, Patrick Barlow, Peter Richardson, Richard Hope, Rob Newman, Chris Bowen, Christian Burgess, Colin Firth, Stanley Coogan, Stanley Townsend, James Wilby, Mark McGann, Hugh Fraser, Reece Dinsdale, Tim McInnerny, Kevin Whately, Brendan Coyle, Tony Slattery, James Coombes, Tim Bentinck, Neil Morrissey, Simon Sutton, John Sessions, Henry Naylor, Ivan Kaye, Kevin McNally, Michael Howe, Simon Dutton, Stephen Dillane, Simon McBurney, Neil Pearson, Ralph Fiennes, John Fortune, Angus Deayton, David Baddiel, Robert Bathurst, Sean Chapman, Clive Francis, Adam Faith, David Essex, Peter Egan, Chris Eccleston, Barry McGovern, Mick Lally, Bryan Murray, Martin Ball, Tom Wilkinson, Michael Kitchen, Richard O'Brien, Simon Slater, Chris Blake, Anthony Andrews, Adam Ant, Alun Armstrong, Chris Barrie, Sean Bean, Nick Berry, Philip Bird, Jim Broadbent, Chris Evans, Tim Brooke-Taylor, Ralph Brown, Simon Cadell, Simon Chandler, Martin Clunes, Jeremy Clyde, Jason Britton, Barry Foster, Rupert Everett, Michael Elphick, Ben Elton, Jason Durr, Hugh Dennis, Tim Dalton, Jon Coy, Peter McEnery, John Kavangh, Johnny Murphy, Hilton McRae, Bill Patterson, Joylon Baker, Tony Matthews, Hywel Bennett, David Jason, Matthew Kelly, Ben Kingsley, Jeroen Krabbe, Chris Langham, Patrick Malahide, Denis Lawson, Leigh Lawson, Simon Williams, David McAlister, Malcolm McDowell,

Chris Fairbank, Ian Redford, Stephen Moor, Bill Nighy, Philip Jackson, James Larkin, Simon Callow, Miles Anderson, Chris Casenove, Jonathan Ryan, Michael Ball and Pierce Brosnan.

A number of actors the Hubbards had already sounded out had declined interest by now, including Tim Curry, Paul Bradley, Rory Bremner, Stephen Fry, Harry Enfield, Charles Dance, Roger Allam, Hugh Laurie, Rufus Sewell (he was not available until January 1995), Rowan Atkinson, Griff Rhys-Jones and John Hannah.

At the same time, the Hubbards were keeping their eye out for potential Borusas, should the Peter O'Toole connection fail. These included some rather 'big' names including John Gielgud, Alec Guiness, Anthony Hopkins, Richard Attenborough, Paul Newman and Ralph Bellamy.

Casting sessions were now up and running, the first taking place, the first on 1 March. Before it got under way, John Hubbard told Phil Segal that Ralph Fiennes's agent had said he was not keen to commit to a long-term US TV contract.

What follows is rough detail of those casting sessions – comments in brackets were those written next to the names during and after the auditions by Peter Wagg, who was over in the UK by now waiting for Phil Segal to join him.

1 March casting session
1030	Christian Burgess (maybe)
1100	Liam Cunningham (yes)
1130	Henry Naylor (no)
1200	Rob Heyland
1230	Bill Armstrong (no)
1330	Chris Bowen (yes)
1400	Paul Bown (yes)
1430	Mark McGann (yes)

2 March
1030	Richard Hope (yes)
1100	Simon Dutton (yes)
1200	James Coombes (maybe)
1230	Tim Bentinck (maybe)
1415	Robert Lindsay (not interested)
1515	Tim McInnerny (borderline)

Many others were either not available to audition because they were working, or would be by the time the production began. More notes about casting Borusa were made that day as well . . .

Available and interested actors are John Gielgud, John Mills, Richard Attenborough, Ian Richardson, Alec Guiness (very interested apparently). Other possibilities to consider include Gregory Peck, Burt Lancaster, Kirk Douglas, Jack Lemmon, Richard Harris.

Many of the older actors from the original listing of potential Doctors were transferred to the possible Borusa list now. Ian McKellen, Joss Ackland, Peter Ustinov, Robert Stephens, Richard Griffiths, Donald Pleasance, Herbert Lom, Christopher Lee, Peter Cushing, Eric Porter, David Warner, Max Von Sydow, Armin Mueller-Stahl, Don Ameche, and even Hugh Grant! More casting sessions were arranged.

3 March
1030	Stephen Hartley (no)
1100	Michael Howe (no)
1130	Andy Bicknell (yes)
1200	Mark Greenstreet (borderline)
1230	Anthony Calf (no)
1300	Paul Venables (no)
1330	Kevin McNally (no)
1430	Benedict Taylor (maybe)
1500	Chris Blake (no)
1530	Christopher Villiers (no)
1600	John Michie
4.30	Peter Birch
5.00	Robert Lindsay

8 March
1445	Nathaniel Parker (no)
1515	Rob Heyland (call back)
1530	Robin Kermode (no)
1545	Valentine Pelka (yes call back)
1615	Paul Nicholas
1630	Daniel Abineri
1645	Peter Woodward
1715	Julian Wadham
1745	Stephen Dillane
1800	John Sessions

At some point after this, Peter Wagg also saw Aidan Quinn (yes) and Neil Morrisey (no) but wasn't able to meet with Philip Franks, Hugh Laurie, Peter Richardson, Trevor Eve or Paul McGann (the last three were currently resident in Los Angeles, ironically enough). This was the first time Paul McGann had been linked with the part.

Wagg also comments that, despite his initial reaction, Robert Lindsay had 'tremendous presence'. On 9 March many of them were called back for a second go, alongside one newcomer, Anthony Head. These auditions, reading segments from the Leekley script, were videotaped, with both Wagg and Segal present.

9 March
0945	Anthony Head
1000	Richard Hope
1030	Mark McGann
1100	Christopher Bowen
1130	Paul Bown
1230	Christian Burgess
1400	Liam Cunningham
1430	Andrew Bicknell
1500	Tony Slattery
1630	Robert Lindsay
1715	Rob Heyland
1815	John Sessions

The videotaped interviews are interesting and it is easy to see which actors were preferred by the producers. A number of the actors 'acted' the part based on a simplistic idea of what the Doctor was like – very zany, very quirky – and one could imagine they saw themselves in a long scarf and floppy hat as they read to John Hubbard (apart from John Sessions who read every part in the script himself, putting on different voices). Only a handful actually played it straight.

By 14 March three names had emerged as the frontrunners: Michael Crawford, Liam Cunningham and Robert Lindsay, although enquires were still being made about Billy Connolly, Paul McGann, Trevor Eve, Roger Rees, Eric Idle and Aidan Quinn. A week on, and Liam Cunningham was now the only 'under consideration' of those seen, because Robert Lindsay's agent let the Hubbards know that he'd been offered a job that would take him away filming until 17 July (the plan was to shoot *Who* from 1 July onward).

By now Albert Finney was added to the Borusa list of maybes, although Peter O'Toole had described the offer made to him as 'acceptable'. The next day, Liam Cunningham was reported to be in Los Angeles for ten weeks from 2 April doing a play, and that put him effectively out of the running as well.

Paul McGann was sought by the production team from very early on in the casting process, but his busy schedule meant that two years would pass before they could work together.

After several weeks of downtime, I received a call from one of the Universal executives, Bill Hamm, who asked if he could set up a meeting between me and another writer who was interested in working on *Doctor Who*. His name was Robert DeLaurentis. I had met Bob several times and we got along quite well. I always found him to be what I like to refer to as a 'thinking' writer. He would have to understand the motivation of a character or the drive of a storyline through mythic lore or literature. I was fond of the way he developed material.

But if Bob had one fault it was procrastination. If you didn't go round and round in circles with him endless times on something he could not mentally stamp it 'approved' and move on. We often sat for hours going round and round. I never lost my

It was also around this time that my partner in all this, Peter Wagg, was getting restless. He had patiently gone through one misfire, one pre-scout trip and one overdeveloped bible, which we had of course done during the Leekley era. Peter came to me one day and dropped a bomb. He announced he was returning to England to live and therefore could not continue to be involved in *Doctor Who*. I was sad but knew and understood that waiting for as many years as Peter had would tax anyone. I was so grateful for all his support.

In some ways, Peter was the only grounding rod I ever had. There were so many times I

It was the strength of such powerful performances as his role in *The Monocled Mutineer* (left) that brought Paul McGann to the attention of *Doctor Who*'s producers. Later, *The Hanging Gale* (below) would further pique their interest.

patience with Bob – I just got bored with him. Don't get me wrong, he's a good writer – I personally just have a problem with guys who have written on the staff of shows for a long time. When you push, though, and do manage to get original thought from someone like Bob, he's pretty damn good!

At this point, I was aware of a rapidly advanced state of apathy towards this project at studio level. Bob's prevaricating thought processes made *Doctor Who*'s development even more arduous. Bob created a show for Universal and NBC called *Man and Machine* that was his idea of science fiction. It wasn't mine, but I knew that the studio would never let me develop another script that required them to spend hard dollars on the project. Simply put, I was always forced to work with writers Universal had under contract. This way, Universal could write off or write down the cost and charge it against the money they had advanced to writers like Bob for remaining exclusive to Universal for a predetermined period of time.

So without fanfare, we went back to work on the script. This time, we ended up so far away from the heart and soul of *Doctor Who* that it was painful. In my heart I felt that I was letting down the fans and everyone else who had fought so hard with me to get this franchise back on its feet. The funny thing is, when you put negative energy out into the universe, negative things happen, and, sure enough, the DeLaurentis version was doomed to fail. Even if the network had approved it, I knew in my heart that the BBC would not.

Chris Bowen – who had already appeared as Mordred in the 1989 *Doctor Who* story *Battlefield* – was another auditioning contender on 9 March 1994.

felt like I wanted to explode and tell everyone to get lost. Only Peter's influence prevented that from happening. In truth, he was the only one I ever listened to. Strangely, however, even though Peter had announced his intentions, little did he know he had one last hurrah left and it was about to come in the form of reprieve for *Doctor Who*. But more on that a little later. Back to Bob DeLaurentis ...

Several weeks after Bob had turned in his draft to the network for review (and hopeful approval), I received a call from Fox, telling me that they did not want to proceed with Bob as the writer. I was stuck. Fox also sent another shocker my way: they asked if we could go back to the Leekley version of the script. Now I have to say that, secretly, I liked Leekley's script very much. Granted, it needed some work, but I always believed John understood the mythic proportions and possibilities of the programme. Looking back,

I think that we could have made a pretty good team.

I had the rough task of telling DeLaurentis that Fox did not want to proceed with him on the project. I felt bad for Bob. It's never easy when someone tells you your work is not appreciated or needed, especially for writers – a very vulnerable breed indeed! But Bob took it stoically. We shook hands, hugged, and that was the end of that.

The events during 1994 were both fast and furious. Calendars were created, charting the proposed time it would take to get the show up and running, with specific dates earmarked – 24 January saw the start of the bible-writing (which ending up costing over $100,000); 31 January was Richard Lewis's date to begin the design phase; 21 March was the pitch to the US network; and so on, with dates marked for each of the individual episode scripts to commence and be delivered, plus shooting dates etc.

Peter Wagg spent much of his time between London and Los Angeles. As executive producer, he was now the driving force behind the day-to-day work, while Philip Segal and John Leekley concentrated on getting the bible done in time. As Wagg sorted out his schedules, ensuring that the Daleks and Cybs would be ready, Philip concentrated on ensuring that certain important stock items were available to them, such as the TARDIS prop. Of course they weren't, which meant added costs of building even the most basic items, which the BBC had decided to sell off or destroy a few years earlier.

By this time a US visual-effects company, XFX, run by Steve Johnson, was pitching to collaborate with Richard Lewis, as was All Effects, while other construction companies, Stetson and also Burmans, were bidding to build the Daleks.

And then a story broke in the British press that was to give all concerned their first taste of what was to come. *The Mirror* announced that David Hasselhoff had been cast as the Doctor. The team were understandably astonished, since Hasselhoff was an actor who had never featured in their imaginations, let alone had any contact with them. They were even more astonished by a selection of the letters the BBC received from fans on the subject, sent over to LA by Tony Greenwood, all addressed to a no doubt bemused Steven Spielberg. Comments ranged from the impassioned and abusive to the impassioned and open-minded. As for *The Mirror*'s promised talking-TARDIS idea, well, apparently it was *'as stupid as they come. After all* The Planet of the Daleks *and the* New Adventure *novels state that the TARDIS has telepathic circuits attuned to the Doctor's brainwave pattern. Also* The Two Doctors *states that the Doctor and the TARDIS have a symbiotic relationship via the Rassilon*

Imprimature otherwise known as a Time Lord's symbiotic nuclei.'

Faced with an in-tray like that, it's no wonder the Amblin and Universal executives, unlike the BBC, who were used to such diatribes, were scratching their heads, wondering what on earth they had taken on. Not least Tony Thomopolous, Amblin's president, who received a number of letters suggesting which past Doctors/companions should be employed. 'The Whovians walk amongst us ...' was his scribbled comment on one such letter. 'Help ...' was on another.

On the positive side, they also had a number of calmer people offering their services to the project as *Doctor Who* experts, reasoning that a 30-year-old show had a lot of history which, while not necessarily needing to be adhered to, should at least not be contradicted. None were taken up, however.

In the middle of March 1994, the Daltenrays team announced their deal with Lumiere and 'an unnamed third party' to make a *Doctor Who* motion picture at the same time as Amblin's TV project. Interestingly, Lumiere themselves actually declined to comment on the reports, suggesting to some observers that all was not well in that camp. Universal got quite agitated over this, wondering why the BBC were effectively granting a licence (albeit not an identical one) to produce something new around the same property. As if that wasn't hard enough, the agents working on behalf of the Daleks' creator, Terry Nation, were asking what Philip considered financially to be 'way out of line'. He was forced to ask Tony Greenwood what the BBC's take on the Daleks was, and whether they were 'crucial to the return of *Doctor Who*. I personally believe we have no show without them.'

The pitch to the networks (NBC first, CBS second) took place in the last week of March, and, with the bible completed, Richard Lewis left the production on 29 March. By the end of April, it looked as if Peter Tortorici, the president of CBS Entertainment, was going for the pitch, although only for a two-hour pilot and six episodes, presumably as a potential midseason replacement for a failed show.

The delays and changes effectively killed the plans to shoot in July; instead a date of 19 September was set as the start date for the pilot. In the middle of May, the CBS deal was off – indeed, it had never really been on. Verbal negotiations between Amblin and CBS had taken place, but as yet there was no written agreement. Amblin were particularly embar-rassed by this, since both Universal and the BBC had been very excited about CBS. By the end of May, they had their hopes pinned on Fox, but even then they knew this could be only for a

two-hour *Movie of the Week*, with an option for a second two-hour movie later. The original plan for whole new series seemed to be an improbability now.

Meanwhile, Philip and Peter were taking an extended period in London, talking to actors, companies, writers' agents (a number of previous *Who* writers, Eric Saward, Johnny Byrne, Malcolm Kholl and Pip and Jane Baker, all contacted Philip about work at various points) and even talking to representatives of musicians who wanted the opportunity to have a bash at revamping the theme tune for the 1990s. Both Cybertech – who the year before had provided the music for the BBC's *Dimensions in Time* effort – and a group called the Future Sound of London were very interested, the latter actually producing a demo version.

On returning to Los Angeles, Philip received a computer-generated image (CGI) of the

Actor and mimic John Sessions not only played both the Doctor and Napoleon in his audition, but improvised nearly five minutes of additional dialogue in his bid for the part.

new-style Dalek from Amblin Imaging. He sent a copy of the tape over to Tony Greenwood – and a clip from this ended up being shown to a rather sceptical general public on the ITV show *Gamesmaster* shortly afterwards.

At this time, the freelance writer and *Doctor Who* fan Jean-Marc Lofficier entered the picture, offering his services to Peter Wagg as a *Doctor Who* technical adviser. Apart from his background in writing, he had authored a number of reference books on *Doctor Who*, most of which were on both producers' bookshelves. Peter passed this on to Philip – having a Los Angeles-based expert seemed a far better idea than having one in London, and Lofficier would provide a useful buffer between the voracious organised fandom and Amblin.

By 28 June, Fox had confirmed they wanted a 'back-door pilot', a *Movie of the Week*, which, if hugely popular, might transfer over to their

From his audition, it is clear that Rob Heyland, best known for his role in the BBC vet series *One by One*, had the potential to be a very good new Doctor.

series department. This meant that the network need order episodes only in batches of 13 rather than the traditional 26, thus cutting down their commitment.

Peter Wagg needed to kick everything into gear very quickly now. Casting became imperative, with Wagg saying his top three choices were the American movie actor Jeff Goldblum ('Jeff doesn't do TV' was his representative's response, but he would read a script), Liam Cunningham and John Slattery, who was on Broadway at the time. He later added Aidan Quinn, Kyle MacLachlan, Matt Frewer, David Strathairn, Rutgar Hauer, Chris Issak, Michael Biehn and Gary Sinese to his list. By the end of July Peter had his cast down to Jeff Goldblum, Aidan Quinn and Kyle MacLachlan (Liam Cunningham having accepted a film that put him out of Wagg's time frame).

Philip was busy trying to get his hands on stock footage of Blitz-torn London for the designers and preparing to tie up a deal with the Irish-born actor, Peter O'Toole. All Effects were given the brief of what was needed in terms of creatures and props (Davros, Daleks, sonic screwdriver, the TARDIS itself …). The promotional log line 'He's back and it's about Time' was adopted. Things were slowly but surely coming together.

However, in London, Alan Yentob was becoming disturbed by the lack of British actor in the running for the Doctor. It had been his one stipulation to Philip and Peter. Philip assured Yentob and Michael Wearing that they had done all they could. A London shoot now seemed out of the question because of the rising budget and delays in getting the network deal – and then there had been the negotiations with Peter O'Toole over playing the part of Borusa. To add to the complications, if they were going to use O'Toole, it would require a five-day shoot in the UK, because he could not leave Britain, and the BBC would have to fund it.

The London casting agents John and Ros Hubbard, meanwhile, were still suggesting new possibilities. They again investigated Robert Lindsay, but he was not available until after March 1995. They also retried for Hugh Laurie and Julian Wadham, who had been seen and liked by Peter Wagg back in March, and who, the Hubbards felt, 'would be brilliant'. A number of agents said that their clients would not be averse to a three- or five-year commitment and these included Jason Connery, Rik Mayall, Ade Edmonson, James Frain, Art Malik, Nigel Havers, Nick Le Prevost, Oliver Cotton, Valentine Pelka, Alexis Denisoff, Mark McGann, Clive Carter, Brendan Gleeson, Chris Blake, Martin Jarvis, Tim McInnerny, Robert Reynolds, Patrick Ryecart, Chris Eccleston, David Essex, Simon Shepherd, Larry Lamb, Gary Cady, William Chubb, James Purefoy, Adrian Rawlings, Greg Cruttwell, Chris Guard, David Hunt and Richard Bourneville.

Nevertheless, the newly revised planned commencement of filming in November was beginning to look more and more likely. And on 16 August another name re-entered the frame. Paul McGann had come out of various telephone calls between the BBC and the Amblin sides – and, although they had discussed him previously, very little had come of it. A copy of the bible was sent to his agent from Philip, plus a run-down of the current plans, should his interest be piqued and he be free from his commitments to the major BBC drama *The Hanging Gale*, in which he starred with his three brothers. The letter explained that it was effectively a pilot and that, if it did go to a series, then production would start in July 1995 for thirteen episodes, to be shot over the subsequent thirty weeks. This would mean that, if it was a success, McGann would be free for three months between seasons to do other work.

Another person Philip contacted – in a somewhat ironic twist, bearing in mind how he came to meet up with Peter Wagg – was the director Alan Parker. He wondered if Parker would consider helming the pilot, some of which might now be filmed in Vancouver, Canada, and some in Denver or Utah. His reply was a pleasant 'thanks, but no thanks'.

Peter Wagg then compiled a list of potential directors. These included Leonard Nimoy, Jon Amiel, Michael Apted, John Badham, Kathryn Bigelow, Martin Brest, Michael Caton-Jones, Brian Spicer, Joe Dante, Brian Grant, Philip Noyce, Jim O'Brien, Carl Schutz, Ridley Scott, Mark Tinker, Ron Underwood, Peter Weir, James Whitmore Jnr, Simon Wincer and Rod Holcolm.

BBC Children's Books then got in contact – the first real hint of the commercial exploitation that would follow. They wanted to do a big glossy '*Making Of*' book, heavily illustrated, but Philip was cautious – put off slightly by the fact that it was the Children's Books department and feeling that picture books would not accurately reflect the direction in which he saw the movie going. In London, during a break from the filming of *The Hanging Gale*, the Hubbards and Peter Wagg met with Paul McGann and videotaped a casting session with him, playing the Doctor with John Hubbard reading the Borusa part, and an American actress called Lisa reading in Lizzie. And that swung it for everyone.

In Coventry, England, at the annual *Doctor Who* convention *PanoptiCon*, Sylvester McCoy let slip that one of his mates, Paul McGann, had been asked to play the Doctor. Intrigued but with an understandable built-in cynicism, the British fans nodded politely. We'll believe it when we see it, they seemed to be saying. Too often there had been definites, absolutes and undoubtedlys given to them about *Doctor*

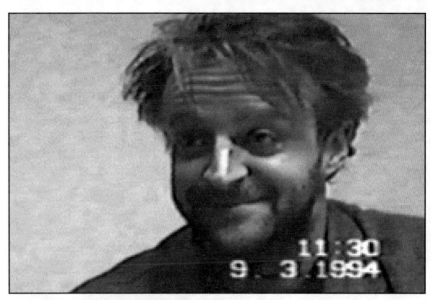

Actor Paul Bown gave a spirited performance for his 1994 audition.

Who's future. One more really made little impact.

Meanwhile, the moment all parties saw the tape they knew they had cast the eighth Doctor. Other actors were still being touted by their agents for the part, including the likes of Simon MacCorkindale and even Tim Curry, but by this time everyone had their heart set on Paul McGann. Which was fine until 26 September, when Philip had to break the news that the project may have to be pulled, owing to script problems. Steven Spielberg didn't like the script and wanted a new writer brought aboard, which meant delaying the whole shoot until February 1995 at the earliest, moving from Utah to British Columbia in Canada. Enter Robert DeLaurentis, with a new script which still didn't meet the requirements and was quickly abandoned, and so, as the production team greeted a new year, they greeted a whole new batch of problems ...

• 1994 •

THE LEEKLEY BIBLE

The attractive and costly leather-bound bible produced for the Leekley project. The symbol on the front is taken directly from the Doctor's note to the Castellan seen in the 1976 adventure *The Deadly Assassin*.

One of the first, and most expensive, things prepared by Amblin was the New Series Document, or 'bible', to be used by prospective writers, directors and actors as a guide to what *Doctor Who* was all about. Lavishly illustrated with production drawings and paintings to give an idea what the alien planets or creatures or the TARDIS interior might look like, it came wrapped in a special leather jacket, with the then new logo and some Gallifreyan script on it. A very plush-looking document, it is also, with the power of hindsight, a very interesting historical one, too. It conveys very simply just how far removed from 'traditional', BBC *Doctor Who* Amblin were prepared to let their new series be.

Essentially, this is a reinvention of the series from scratch, leading off from John Leekley's pilot script and setting up what may as well have been an entirely new programme that merely used the original series' name and some of its trademarks as useful marketing tools. Let's be honest here: a majority of die-hard *Doctor Who* fans would have loathed a series created along this format, and yet commercially it is undeniably a very shrewd idea. With no 'kisses to the past', it was far more likely to appeal to a US network looking for a new science-fiction format than one that had a 30-year back-story which the average American viewer would have no chance of understanding.

Leekley himself wrote the bible, along with input from Philip Segal and Peter Wagg. It takes the form of a document created by the Doctor's grandfather, Barusa (obviously this is a case of borrowing, and misspelling, an established *Who* character name – indeed, occasionally in the bible it is correctly spelt Borusa), and goes through the new show's set-up. It ends with a run-down of a number of potential stories.

Whether Amblin automatically had the right to borrow story titles/content willy-nilly from past *Doctor Who* stories is a bit of a grey area. Certainly they believed they did and asked more than once for this to be clarified. No answer was ever forthcoming. So, had Amblin gone ahead, just who would have paid Eric Saward for the reuse (and misuse) of *Earthshock,* Terrance Dicks for *The Horror of Fang Rock,* Donald Cotton for *The Gunfighters,* and so on? In the end, most probably the BBC, which could have been potentially the most expensive cock-up they could make, so it was lucky for all concerned that it never actually got that far, that the Leekley side of things fell through, that the series died a death and no one actually had to worry if the writers Mervyn Haisman and Henry Lincoln would object to having Professor Travers become Sir Edmund Hillary and the Yeti being cute and shy rather than aggressive and robotic.

Reprinted here, then, is that bible in all its textual glory, complete with Barusa/Borusa typographical variants and Leekley's own, rather bizarre, idea of when police boxes first came into existence. Bet you didn't know they had them in America as well …

The Chronicles of Doctor Who?

I AM CARDINAL BARUSA … TIME LORD OF GALLIFREY

This is my official insignia, and my personal glyph. Having transcended the confines of body, I exist now amidst the crystals of the Domed City of Gallifrey, which resonate with their beautiful sounds … much like the wind chimes along the seas of the Blue Planet … the place you call Earth.

I have decreed that my adventures with the Doctor and his flying ship, the TARDIS, in our quest to find his father Ulysses the Explorer, be written down by a scribe. I have instructed him to write these chronicles in the language of the Blue Planet, in long flowing script, because I believe that is the way the Doctor prefers it. Our own hieroglyphics of Gallifrey can't capture the real adventure of it all, our glyphs are far too precise … they are meant to convey the logic of the law, and the science of time travel, which are the two proud hallmarks of Gallifrey. This odd elliptical language of the Blue Planet is far more appropriate to the Doctor, who seems to prefer humour over efficiency.

The Doctor wishes the people of the Blue Planet to know of our travels … to see for themselves that these worlds we have visited are not so

distant after all. Those companions who travelled with us in our adventures can attest to this … if they will be believed by humankind …

TIME TRAVEL

This is the supreme gift of Rassilon, the founder of our dynasty, who, millennia ago harnessed the power of a Black Hole. This fathomless power brought to the Time Lords mastery over the fourth and fifth dimensions. We found that we could travel back in time. The Time Lords of Gallifrey monitor and record the significant events on the planets in this Galaxy and beyond, throughout time and space. They are recorded in the Matrix … as well as all of the life experiences, feelings and memories of the Time Lords, themselves. The Matrix is our record of life in the Universe, contained in the Panopticon. This is our heritage and our duty.

Until the TARDIS ships were perfected, some of our early Time Lords were lost in time, and never returned. We have found a few, by accident … but many will be travelling for an eternity. Unable to get back home to the Domed City, that jewel under glass … or to the windswept mesas and bottomless canyons of Gallifrey.

The most legendary Time Explorer was Ulysses, a hero among the citizens of Gallifrey. His fate is unknown to the general populace … but not to me.

Ulysses the Explorer was my son. And, in turn, Ulysses had a son … who, in later lives, was

An artist's impression of the Leekley Gallifrey – a beautiful planet with the massive Time Lord city encased in a protective crystal dome. Perhaps the spire in the foreground is based on the Dark Tower of Rassilon from the 1983 adventure *The Five Doctors*?

Philip Segal and Pete Ware took a trip to Utah to recce potential locations for Gallifrey. Most of the sequences featuring the Doctor finding the scrolls and facing a Dalek creature would have been shot here.

called the Master. The Master's ruthless ambition was to wrap himself in the Sash of Rassilon ... worn only by the President of the High Council ... the Sash I had worn for so long. Rather than using our immense powers for the spread of enlightenment to all races, The Master wished only to conquer and rule.

IN THIS TIME OF DANGER AND TURMOIL

The Doctor and the Master were the two greatest minds to emerge in the millennia since Rassilon. It was strange that two such towering figures were born in the same era of time, as if somehow brought forward by nature ... as if by

the planet itself. And as the years went by, the Doctor grew in his powers ... of intellect and telepathy. After seven regenerations, he seemed to us, the Time Lords, to be the only leader capable of standing up to the Master and his followers.

However, there were those that distrusted his exuberance. The Doctor was as irrepressible as when he was a youngster. Although the Doctor was by then 800 years old, he had the body of man 30 years old ... and he was still rebellious and curious, usually beyond our patience.

He would often time travel to the Blue Planet Earth and, against our strict rules and traditions, would meddle with history ... interfering with the affairs of other worlds ...

• Entry remark ... I am reminded by my scribe that there may be a confusion concerning our Gallifreyan ability to regenerate. In the terms of the Blue Planet, it is both a death and a rebirth. It is very sacred and profound to us ... also agonisingly painful. Regenerations are triggered in several ways ... old age ... mortal accident ... by decree of the Time Lord Council ... or by will.

A regeneration produces a completely different body, chosen by the unconscious much like a dream is chosen ... and it profoundly affects one's personality and memory. I, for example, in an earlier regeneration, became a megalomaniac. Happily it was a phase that passed ...

HE WAS CALLED DOCTOR

There may be a confusion concerning the word 'Doctor'. On the Blue Planet, that word is used for medical advisors. The Doctor feels that medical practitioners are quite useful, like automobile mechanics, which are a group he very much admires. But on Gallifrey, a Doctor is one who has mastered all fields of knowledge.

The Doctor is also a tinker and a lover of inventions. For many yeas, he has escaped the clutches of intergalactic bounty hunters, monsters, and killing machines with his ingenuity and quick wits. But I am obliged to admit that the Doctor is also irascible, eccentric, and exasperating.

He is very secretive. One minute everything is going splendidly … and suddenly he will shut you out if he does not wish you to know the plan he is devising. He can be happy, even giddy, but can quickly turn dark and brooding if he has picked up some obscure hint of danger or deception. This is how a fugitive stays alive.

He seems to be unable to simply travel from point A to point B. He loves oblique tangents, and can easily be diverted from his apparent mission.

Only later do you realise he never intended to go to the first location anyway … it was all planned.

The Doctor preferred not to use force. Although he was a master of the martial arts, and usually used the force of the enemy back against the enemy. However, the truth must be stated that he occasionally relished a good fight … He is also the most stubborn man in the Galaxy … and certainly not modest.

Here, for an example, is a journal entry from the night before the Battle of Waterloo …

• June 17, 1815 … The Doctor is in the tent of Emperor Napoleon … sharing an excellent glass of brandy, and trying to convince him of the necessity to protect his flanks. Napoleon has interrupted …

NAPOLEON: You seem well versed in military history, sir. Who are you?
THE DOCTOR: I am the Doctor
NAPOLEON: What sort of Doctor are you?
THE DOCTOR: I'm not a Doctor … I am the Doctor. The definite article, you might say …
NAPOLEON: And what are you the doctor of?
THE DOCTOR: A great many things. Temporal engineering, metaphysics, archaeology, history, quantum mechanics, astronomy, medicine … the things one must know.
NAPOLEON: I have never heard of quantum mechanics …
THE DOCTOR: It hasn't been invented yet.
NAPOLEON: That's very impressive …
THE DOCTOR: Well, you see I'm a genius.
NAPOLEON: Temporal engineering? Can you engineer time?
THE DOCTOR: (grins) Let's just say that I'm a tinkerer. Now, back to my concerns about

Waterloo … As the Master has always said, the Doctor's chief weakness is his curiosity. He can't help meddling in the business of other worlds and cultures.

• Journal Entry, 4 am that morning … The Doctor walks out of Napoleon's tent, and into the TARDIS … shaking his head. I have just illuminated the crystals, and am running through the circuits …

THE DOCTOR: Napoleon has had too much brandy … he's not thinking clearly …
BARUSA: It is strictly forbidden to meddle in the affairs of other races …
THE DOCTOR: (noticing my work) What are you doing?
BARUSA: I have been working on the repair of the dematerialisation circuit in order to activate the chameleon device.
THE DOCTOR: Why are you messing with that?
BARUSA: This Type 40 you 'borrowed' is a great and classic ship. Just possibly, if I can repair it, we can be rid of this ridiculous exterior, this Blue Police Box.
THE DOCTOR: I like it.
BARUSA: How can I make you comprehend that a London Police Box will seem a bit out of place in a great many places in the Galaxy? … For example, outside Napoleon's tent.
THE DOCTOR: He thinks it's a portable out-house … he likes the idea. He's forward thinking …
BARUSA: It belongs in the London Museum, in the section for obsolete and silly artifacts of the Victorian era.

He ignores me. The good Doctor is quite sentimental … the worst trait conceivable for any Gallifreyan. I believe he keeps his ship in the outside dimension of a Police Box just to irritate me …

THE DOCTOR: Tomorrow, forty thousand men will die, their blood draining into the grass … for a mistake he is about to make. I can stop it.
BARUSA: There are strict rules about this sort of meddling.
THE DOCTOR: (goading him) Rules are meant to be broken.
BARUSA: After almost two thousand years, I should have peace in my golden years. Instead, we have been dodging Dalek killing machines, trying to keep our scalps from ending up on Cyb lances … and here you are trying to change the entire history of civilisation.
THE DOCTOR: (grinning) Things are never dull …
BARUSA: We have a quest … to find your father. Shall we get on with it?!
THE DOCTOR: (nodding) So … what are we waiting for? Power up the Crystals, Cardinal … let's go exploring …

As the great ship vanishes with a eerie whoosh, the Doctor looks back at Napoleon, standing outside his tent, staring off at the field where the

The Utah locations were also perfect for John Leekley's vision of the desert wasteland of Skaro.

The Leekley bible was beautifully illustrated with drawings and paintings of the proposed TARDIS interior sets. This version of the Console Room also incorporates the Gothic cathedral look of the Cloister Room as seen in the final movie, made two years later.

Battle of Waterloo will commence in the morning … tired and worn out from endless campaigns … staring into the night and fog …

THE DOCTOR: (to himself) Forty thousand. Humans are such a mystery …

THE CHRONICLES OF DOCTOR WHO

In that time, so long ago, when I first ventured forth with the Doctor on his adventures in our Galaxy and beyond, things were not so hopeful for my world of Gallifrey as they are now. In those days, all around our fabulous Domed City, which sits like a cluster of jewels under glass, the vast mesas were ripping open, forming gigantic canyons which threatened to tear the entire city apart.

It is a mystery, even to us Time Lords, why the geologic forces of our planet reflect exactly our own cumulative consciousness. We, and our tragic planet, are one and the same.

Within the Domed City, the forces of darkness, led by the Master, threatened to tip the balance of power among the Time Lords. The Master's dark dream was the domination of all life forms in our Galaxy. Like a stained liquid, his teachings had seeped into the cold logic of the bureaucrats and law makers. Our ancient wisdom had been lost.

The time came in which we were forced to decide the future of or planet. In the Panopticon, the Time Lords met. I announced what had long

been rumoured, that my twelfth and final regeneration was about to happen.

These were my words, from the record … 'According to our ancient custom, my heir will wear the Sash of Rassilon upon my death. The Master is brilliant, but he is cruel and ambitious. He is the perfect embodiment of our worst as a race … without feeling or affection.

It is the Doctor's thinking which has begun to change the way we are …. to turn our fate from Darkness … to save our planet. Without strong hearts, we will evolve to become like the Master. Our Gallifrey, so beautifully stark, so solemn with its quiet mesas and its harsh sun-burnt canyons, will shatter unless we turn from the Master's dreams of domination … The Doctor offers a change … he is admired for his exuberant character, his energy, and fullness of life. He and his Time Lord supporters are our only hope.

I therefore propose we break with our traditions … that the Doctor, although he is an orphan from a clan that has died out, take my place as President of the Time Lords and wearer of the Sash of Rassilon upon my death …'

The Time Lords were bitterly divided … between the supporters of the Master … and the supporters of the Doctor, who offered a new vision, a revival of the classic era … of exploration, science, and peace.

The Doctor finally stood to speak. He accused the Time Lords, himself included, of dereliction of their sacred oath … which was to nourish all the races and bring harmony to the Galaxy and beyond. He said that they had ruled this Galaxy for so long that they had become the perfect bureaucrats … cold efficiency had replaced wisdom … they had lost their hears and souls.

The Time Lords were shocked and outraged. No one had ever challenged them in this way. In their indignation and fury, they exiled the Doctor forever.

The Doctor left the Domed City, and set off into the barren and inhospitable desert … The Master demanded to be given the Sash … and upon my death, it came to pass. Being of my bloodline, and that of my son Ulysses the Explorer, the Master was entitled to be President. But the Doctor was always more favoured by our people. For these reasons and more, the Master reserved his purest venom and hatred for him … and plotted his destruction.

IT WAS WRITTEN AND FORETOLD

For weeks and months, The Doctor wandered in the desert wilderness … searching for the Tomb of Rassilon. Even the Time Lords are not allowed in this forbidden zone. Against the ferocious winds hurling sand, he searched the caves on the face of the cliff, from which the Tomb had been carved. He went for weeks without eating or drinking, using his powers of physiological control to reduce his breathing, and to halt one of his two hearts to conserve his life.

But it was not enough, even for the Doctor. He was found, near death, by the tribal peoples of the wilderness … called the Outcasts. He was nursed back to health by them, and when they learnt who he was, he was shown the hidden caves which are the entrance to the Tomb of Rassilon. It is they who are the true keepers of the Tomb. Their reputation for ferocity is due to their complete dedication to Rassilon … The Doctor told us later that he was called by the voice of his father … finally he found what he was searching for. By crawling deep into the heart of the mountain, which was in reality the heart of the Tomb of Rassilon, he discovered an earthen pot … and inside were the Sacred Scrolls. He had found what no man had seen since Rassilon had placed it there, millennia ago. The Doctor has never revealed their place of hiding.

THE TRUTH MUST BE KNOWN

I was unaware of these events, as at that time I was dying. I had clung to life as long as I could … knowing that the Master was waiting, like a wolf at my door.

The Doctor secretly smuggled himself back into the Domed City … and came to see me on my death bed. He told me of the scrolls and said this about their contents … it was written and foretold that whoever finds the Scrolls shall lead the people of Gallifrey out of the Darkness, and prevent the planet from shattering.
The Scrolls revealed that the answers would not lie in Gallifrey itself … but beyond our world, beyond the Galaxy. His telepathy told him that the answers would lie on Earth … It was then that I admitted the truth of his birth … it was time that the truth be known. The Master and the Doctor are both of my bloodline. They are half-brothers.

They were born to my son Ulysses the Explorer, who has been missing for centuries from Gallifrey. The two brothers are born of different mothers … which is why they look so different. The Doctor was born on the Blue Planet … his mother was human.

The Doctor watched over me a long time … he seemed to already have sensed this. Finally, he asked me why I had not told anyone of this in the past.

I said, 'The Master is the elder, born of Gallifrey, and therefore the rightful heir to the Sash. You could never prove you were also the son of Ulysses … in fact, because your mother was from the Blue Planet, you would have never been allowed to be a Time Lord. Everything you have to offer us would have been lost … you would have become an Outcast, sent to the wilderness to live among the savages …' Then he nodded, smiled, and held me a long moment. He said, 'I have to find my father …' He kissed my cheek … and said goodbye. It is an affection we on Gallifrey never do. It was strange and wonderful.

The eventual TARDIS set as built for the 1996 TV Movie used many concepts created for the 1994 feature bible. Philip Segal was always very keen on the TARDIS being all wood and brass, very Heath Robinson meets Jules Verne – directly inspired by the Primary TARDIS console room first seen in the 1976 adventure *The Hand of Fear*.

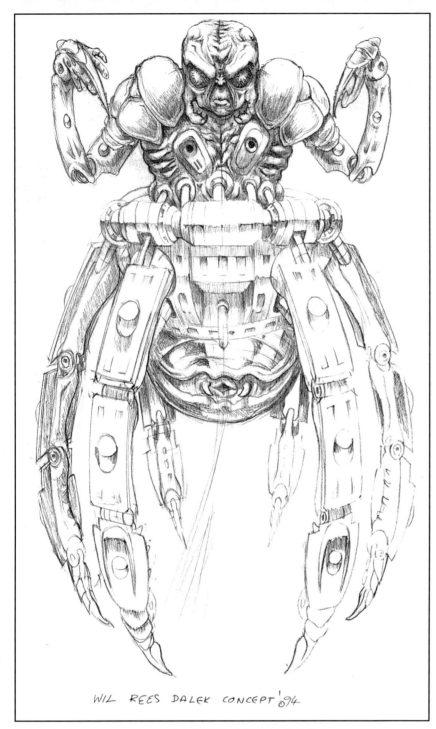

WIL REES DALEK CONCEPT '94

A modified Dalek creature in a variant Dalek casing.

inoperable. He didn't seem to care.

At the moment of my death, as my soul rose above my body, freed at last from the endless cycle of return, I was drawn inexplicably toward the Doctor … my spirit fused with the Doctor's TARDIS, just as it vanished back in time and space, toward the Blue Planet.

I found myself carried along on a great adventure … in control of the Doctor's ship … The Master began a hunt for the Doctor through the Galaxy. However, among the people of Gallifrey, once cannot kill one's own blood relatives … it would mean the destruction of the killer himself. That is how we are.

Unable to personally destroy his own brother, the Master sent his killing machines … the Daleks, to find him. An intergalactic pursuit … And thus began the odyssey of the Doctor, this strange man … this fugitive Time Lord in search of his father. And myself … existing only in the resonating crystals of the great TARDIS.

The story of the Doctor is intertwined, strangely enough, with the Blue Planet …

THE BLUE PLANET

Time has brought mountains to the sea … and seas have dried to dust and blown away. Planets have turned themselves inside out, lava has flowed for aeons, new mountains have risen. The rains began, forming the endless oceans. And this little planet, in a far corner of the Milky Way, turned blue.

I have seen these things with my eyes. Together with the Doctor, I have travelled back, all the way to the beginnings of history on the Blue Planet. We have seen the roar and the spectacle of humankind. The Doctor is a part of their history … he belongs equally to the Blue Planet and to Gallifrey.

The Doctor, my grandson, was unique to us. In so many ways. And it is fitting and proper that he would have begun his life in adventure and romance and tragedy. He is the only Time Lord that ever lived who was born on another planet. Although he was never told this, I think he somehow knew.

The essential conflict between the Doctor's birth on the Blue Planet and his origins in Gallifrey explains his odd personality contradictions. He is of two worlds.

I remember when he was a boy on Gallifrey, after his early and tragic first death, he would stare for hours into the night sky, at a small system known as the Solar. He never knew why the Blue Planet called out to him. What did he seek there? Like the vague remembrances of a past life, what he didn't know was that his first regeneration took place on the Blue Planet.

INTERGALACTIC FUGITIVE

Because the Time Lords were now under the control of the Master, they voted to condemn the Doctor to total disintegration, making him a wanted man … a fugitive. The Master could never let the Doctor return. He had to destroy the Doctor simply in order to keep his place of power.

The Time Lords hunted for the Doctor. To escape Gallifrey, he 'borrowed' an old TARDIS … a Type 40. This is our time capsule, which can convey the Explorer to any planet or ship in the Universe, at any time in the past. It was in need of repairs … the steering mechanism was faulty and its chameleon cloaking device was

I blame myself for this longing he could not name. As President of the Time Lord Council, I had the responsibility to hold my shattering planet together. I knew even then that one day the Doctor would wear the Sash … The people of Gallifrey only knew that the Doctor's father never returned from his voyages. They assumed the Doctor was an offspring from one of our space colonies.

They never knew the truth … that his mother was a human … an extraordinarily beautiful and bewitching woman from the Blue Planet. Her name was Annalisse.

His father, Ulysses, having fallen in love, never returned to me … or to our sacred soil … not even in death. He gave up his status as Time Lord, as well as his immortality to be in the arms of a simple peasant girl. Ulysses was my son … but I never understood him. His spirit was not of Gallifrey. Ulysses could have worn the Sash of Rassilon, but chose instead to be an explorer travelling through time. He was the most rebellious Time Lord in history … until his son the Doctor. I suppose you could say that the Doctor comes by it honestly … I have asked the scribe to decode my journal entry on the night of November 23, 1994 …

The TARDIS has brought us to a dusty corner of the basement of the Cairo Museum, in Egypt. These are the last coordinates we ever received from Ulysses the Explorer. We have found a sarcophagus, once buried in the great pyramid of Giza … the hieroglyphics painted on the outside reveal it was created for the pharaoh Cheops. The face painted on the outside is that of Ulysses … It appears to have been Ulysses who taught the ancient Egyptians to construct such magnificent wonders as the pyramids. It was like him to do so … It seemed to us that it was the fate of his son, the Doctor, to find his remains … but it was not to be.

When we opened the sarcophagus, it was empty … inside was only an inscription, in the hieroglyphics of Gallifrey, a message from Ulysses … 'To my son, who will search for me. Forgive me for leaving you behind. One day we will find each other again …' Oddly, the Doctor seems very pleased … he is seated among the other mummies, smoking a cigar and relating the events of his life. He seems to believe the mummy next to him is listening.

THE TARDIS

The Doctor roams the Galaxy in a great ship known to its inventors, us Time Lords, as a TARDIS. The letters stand for Time And Relative Dimensions In Space and is far more than just a time machine. It is capable of transporting its operator and passengers through time and space to any planet in the Universe and to any point in that planet's history.

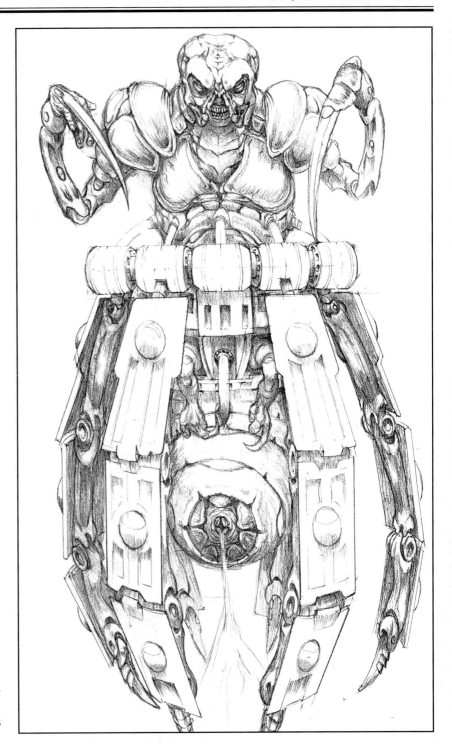

The Doctor's is an old 'type 40' TARDIS built as a mobile research laboratory which would carry its crew of scientists to survey distant galaxies, explore new worlds and observe astronomical events. The type 40 TARDIS has since been superseded by more efficient and better equipped models.

The chameleon circuit, a device incorporated into the ship's circuitry, scans the landing site and alters that site just prior to materialisation. Under normal circumstances, the TARDIS would look like a cactus, a stone pillar, or anything else which would blend with the surroundings of the planet on which it had landed. Unfortunately, after the Doctor's visit to Earth, the mechanism failed to function and ever since, the TARDIS has

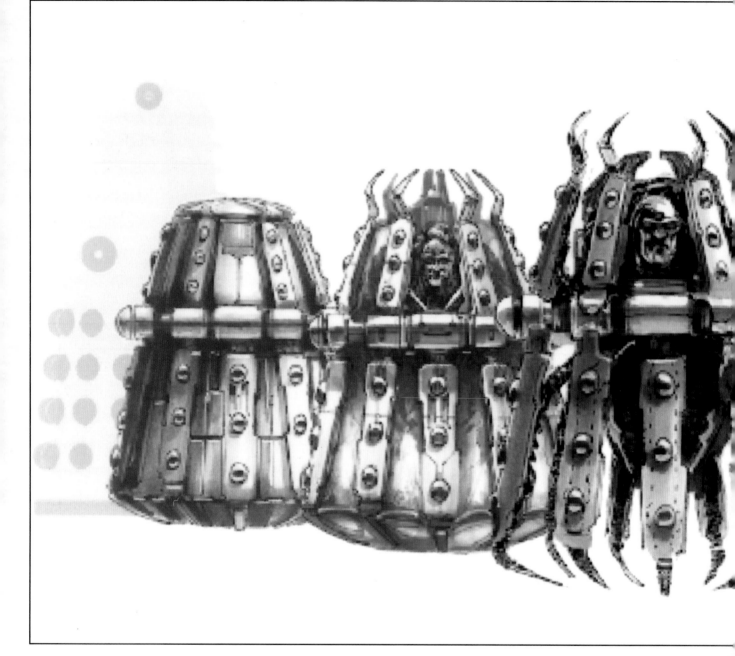

remained locked in the form of a Police Box, found in America and England in the time period of the late nineteenth century … the Doctor's favourite time on the Blue Planet.

The TARDIS is infinitely bigger on the inside than the outside. This is due to one of the key discoveries made by the Time Lords, that of temporal physics. On entering the TARDIS through the outer door, one actually crosses a bridge into another dimension. The exterior of the TARDIS 'exists' in the real world, but the interior is within a different relative dimension. The TARDIS has five chambers … controlled from the five sided console in the centre of the great ship …

1. Captain's Quarters … the Doctor often chooses to plot his navigation course from the Captain's Quarters. Seated at the Magic Lantern, he has a 360 degree view of the Galaxy which

surrounds him. The Doctor's library and living quarters are at the entrance and exit of the TARDIS.

2. Engineering … in this vast space is the time vector generator, dematerialisation circuit, quantum accelerator, and a dynomorphic regenerator. The Environmental Systems maintain such things as temperature, gravity and atmosphere within the TARDIS.

The gigantic crystals which power the all the generators are located in the centre of the main console, and extend outward and upward … into deep space and beyond …

3. Science Laboratory … the TARDIS is totally indestructible and if its exterior is attacked it will dematerialise instantly, rematerialising close by, out of danger, if the Doctor has set the H.A.D.S. (Hostile Action Displacement System).

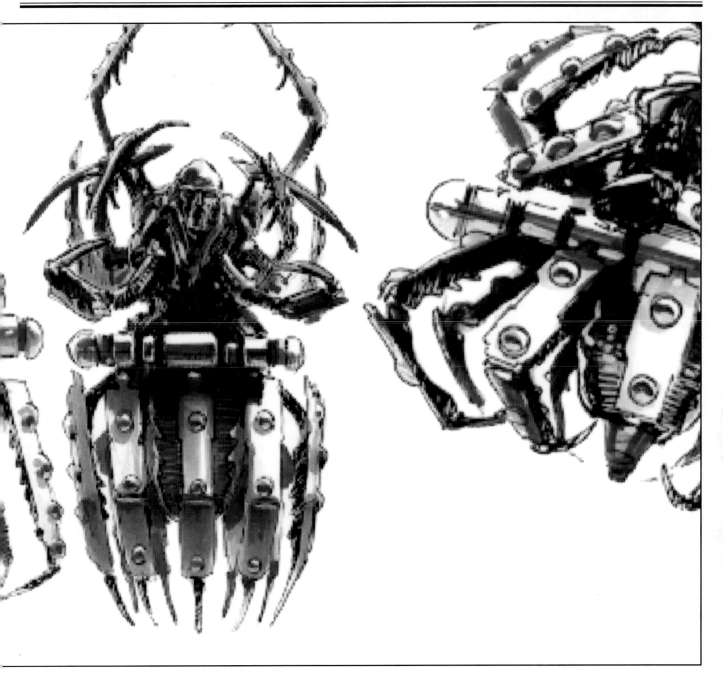

4. Cloisters … Of the five chambers in the TARDIS, the Cloisters is the most spiritual. The walls are stained glass, depicting the mythology of Gallifrey, most of it lost to the people of my planet. It is here that the Cloister Bells are located, the sound of which can heal the sick and dying, in body as well as in spirit. And it is in the Cloisters that I, Cardinal Barusa, appear in hologram form, to speak with the Doctor … it is the place the Doctor goes to think and dream …

5. Cosmos … this is a simple wooden railing which overlooks the Galaxy, through a vast and invisible lens. It is a vision of wondrous beauty as he travels through the Galaxy.

THE DALEKS

• Journal Entry, Time Space Coordinate 5725.1 … the Doctor has been captured by the Time Lords. He and our TARDIS have been propelled

back to Gallifrey, and he has been brought before the Master and the Council … I fear he will be destroyed …

• Journal Entry 5725.2 … Strange events. The Master, now fully in control of the Time Lords, has embraced his brother in front of the Council. He has negotiated a reprieve for the Doctor, who will be allowed to travel freely in time and space … with the proviso that he perform certain duties for the Time Lords when called upon for service … the Doctor is wary …

The Master tells us that creatures called Daleks have swarmed across the far end of the Galaxy, killing entire races of people. They must be stopped. He has asked the Doctor to travel back in time, to the planet Skaro, to the time of the creation of these creatures … and prevent them from ever being made. The Doctor has agreed …

• Journal Entry, Time Space Coordinate 4244.1

The Daleks were far more independent and mobile in Leekley's script. One is seen here emerging from within its Dalek casing, which then becomes airborne.

Had the movie spawned a series, Leekley would have drawn on the extensive *Doctor Who* mythos for subsequent story ideas. Primary among these was Robert Holmes' 1977 adventure *The Talons of Weng-Chiang*, which saw the Doctor in Victorian London – one of Philip Segal's favourite historical periods.

… We have landed on the planet of Skaro … and are horrified to find that this land, once lush and fertile, is now a vast wasteland with bomb craters miles across filled with vaporised cities. The Time Lords were accurate in their predictions … the inhabitants, the Kaleds and the Thals, have destroyed their world. Of all the planets in the Galaxy, the planet of Skaro was most like the Blue Planet … two continents, separated by a vast ocean. Our instruments indicate that the seas are poisoned and dead, the great cities on both continents are rubble, and the land is so hot with radioactive dust that nothing could survive on the surface for very long. We are leaving the TARDIS to investigate, protected by Aura Force Fields …

• Journal Entry 4244.2 … We have found the Kaleds. Like their enemies the Thals, they have been forced underground into mine shafts and underground silos that were once used to launch the neutron missiles. And still they wage their savage war … the hatred passed from generation to generation here, deep underground.

The two humanoid races of this once proud land, the Kaleds and the Thals, unable to live together in peace, turned away from integration of the races and divided the planet. Segregation nurtured mutual fears and hostility … and they began a vicious thermonuclear war which has been waged implacably for hundreds of years.

• Journal Entry 4244.3 … the Doctor has been allowed to speak before the Kaled High Council. He has informed them that he is a Gallifreyan ambassador of peace from the future … he tells them of the Daleks which will somehow be created on Skaro, and will slaughter millions upon millions in all parts of the Galaxy. Although they seem numb from the centuries of warfare, they wish to help. We are allowed to meet with their military and scientific leader … Davros.

Among the Scientific Elite Corps, Davros is the most eminent and the most brilliant. Like so many of the Kaleds, he is a mutant, having survived a Thal neutron bombardment. His whole body seems crumpled down, as if gravity were exerting an enormous force down on him. His eyes, ears, voice box, and left arm have been replaced with vat-grown bio-mass plastic. The rest of his body is not visible, hidden by the extraordinary protective shell he exists within. A pitiful sight … a mind so powerful, and body so deformed and twisted. Davros's life support system is powered by a tiny nuclear reactor … without it, he would instantly die.

He has received the Doctor with a curiously calm manner. He has agreed to cease work on new weapons for war and has poured all of his energies, as well as the Scientific Elite Corps, into designing life support systems for the Kaled nation. The babies are all born genetically deformed.. they look less humanoid, and more insect like.

• Journal Entry 4244.4 … Davros and the Doctor have finished their experiments … the genetic mutations among the Kaleds are irreversible. They are evolving into a non-humanoid race … they are becoming enormous spiders.

Davros works night and day, seeming never to sleep, to design what appears to be the ultimate shield for these creatures.

The Doctor suspects that the endless rows of vats are actually incubators … embryo mutants. That Davros is using genetic designs of his own creations to create the new race of Kaleds … and the shield he has designed is actually armour … genetically attached to the Kaleds as they grow. He is mass producing the ultimate survivors … the ultimate killing machines. Without feelings or desires other than to kill to defend their hellish race. Davros is creating the Daleks …

• Journal Entry 4244.5 … Much has happened

since the last entry … terrible things. The Doctor informed the High Council of the attempt by Davros to create the Daleks … and Davros learning of this, has betrayed his own race. To keep his experiments from being halted, he has revealed to their enemy the Thals the exact locations of the mine shafts and missile silos. The Thals have bombed them … all Kaleds other than his mutated army of creatures, were destroyed. A whole race is lost … the Doctor and I have escaped back into the TARDIS. The Doctor is feverishly working on a plan to gain access to the bunker where the embryos are stored …

• Journal Entry 4244.6 … The first wave of Daleks has been unleashed on the Thals … Davros is a wonder of betrayals. The Thals have been fried by microwaves and hacked to pieces by these monstrous creatures. However, the Doctor has gained access to the Incubator Bunker … it's a trap … Davros has captured the Doctor … he was about to feed him to the Daleks …

• Journal Entry 4244.7 … the Master has appeared … he reveals to the Daleks how Davros betrayed their race and murdered their people. Davros has been horribly murdered … The Master cunningly used the Doctor to bring about this moment in history so he, himself, could take control of these perfect killing machines … Before they could rip apart the Doctor, he has revealed his own plan. He has blown up the Incubator Bunker and escaped into the TARDIS … the Master and his Daleks in pursuit.

Within the TARDIS, the Doctor has reversed time, to the moment he first arrived on Skaro. Now, with the push of a button he can wipe out Davros' power source, he can destroy Davros and his research … eliminating the Daleks from history.

But astonishingly, the Doctor can't bring himself to push the button … he feels he has no right to alter the history of the Galaxy in this way. The existence of the Daleks caused the multitude of planets and races in the Galaxy to unite against the Daleks … and this unity created the future of harmony.

Some things are not for men to decide … we are not God.

ADVENTURES ON DISTANT WORLDS

• I have asked my scribe to make a random selection of my adventures with The Doctor. As I read through them, I am reminded of the words of the Doctor, 'Things were never dull.'

THE PIRATES

Borusa is convinced that the Doctor's father Ulysses was once the famous Blackbeard. Delighted at this prospect, the Doctor lands the

time machine on the coast of 18th Century Spain … and unwittingly falls into the hands of pirates searching for treasure. Realising that the pirates' treasure map reveals the whereabouts of Bluebeard and his treasure, he escapes with the map and the pirates in pursuit … The Doctor arrives at the 'X marks the spot' in the treasure map to find the legendary Bluebeard retrieving his chest … and are set upon by the pirates. Fighting side by side in a swashbuckling finale on the beach, the Doctor and Bluebeard are victorious … the Doctor turns to finally ask him if he is indeed his father, only to see Ulysses vanish over the hill on an Arabian horse … gone …

THE TALONS OF WENG-CHIANG

The TARDIS in present day New York, where a series of murders have been committed by the Chinese Tong of the Black Scorpion, led by Weng-Chiang.

Weng-Chiang is in reality Magnus Greel, a war criminal from the future, whose experiments backfire and whose body needs the energy of others to survive. Hooking up with an NYPD cop, they trace the location of Greel's lair and bring the murderer to justice.

EARTHSHOCK

(The Cybs are the pirates of the galaxy … slash and burn marauders from the planet Mondas. Having ruined the environment of their own planet, they have become cybotic, made up mostly of vat-grown plastic. Since much of their bodies is manufactured, they are very handsome and quite vain. The Doctor often uses that vanity against them. One of the few things that can kill a Cyb is having gold dust thrown into its breathing apparatus …)

In 1994 the Doctor investigates the death of palaeontologists murdered under mysterious circumstances while studying dinosaur remains in an underground cave in Wyoming. He discovers that the deaths have been carried out by the Cybs to protect the location of a bomb capsule, which has been planted in the cave … it is capable of destroying Earth.

He disarms the bomb but is taken captive by a Cyb raiding party who forces the Doctor to take them on board his time machine. The Cybs and the Doctor engage in deadly combat …

THE HORROR OF FANG ROCK

The Doctor and Borusa are attracted by streaks of light that are passing through the galaxy. They follow and find themselves near a lighthouse on the Lands End, England in 1906. An eerie fog rises from the sea, forcing a passing clipper ship to run aground. The survivors are rescued by the Doctor. The captain of the clipper is mysteriously murdered and the Doctor is suspected because

More concepts 'borrowed' from the BBC's *Doctor Who* canon included adaptations, some looser than others, of (from top): *Horror of Fang Rock* (more 19th century romps); *The Celestial Toymaker* (in which the powerful villain would be revealed to be a pawn of the Master); *The Abominable Snowmen* (far more educational than the original, without any furry robots or glowing spheres); and *The Ark in Space* (fusing the original with an *Alien*-inspired set-up).

Mixing *Mad Max* imagery with Native American Indian paraphernalia, the Cybs were a vastly different interpretation of the Cybermen – a race of nomadic galactic plunderers and scavengers who had added cybernetic parts to their bodies.

of his unexplained arrival. The Doctor believes that an alien ship has crash landed and the alien has absorbed the body of the lighthouse-keeper to send a beam of light for a rescue party.

The Doctor is forced to prove his innocence and destroy the alien and its Mother ship.

THE CELESTIAL TOYMAKER

It is 2525. The Doctor's time machine is mysteriously pulled off course and materialises in the domain of The Toymaker, an evil force who dominates a fantasy world.

The Toymaker renders the TARDIS inoperable and forces the Doctor to play a deadly mind game which, if lost, will result in the Doctor's imprisonment forever.

While the Doctor is entangled with the Toymaker, Borusa makes a chilling discovery – the Toymaker is controlled by the Master, who has concocted this duel in an effort to destroy his half-brother …

DON'T SHOOT, I'M THE DOCTOR

While travelling through time and space, the Doctor gets a severe toothache. He decides he'll set coordinates for the Blue Planet Earth, where he knows he can get help. However, an error in his calculations sets the TARDIS down in Tombstone on 26th October, 1881.
The only doctor available is none other than the

infamous gunslinger, Doc Holliday, who is feuding with the Clanton family. Both doctors strap on their guns to help Wyatt Earp against the bushwacking Clantons in the shoot-out at the OK Corral.

TOMB OF THE CYBS

The TARDIS rematerialises in the future on the freezing planet Telos, where the Doctor meets an Earth-led expedition excavating a tomb where the last Cybs are rumoured to have been buried when their planet was destroyed. But the Cybs are revived by a rise in the temperature engineered by the Doctor's half-brother the Master. The party escapes from the tomb but the Cybs are on the loose …

THE YETI

It is 1953 and the Doctor has landed in Tibet to seek advice of his father's whereabouts from his old friend the Dalai Lama. His visit coincides with an expedition of Sir Edmund Hillary to conquer the summit of Mount Everest for the first time in history. The Dalai-Lama informs the Doctor that the Yeti, the huge mythical creatures that are claimed to exist in the mountains will feel threatened by the intrusion on this, their last place of solitude. The Doctor is intrigued … They hear gunshots and a fierce battle ensues, no one gets a good look at the Yeti, only glimpses of their ferocious bodies and terrifying screams. Several members of the team wish to hunt down the Yeti in the morning … the Doctor is opposed, preferring to meet with them instead. Suddenly they are surrounded by the beasts, but they are not monsters after all, they are in fact ancestors of humans … the Neanderthals … the last of their race having been driven to this remote place of hiding for thirty thousand yeas.

The Doctor communicates with the Neanderthals and finds them gentle and shy. He pledges with Hillary to protect them by keeping the myth of the Yeti, as savage monsters, alive.

ARK IN SPACE

In our future, the TARDIS materialises on a fully automated space station for supplies. It appears to be empty and deserted, but in reality it contains the whole future population of Earth stored away in deep freeze until the Earth, ravaged by disease, is again inhabitable. Due to a fault in the machinery, they have failed to awaken on schedule.

Aeons have gone by … The Doctor discovers that the station has been invaded by giant insect-like creatures who had laid their eggs in the leader of the Ark, Noah. They have assumed the personality and control over the body of Noah, planning to take over Earth. Struggling for control of his own mind and body, Noah leaves the safety of the Ark, and sacrifices himself … blowing up the insects inside him. The Doctor awakens the population … and they make preparations to return to Earth.

THE QUEST

At the end of our travels, when the Doctor had finally found his father Ulysses, who had wandered for aeons, lost in time, the were reunited with great joy. It is truly said … 'the son is father to the man'.

When they returned to Gallifrey, they brought with them all the strength and curiosity that had been lost. They brought passion and, even more importantly, compassion. They brought us back from the edge of the precipice, back to the wisdom of the heart.

With his father there to prove his lineage, and no longer a fugitive, the Doctor now wears the Sash of Rassilon. The Time Lords are once again vibrant with colour, united in the dream of ridding the Universe of the enemies of life … once and for all.

The bottomless crevasses which had threatened to shatter our planet apart are closing again … the land is healing. We are now one … and we are bringing peace and harmony to the Galaxy. I remember something the Doctor once said about the pyramids of Egypt on the Blue Planet … those lone sentries of the desert, who remain constant through the millennia. 'Time is the one

thing that men fear the most. But Time fears the pyramids.' This is why he so admired the wonders of Egypt. The Nile flooding its banks, year after year since the dawn of time, leaving silt for the fertility of man. The Sphinx, which stares unblinking into the desert, guiding lost souls.

These things were like old friends to the Doctor, he travelled back to the beginnings of things to know the why of them. The Doctor is like the Sphinx … he does not fear Time. Time fears the Doctor.

I understand now why the Doctor went out into the Galaxy. The quest was to find his father … to take his rightful place … but it was more than this.

It was also a journey to the centre of his own cosmos … somewhere under the brilliant yellow sun of The Blue Planet … and the twin red suns of Gallifrey.

It is said that you cannot know where you are going, if you don't know where you have been. And occasionally, even to this day, when you least expect it, the Doctor will suddenly be missing from his place with the Time Lords … and also missing will be his ancient TARDIS. He will be travelling back to the Blue Planet … back through vast regions of time and space … simply for the adventure of it all …

This final version of the bible was finished in late March 1994 and distributed. However, there had been revisions made to the earlier drafts on a number of occasions. For instance, in the Napoleon section, Borusa's dialogue is longer:

THE DOCTOR: Tomorrow, twenty thousand men will die, their blood draining into the grass … for a mistake he is about to make. I can stop it.
BARUSA: It will change the entire history of civilisation ….
THE DOCTOR: You insisted I help the Greeks design their public buildings …
BARUSA: It was a public service … the Acropolis and the one down the street, the Parthenon … lovely work …
THE DOCTOR: I wanted to light those buildings with solar powered arc beams, but you pooh-poohed the idea …
BARUSA: I felt it would be meddling too much in their development as a culture. That took a few thousand more years for them to design … (HE GOES ON …) For my first 12 regenerations, things were harmonious and dignified. After almost two thousand years, I should have peace in my golden years. Instead, we are battling Sea Devils, introducing ourselves to Yetis, dodging Dalek killing machines, trying to keep our scalps from ending up on Cyb lances, and you are running after the most immoral woman in the Galaxy, that Time Lord wench, the Rani.
THE DOCTOR:(grinning) Things are never dull …

The Cybs featured heavily in the proposed *Doctor Who* series – including a visit to their Telosian tombs, as seen in the 1967 adventure *The Tomb of the Cybermen* and revisited in 1985's *Attack of the Cybermen*.

Finally, there were a number of other adventures that did not make it into the final version of the bible. These first three are from the rough draft of the bible, where they sat alongside *Ark In Space*:

THE CYBS

The Cybs are the pirates of the galaxy ... slash and burn marauders from the planet Mondas. Having ruined the environment of their own planet, they have become cybotic, made up mostly of vat-grown plastic. Since much of their bodies is manufactured, they are very handsome and quite vain. The Doctor often uses that vanity against them. One of the few things that can kill a Cyb is having gold dust thrown into its breathing apparatus ... The first time the Doctor encountered the Cybs, it very nearly meant his destruction. While travelling back in time to the twenty-first century, the Doctor receives a distress signal from an Earth outpost on Mars. A Cyb hunting party has attacked a caravan of the humans ... taking slaves and women to increase their numbers. The Doctor hides them in a gold mine while he goes after the Cybs to save the women and children who were captured.

THE SEA DEVILS

Doctor Who travels back in time to the drilling of the first off-shore oil rigs in Louisiana. There have been mysterious disappearances of rig workers and ships in the Gulf. He discovers that the oil drills have broken through the ocean floor into huge underwater caverns, awakening the Sea Devils ... reptilian creatures who ruled Earth for millions of years during the dinosaur era, and who went into hibernation when the meteor showers enshrouded the world. Now disturbed, they are gathering to retake Earth as their rightful home. The Doctor refuses to help destroy the Sea Devils, who call themselves Silurians, deciding that they were here before man and have a right to coexist. But the Master has also arrived to provoke the Sea Devils to trap the Doctor. The Doctor is forced to drive the Sea Devils back into the sea, exploding their caverns, retrapping them ... to hibernate again until the two races are ready to coexist.

THE OUTCASTS

Something has gone terribly wrong with the crystals in the TARDIS, and Cardinal Barusa, who exists only in the crystals, is dying. The Doctor suspects hat the Master is behind the power drain, drawing them back to him. The Doctor is forced to return to Gallifrey to save Barusa, and lands in the wilderness. He comes upon the Cybs attacking the Outcasts, those natives who live outside the Domed City. He comes across a hunting party of Cybs who had ambushed a caravan of the Outcasts ... to take slaves and women. The marauding Cybs from the planet Mondas, their own planet, which they poisoned

Determined to keep Terry Nation's Dalek concepts, if not their BBC execution, Leekley was keen to show Davros as their creator. Still a crippled scientist, this Davros was far more human and, ultimately, far more malevolent. However, just like his BBC counterpart, he also underestimated his own creations ...

BARUSA: We have a quest ... to find your father. Shall we get on with it?!
THE DOCTOR: (nodding) Power up the Crystals, Cardinal ... let's go exploring ...

Later on, in the journal entry describing the Egyptian escapade, Barusa reports that the Doctor cracks a joke:

Oddly, the Doctor seems very pleased ... he is seated among the other mummies, smoking a cigar and relating recent events. He seems to believe the mummy next to him is listening. The Doctor just said ... 'My dad has apparently flown the coop. Do you mind if I call you mummy?'

and destroyed, are cybotic … made up mostly of vat-grown plastic. He saves the Outcasts, and leads them, like Lawrence of Arabia, against the Cybs. With the Cybs in pursuit, he allows them into the Domed City … They wreak havoc, allowing him time to defeat the Master's Grid Lock, releasing the TARDIS … and saving Barusa.

(One cannot help but wonder whether, with the plan to get Peter O'Toole to portray Barusa, the *Lawrence of Arabia* line was something of an in-joke.)

On 21 March, Leekley came up with some more adventures, such as *The Celestial Toymaker, Don't Shoot, I'm The Doctor* and so on. Although a number of these appear in the final bible verbatim (*The Talons of Weng-Chiang* and *The Horror of Fang Rock*), others, such as the Toymaker story and the Wild West one, have subtle differences, and there are some others that were dropped:

THE LAND OF FEAR

Attempting to learn something about his father, who he knows once met Robespierre, the Doctor lands the TARDIS in a forest clearing 20k from Paris during the reign of terror in 1790. Masquerading as a citizen, he slips into town and during his investigations, runs into English master spy James Stirling, who is plotting Robespierre's assassination. In a conversation with Borusa, the Doctor is convinced to interfere with Stirling's plan.

THE CELESTIAL TOYMAKER

[This is as we see above, except for the final sentence:] While the Doctor is entangled with the Toymaker, Borusa make a chilling discovery – the Toymaker's domain is a time vortex, controlled by the Master, who has concocted this dual in an effort to destroy his half-brother.

DON'T SHOOT, I'M THE DOCTOR

[Again, this synopsis is, as the one above, except for the last sentence:] When Borusa learns of the Doctor's attempt to interfere with the massacre at the OK Corral, he telepathically convinces Marshall Wyatt Earp to arrest him, thereby allowing the famous shoot-out to occur.

THE PIRATES

Borusa is convinced that the Doctor will find his father in a remote part of 17th century Spain. Agreeing to Borusa's suggestion, the Doctor lands his time machine and unwittingly walks into pirates searching for treasure.
The Doctor meets a church warden who may hold a clue to his father's whereabouts. But before he can find out, he stumbles upon a treasure map that the pirates desperately seek. The Doctor is forced to flee when the pirates

discover he has the map and murder the warden.

TOMB OF THE CYBS

The TARDIS rematerialises in the future on the planet Telos where the Doctor meets an Earth-led expedition excavating a tomb where the last Cybs are rumoured to have been buried when their planet, Mondas, was destroyed.
But the Cybs are revived by a rise in the temperature engineered by the Doctor's half-brother, the Master. The party escapes from the tomb, but the Cybs retaliate by sending Cybermats – little mechanical creatures trained to attack. The Doctor freezes the Cybs into inactivity again.

THE CLAWS OF AXOS

In 1994, an alien spaceship containing the Axons: a race of beautiful and friendly humanoids, lands on Earth. They ask for hospitality as their planet has been crippled by a solar flare. The Doctor is suspicious and discovers that the Axons, their ship and a substance they brought called Axonite are all part of a single, collective parasite – Axos – devised by the Master to absorb all living energy on Earth. The Doctor forces Axos into a time loop, exiling it forever in the time vortex.

THE DAEMONS

Against the advice of a local witch, a prehistoric Earth mound in Salem, Massachusetts, is opened, releasing a mysterious force that kills the team of excavators. The Master has used psionic science to unleash the power of a Daemon, a creature from outer space who came to Earth a very long time ago. When the Doctor realises the extent of the Master's involvement, he comes to the villagers' rescue.

SHADA

The Doctor takes Romana, a Time Lord in her own right, to visit her uncle – a retired Time Lord living incognito on the Blue Planet in 1994.

Romana's uncle tells the Doctor about an ancient book of law containing the time/space coordinates of a secret prison planet called Shada. The Doctor believes his father may be held there.

He decides to try and reach this mysterious planet but his plans are thwarted when the ancient book disappears. While searching for the book, the Doctor is plunged into a deadly game when Romana's uncle disappears.

EARTHSHOCK

In the 25th century, the Doctor investigates the death of palaeontologists murdered under

More BBC revamps were planned, including (from top): *The Claws of Axos*; *The Daemons* (relocated to Salem, site of the infamous Witch Trials); and *Shada* (which saw Professor Chronotis become an uncle to Romana, and holding a clue to the whereabouts of the Doctor's lost father).

The stunning visualisation of the TARDIS central console at one end of the cathedral-like TARDIS interior.

mysterious circumstance while studying dinosaur remains in an underground cave. He discovers that the deaths have been carried out by the Cybs, to protect the location of a bomb capable of destroying Earth. He disarms the bomb and follows its radio signal to a gigantic space freighter which has been taken over by a Cyb raiding party who intend to direct it to Earth.

After locking the freighter on its deadly course, the Cyb leader forces the Doctor to take him on board the TARDIS. The Doctor destroys the Cyb leader and reroutes the freighter into a time spiral, saving the Blue Planet.

OK, so just to recap: Cybs are from Mondas, they are cybotic (Leekley's favourite new word, it seems), and the Master is the Doctor's half-brother. Oh, and Earth is the Blue Planet.

After the bible was completed, work started on some story outlines proper. The only one to go some way was *Don't Shoot, I'm The Doctor*, roughly based upon the 1966 *Doctor Who* adventure *The Gunfighters*, which had starred the very first Doctor, William Hartnell.

The 1966 story by Donald Cotton was a bit of a romp. Owing far more to the '50s movie *Gunfight at the OK Corral* than actual history, *The Gunfighters* is a rare piece of *Doctor Who* – essentially it's a comedy, with some rather black overtones. John Leekley, however, was rather fond of this era of history. His research was more meticulous, with lots of handwritten notes made after arduous days researching the actual gunfight via the Gene Autry Western Heritage Museum, learning about the people involved and the facts leading up to it. Indeed, the only things changed by the addition of the Doctor are the suggestion that the writing on Les Moore's tombstone was his and that it was

Frank McLaury who shot off Holliday's holster.

As the story progressed, many alterations were made (Kate Elder fluctuated between being Holliday's lover and wife – the latter being the more accurate); the Doctor initially escapes jail with his sonic screwdriver before the yo-yo is created as a *deus ex machina* to get out of that predicament. Reproduced here, then, is the third draft of the outline, written towards the end of May 1994 (the first draft was done on 10 May). It didn't actually get as far as being scripted, but as an idea of how a *Doctor Who* series might have gone during the Leekley era, it's a fascinating bit of *Who*-lore.

Don't Shoot, I'm The Doctor

This episode takes place against the backdrop of the rapidly building tension in Tombstone, Arizona, in 1881, which finally escalates into the climactic shoot out at the OK Corral.

The A story and emotional heart of the teleplay however centres around Doc Holliday's wife, Kate, and the dramatic impact the Doctor's presence has on her life.

The B story involves the by now legendary mythology surrounding the 'fictitious' character Les Moore, 'who was shot in the back by a 44.' The visual tone is a cross between *Silverado* and *Back to the Future 3*.

By the end of the show, the Doctor experiences first hand the destructive consequences when two warring factions split a community apart … a parallel to his own home, Gallifrey.

ACT ONE We open on a dark cavernous place full of cobwebs and rats. The chase is on. Our hero is being pursued by a hideous character

wielding a pair of rusty old forceps. As the chase builds to a heart stopping climax, our hero plunges off a precipice into black infinity … and we cut to: The Doctor falling from his hammock in the TARDIS, waking rudely from the nightmare as he hits the deck with a welcome but painful start. But the pain is soon replaced by a recurring toothache that provoked the dream in the first place.

Borusa irritably suggests that he's behaving like a child and the sooner he faces up to the inevitable, and has the troublesome molar removed, the better it will be for both of them. The Doctor, surprisingly, agrees. But instead of secretly returning to Gallifrey, where the tooth can be sonically removed, the Doctor haughtily sets the time travel coordinates for the Blue Planet … where he can be treated by a civilised dentist!

The TARDIS duly materialises on Earth and the Doctor leaves the Police Box to discover that he's got it wrong again! Instead of twentieth century Earth, he's landed just outside Tombstone Arizona, in the year 1881! Inquisitive as ever, and nursing his throbbing jaw, our hero decides to stroll into town … and we cut to:

A tense moment inside the lunchroom of the Alhambra Saloon. The atmosphere is electric as two men confront Ike Clanton, who is being 'called out' for making threats against the Earp family.

One of his accusers, (whose back is to camera), is not satisfied with Clanton's response: 'You son of a bitch, if you ain't heeled go and heel yourself.' The Doctor meanwhile approaches Boot Hill, where a funeral is in progress.

He talks to one of the entourage and asks if the

local dentist is at his practice. The man's reaction – a mixture of nervous laughter and transparent fear – leaves the Doctor somewhat bemused.

(During the course of our story, Boot Hill and funerals will be a running thread to underscore the wildness of the town and provide a dark comic edge as we slowly realise that the mourners are always the same odd group of characters: like rent-a-witness at a Las Vegas wedding).

The Time Rotor of the console would be seen to descend deep within the bowels of the TARDIS when in flight. The idea of the rotor being crystalline was retained for the TV Movie.

Holliday's offer to go to his 'surgery' for repairs. His apprehension at seeing the dental equipment is more than off-set by the presence of Holliday's gorgeous lover, Kate.

Holliday leaves Kate tending to our hero's wounds to 'take care of some unfinished business.' On the Doctor's questioning look, Kate starts to explain … It appears that trouble has been brewing between the Earp and Clanton families for some time – but it's now getting out of hand. She believes that Holliday is simply trying to keep a lid on things in the face of the Clanton's supposed broken promise to the Earps regarding a pact over the Benson stage robbery. But his behaviour is very erratic. One minute he's kind and cheerful, the next angry and violent.

As Kate talks and tend to the Doctor's wounds, we sense a sexual chemistry developing between them.

Leekley went to extraordinary lengths to make *Don't Shoot, I'm the Doctor* far more historically accurate than the 1966 adventure *The Gunfighters*, upon which it was very loosely based.

Back in the saloon, the argument with Ike Clanton reaches an uneasy conclusion with the arrival of Marshal Virgil Earp, who pulls one of the men aside (who we learn is his brother Morgan) and leads the pair away to a final taunt from Morgan: 'You can have all the fight you want now!' And we cut to:

The Doctor entering Freemont Street, and attracting the attention of a couple of horse riding, drunken cowboys, who see some sporting possibilities with this weird-looking stranger.

With a hoop 'n' a holler, they spin their lassos and proceed to rope-drag our hero at high speed down the street … causing him to temporarily forget his toothache.

As they approach camera, two boots step ominously into frame, causing the boys to haul on their reins in an explosion of flying earth and snorting nostrils … dispatching the Doctor, who ploughs through the dirt and finally comes to rest at the feet of the mysterious figure. Cut to:

An extreme close-up from the Doctor's POV, as a craggy weather-beaten face with broken and stained teeth leans into the lens … And we realise it is the man who has just threatened Clanton! FADE TO BLACK

ACT TWO The 'man' is none other than Doc Holliday, Tombstone's resident dentist.

Our Doctor struggles to his feet and accepts

(During this Act, we intercut scenes of Ike Clanton roaming the streets and bars looking for a fight, now armed with a pistol, and burning form Holliday's insults).

Kate meanwhile is baring her heart to the Doctor. She thinks that Holliday and Tombstone are about to self destruct … and even though Holliday abuses her, she is still fond of him. She has no one else to turn to – can the Doctor help? Our hero agrees to 'do what he can,' and sets out to find Holliday. But before leaving, asks Kate if she can arrange a change of clothes – he will look less out of place and his own are ripped and dirty from the rope dragging incident.

She readily concurs and takes him back to their boarding house to loan him some of Holliday's, which she thinks will be a good fit. (Here we build the sexual undercurrent in a fun scene as the Doctor undresses). Kate is amused as she watches him transfer odd items from his pockets … such as jelly babies and the sonic screwdriver … and is particularly curious about a little round drum with string which he uses for testing local gravity … and calls a yo-yo.

And with that he leaves Kate shaking her head, saying to herself, 'Who is this man?'

The Doctor finds Holliday at the Eagle Brewery, where he is indulging in his favourite pastime … drinking and cards. He reacts instantly to the Doctor wearing his clothes and becomes even more incensed when our hero tries to talk to him about Kate's concerns.

'What do you know about the Clantons?' barks Holliday, grabbing the Doctor by the neck. 'Only what Kate has told me,' he replies. 'She's been shooting her mouth off again?' snarls Holliday, who ends the conversation by telling the Doctor to keep his nose out of other people's affairs … upon which he is unceremoniously thrown out of the bar.

Holliday is now highly suspicious about this stranger and his intentions toward Kate.

Picking himself up for the second time, the Doctor returns to the boarding house and tells Kate about his failure to communicate with Holliday … he did what he could, but Holliday just didn't seem to understand his line of reasoning. Anyway, all he really wants is to get his tooth fixed, but now he doesn't feel at all happy about being in Holliday's dentist chair! Kate thanks him anyway and says that nothing more can be done that evening … it's already way past midnight … and so she arranges a room for him at the boarding house.

With thoughts of Kate taking his mind off the uncomfortable mattress, the Doctor falls asleep. Holliday meanwhile is leaving the Brewery, still brooding over the interference of the Doctor, and decides to have it out with Kate when he gets home.

As the Doctor turns over with a snore, we see the shadow of a man at the bedroom window, forcing the catch and letting himself up. With a voluminous snore and just before the gunfire erupts, the Doctor throws up the blankets, deflecting the barrel … and the shots blast safely into the headboard.

We realise that the man is Ike Clanton … who thinks our hero is Holliday! Clanton retrieves his gun in the seconds of confusion, and with the Doctor in his sights snarls: 'Whoever you are, you're one of his kind. Tell Holliday he's a dead man, and if you don't leave town, you'll be sharing a plot next to him on Boot Hill.' As he backs toward the window, the door is suddenly kicked down and in bursts Holliday looking for a fight. And he couldn't have found a better place … all hell breaks loose as the Doctor unhappily finds himself once more at the centre of the action.

The noise has already woken up the whole house and as the three set to, lights start to go on all around the neighbourhood. At which point, Kate jumps into the fray, distracting Holliday long enough for Clanton to escape through the open window.

As the Doctor surveys his devastated room, Virgil Earp steps though the door and brutally knocks

him unconscious with the handle of his Colt 44.
FADE TO BLACK

ACT THREE The Doctor wakes with a sore head to find himself locked in a jail cell with a scowling Holliday. It occurs to him that even an adventure on Mondas with Cybs and Daleks would be a veritable picnic compared to this. He decides to pretend to be unconscious for a while. And we cut to:

Wyatt, Virgil and Morgan Earp convening on Allen Street to hear from several locals that Ike has boasted he will kill them on sight. They decide to split up and go looking for him with a plan to disarm and arrest him.

Back in the jail the Doctor hears Holliday, who by now is raging like a bull, arguing with a prisoner in the next cell. As he takes in the scene, he sees a notice board behind the sheriff's desk … written in chalk under Cell 1: Doc Holliday and ? Under Cell 2 is the name Les Moore.

Meanwhile Wyatt Earp has found Tom McLaury, a friend of Ike's, and another confrontation erupts as Earp pushes McLaury to challenge: 'If you want to make a fight, I will make a fight with you anywhere!' Earp responds by drawing his pistol and hitting Tom McLaury twice around the head. Tom falls to the floor, where he is left by Earp.

At this point, McLaury's brother Frank and Clanton's brother Billy ride into town.

At the jail, just about everybody's had enough. As Holliday threatens Moore, Kate runs in to announce the new arrivals, her worst fears are about to happen.

Holliday tells her to get the key and let him out … it sound like the Earps will need this support.

Kate unlocks the cell, but before the Doctor can 'wake up' and get to his feet, Holliday slams the door shut with: 'I've some unfinished business to attend to, then I'm coming back to deal with you.' When Kate remonstrates, Holliday slaps her several times across the face and tells her to 'keep out of it,' dropping the cell keys in the process.

Holliday leaves dragging Kate with him and after sending her home, walks into Billy Clanton and Frank McLaury. Demonstrating a complete change of personality, he shakes their hand and says how pleased he is to meet them.

In about 20 minutes, both Billy and Frank will be lying dead in the dirt at the OK Corral.

The Doctor needs to get out of jail fast, and runs to the cell door to shout for assistance. He notices the keys on the floor … but they are just out of reach! Searching his pockets, he pulls out

It was pure coincidence that the Doctor's costume in the 1996 TV Movie was apparently based on the outfit of frontiersman Wild Bill Hickock.

his trusty yo-yo and finally manages to roll it out, locking the drum between the teeth of the key and dragging it in! He grabs the keys and unlocks the door.

Les yells to let him out too. Having done so, and before he can leave, Les holds him back and suggest they change clothes. He thinks the switch will confuse their identification and help the escape. His real motive however, I that he thinks Holliday will mistake the Doctor for him, and take the heat following their argument in the cells.

The Doctor changes clothes again, but is not quite so happy with the results ... especially the boots which are about two sizes too big! As Les emerges from the jailhouse, the Doctor pauses by the notice board and wipes out their names. He sees a stick of chalk and absentmindedly puts it in his pocket as ... A single shot rings out, and through the window he sees Les Moore crumple to the ground ... shot in the back! With that, the Doctor picks up a gun and holster from the sheriff's armoury, straps it to his waist, and walks outside ... FADE TO BLACK

ACT FOUR Events now move swiftly and we will increase the editing style, gathering pace through the Act.

The Doctor decides to go and make sure that Kate is all right before finding Holliday.

Meanwhile Frank McLaury and Billy Clanton are joined by a friend, Billy 'The Kid' Claiborne, on Fourth Street. They hear about Tom's beating at the hands of Wyatt and go looking for Ike and Tom to persuade them to quickly get out of town.

The Doctor talks to Kate and says that he thinks Holliday just shot Les Moore by mistake, believing it was him. She pleads with our hero to try and stop the madness.

(Threading through the following sequences, we will intercut the movements of the townspeople. Word of Ike's clash with Holliday and their ensuing fight; Tom's buffaloing by Earp; and the arrival of the brothers, lead everyone to expect an imminent clash).

The Clantons, McLaurys and Claiborne meet-up at the gun shop of George Spangenberg. Wyatt Earp chooses this moment to revive his temporary marshal appointment and remove Frank's horse from the sidewalk which is breaking the law ... further increasing the tension.

The Doctor makes his way to the OK Corral. Virgil Earp is told what's going on at the gun shop and joins his brother; forcing the Clantons, McLaurys and Billy Claiborne to move on.

Sheriff Behan is having a shave at Barron's Barber

In Leekley's script, the Clantons were a lot closer to the real family than the cigar-chewin', hard-drinkin' (but vastly amusing) caricatures in Donald Cotton's original *Doctor Who* story.

Shop, when a woman runs in and tells him of the impending trouble. He hightails out ... Finding Virgil and Holliday standing on Hafford's corner as the Clanton party cross the street and enter the OK Corral. Behan tells Virgil to disarm them. He refuses, and so Behan makes his way to the Corral and asks Frank McLaury to give up his arms.

The Doctor arrives on the scene, much to Holliday's amazement, and tries to talk him out of the seemingly inevitable confrontation. Holliday has by now had enough of this troublesome stranger and is ready to finish him once and for all.

As he reaches inside his long grey overcoat for his shotgun, Virgil drags him off to join his brothers, who he fears are now dangerously outnumbered.

Behan and the McLaurys start to make their way to the sheriff's office, when they pause with the Clantons and Billy Claiborne.

Wyatt, Virgil and Morgan Earp, together with Holliday, come round the corner. Behan tries to stop them, but they brush straight by. Within a matter of seconds the four reach the fifteen-foot-wide lot and face-off with the cowboys.

The action happens instantly, triggered by Holliday who takes advantage of the opportunity to settle his score: 'You sons of bitches, you have been looking for a fight and you can have it.' He draws his nickel plated pistol and the shoot out begins. Billy Clanton is killed by Morgan Earp; Tom and Frank McLaury are killed by Holliday.

In the mayhem and confusion, Ike decides to 'do a runner'. But he is spotted by Holliday who fires two quick shots. Ike falls over and Holliday runs after him ... away from the main group.

Reaching the prone victim, he levels his gun at point blank range. But when the hammer hits ... the chamber is empty! As he prepares to draw his second revolver, the Doctor steps out from the Corral barn with his gun drawn. But instead of shooting Holliday, he blasts his holster off with one bullet! A perspiring Ike scrambles to his feet and rushes past with a hasty 'thank you.' The two men are now one-on-one, and start a furious hand to hand battle that spills into the barn. The Doctor, who normally abhors violence, has on occasions relished a good fight ... and this is one of them! (The choreography however will not be a bloody slug-out, but more a staging of the various props found in a barn. The Doctor finally emerges victorious ... but not before loosing his troublesome tooth in the process!). The fight comes to a conclusion with the two combatants climbing up a ladder. Holliday grabs the Doctor's boot, which after a kicking struggle, comes off ... sending Holliday, still holding on to the ladder, arcing gracefully backward through the air,

ending in an almighty crash to the ground ... leaving him unconscious.

As the Doctor gathers his breath and wonders how to get back down, we hear a whistle from outside that would make a New York cabby stop. Opening the double door loading gate, The Doctor looks down to see Kate on horseback. Grabbing the hoist rope, The Doctor closes his eyes and launches himself out ... to land on the back of the horse with a bone chilling jar. Holding Kate's waist for dear life and not a little pleasure, they ride out of Tombstone at speed.

As they pass Boot Hill a burial is in progress. The Doctor tells Kate to stop. She wants to press on so that she can get back before Holliday recovers, but he is adamant. Reaching the mourning party, the Doctor sees a plain gravestone. Spotting the same man he encountered on the way into town, he enquires about the dead man ... it is Les Moore.

The Doctor thinks for a moment and then removes the chalk from his pocket and writes on the headstone the famous inscription: 'Here lies

the body of Les Moore. Shot in the back by a 44. No less, no more.' Rejoining Kate, they ride off to the TARDIS and the Doctor dismounts ... it is an awkward and emotional moment for both of them.

Kate asks, 'Who are you?' 'Just a traveller passing through,' replies the Doctor.

The Doctor reassures Kate that everything will be all right from now on ... 'trust me.' And for some reason she does. They embrace and The Doctor enters the police box. FADE TO BLACK

CODA Over a picture of Les Moore's grave stone, with the rain washing away the Doctor's inscription, we roll the end credits.

Starting with ... John Henry 'Doc' Holliday died six years later of tuberculosis.

Kate Holliday changed her name back to Kate Elder and remarried, living happily and raising three children ... and never forgetting the tall stranger who touched her life.
FADE TO BLACK

One suspects that, had it gone into production, *Don't Shoot, I'm the Doctor* would have had far more convincing Wild West locations than these budget-restricted but imaginative and well-made sets from *The Gunfighters*.

> **LIZZIE**
> Who are you?
>
> **DOCTOR**
> I am the Doctor.
>
> **LIZZIE**
> What are you the
> "doctor" of?
>
> **DOCTOR**
> Many things. Temporal
> engineering, metaphysics,
> archeology, history, quantum
> mechanics, astronomy,
> medicine…
> the things one must know.
>
> **LIZZIE**
> I have a PHD in physics, and I
> have never heard of temporal
> engineering…
>
> **DOCTOR**
> It hasn't been invented
> here yet.
>
> **LIZZIE**
> Can you "engineer" time?
>
> **DOCTOR**
> Let's just say that I'm
> a tinkerer.

*From the First Draft
of Doctor Who
by John Leekley,
24 August 1994*

• 1994 •
THE LEEKLEY SCRIPT

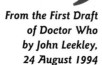

The genesis of *Doctor Who* in the Leekley version is as convoluted as the script itself. The final draft is in fact a complete reinvention rather than a retread of *Doctor Who* and, should a producer ever wish to merely use the concepts of *Doctor Who* and ignore the thirty-five-year mythology, they could do a lot worse than look again at this script. (In much the same way, Brian de Palma's 1996 theatrical film *Mission: Impossible* borrows the thematics of the 1960s television show but reinvents them, doing away with the necessity of understanding the original – a criticism levelled at some other remakes such as *The Avengers* and *The Saint* – or the need to retread the same ground – *à la Lost in Space*). However, the potential in the Leekley script is there and, although it offers up one of US television's more predictable obsessions (that of the 'family', in this case bringing the estranged father and son together again), it does at least move away from the equally predictable 'moral of the week' that plagues much other US prime-time 'family audience' drama.

But how did it get there? Leekley's first story proposal, dated 15 July 1994, sets out the basic storyline that remained relatively unchanged from then on.

On the planet Gallifrey, the Daleks are attacking. Throughout the galaxy these mindless killing machines are rampaging and, within the Domed City, Cardinal Borusa, the President of the Time Lords, fears that his time is up. He is dying, and wants Gallifrey to be led by a dynamic younger leader, with an instinct for surviving the coming battle. The Master, Borusa's son, sees himself as the obvious candidate, but there are as many Time Lords who are terrified of him as there are those who support him. Many would prefer the Doctor, Borusa's grandson, but he is nowhere to be seen …

The Doctor is in fact exploring the outer reaches of Gallifrey, a wasteland populated by the Outsiders. With a couple of them, he searches for the long-lost and mythical Scrolls – but is attacked by a spider-like Dalek. Using a transmat, the Doctor escapes back to the Domed City and faces off with the Master.

The arguments cause Borusa to collapse and he is taken away to his chambers, where he will die. The Doctor attends him and learns that his father, the great Time Lord explorer Ulysses, had a relationship with an Earth woman and that he, the Doctor, is their son. The Doctor, having lost control of the Time Lords to the Master, sets off in his father's long-abandoned TARDIS to find the missing explorer and learn more about his past. When Borusa dies, his life essence is caught up in the crystals that power the TARDIS and he becomes one with it, a disembodied voice to accompany the Doctor on his quest. The Master, meanwhile, wants the Doctor tracked down and executed …

SEGAL'S DALEKS

While John Leekley was preparing his drafts of the storyline, Philip Segal, using his fan's knowledge, came up with this document – a sort of instant guide to the Daleks, as 'remixed' for the 1990s by Amblin!

Skaro – The Dead Planet
A brief history of the Daleks

It is the twelfth planet in a solar system not too far from Earth. It was the home of the Kaleds and the Thals. Ravaged by a neutronic war between the two races, Skaro was made largely radioactive.

Obviously we want a strong resolution to our two-hour in terms of what happens to the Daleks, but some things crossed my mind about the Daleks that relates to the series that might be fun to weave into the two-hour, assuming we have the time and the space! It struck me that the Daleks would, for the series, rise up again against the Doctor. In the original series they were second only to the Doctor in terms of popularity.

We know that Davros created the Daleks sometime after the wars.

His reason for creating the Daleks was that he would have a race of killing machines that would be capable of exterminating all forms of life. This, in Davros' mind, would ultimately make the Daleks the supreme power of the universe.

At some point in the Dalek time stream, the Doctor was sent by the Time Lord Council to Skaro at a time prior to Davros creating the Daleks. His mission was to make sure the Daleks never existed. The Doctor was successful in penetrating the Daleks' stronghold but decided against carrying out his mission. His reason was that he felt by stopping the Daleks from coming to be, millions of other races in the universe who joined forces and rose up against the Daleks would not have done so. This very act may deprive the universe of creating relationships that in some way improved life. A sort of Gallifreyan Darwinism! According to the record, some time in Earth's future it will be invaded by Daleks. (Could be a great season two opener! … I think big) It is also known that sometime after our story happens, the Daleks are attacked by an invasion force from another planet and thought to be totally destroyed.

What happened to Davros?

Right after the wars ended and just about three hundred years before our story begins, Davros survives an assassination attempt on his life and flees to the planet Nekros. While on Nekros, Davros posed as the Great Healer and used the bodies of Nekrolians from the Great Mortuary to create his new Imperial white Dalek army. Now what happens is that the Daleks from Skaro who survived the invasion go off looking for Davros on a tip that he was still alive and kicking. They eventually find him and take him prisoner when he refuses to help. They all relocate to Skaro II and rose up once again. Now, after a long period on inactivity, sometime between the 32nd and 38th centuries, the Daleks restore Skaro to its former glory. They also refine time travel using a rare special metal called tarranium. They were once again able to build very crude time machines. Their first mission once able to travel through time was to end a small group of Dalek assassins back in time to kill the First Doctor.

What does Skaro look like?

For what it's worth, here are my thoughts on 'look' for Skaro. First, if we think of this as a planet that has been ravaged by bombs for centuries and is still trying to recover, it is still very much a 'dead' planet. And I like this notion. Visually, from a production point of view, we have an asteroid/Skaro, Gallifrey, Earth (to include war-torn London 1944 and present day). So for Skaro it might be fun to look at something stark and barren. Since our Daleks don't have the problem of mobility the way the old ones did, our Daleks don't have to worry about moving on flat surface. However, it would seem logical to me that their living quarters would look like giant anthills! Or even take the shape of some kind of hive. You would have a queen or king Dalek, and soldiers and drones could be fun. The point is that by creating some kind of structure to their civilisation, we make it easier for the audience to see how the Master would like to get his hands on this army. Without any kind of structure, we run the risk of it looking disorganised and not very powerful. For some reason I think of organisation and hierarchy equating with power!

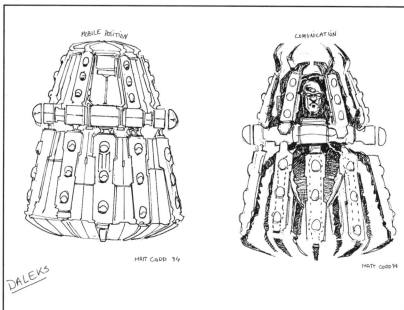

The earliest design sketch for the new Daleks, by Matthew Codd.

The Doctor arrives in England, during the Blitz. He meets an American WAC, Lizzie Travis, and eventually almost convinces her that he's not a spy for the Nazis out to assassinate Winston Churchill, and instead uses the Scrolls he found on Gallifrey to locate his father's last location – in the Egyptian Room of the British Museum. But the sarcophagus is gone and, when the Doctor eventually finds it, it contains a note to him from his father, who guessed he would try to find him.

Lizzie, still suspicious of the Doctor (mainly because there is a spy in the American camp), follows him to the TARDIS and finds herself transported back 4,652 years to Ancient Egypt, where the Doctor realises the Great Pyramid was built by his father to transmit a beacon to Gallifrey.

In deep space, the Cybs patrol the spaceways, eking out their existence as scavengers and murderers. Glock, Kiowa, Bushido and Cyber Dog are being entertained by belly dancers, whom they brawl over. Then their ship receives a signal from ancient Egypt and they head there, just as the Doctor and Lizzie are about to find Ulysses, disguised as a dead pharaoh. Then the Cybs attack.

Lizzie, meanwhile, is trapped with a regenerating Ulysses wrapped up inside the sarcophagus, just as the priests seal the tomb. When Ulysses has recovered, the two of them find their way to the TARDIS, where Ulysses meets the image of Borusa, his own father. Then, using the TARDIS transmat, Ulysses finds himself with the Doctor, fighting off the Cybs.

For a brief moment father and son are reunited, but Ulysses then tricks the Cybs into following him into the transmat, and this takes them all through time to the sixteenth century, where they emerge aboard a sailing ship. Determining to find him again, the Doctor takes the TARDIS, with Lizzie and Borusa, to Gallifrey, where the Praetorian Guard capture them. The Doctor is astonished when the Master acts like his oldest friend, offering him his freedom if he will find a way to destroy the Daleks.

The Doctor and Lizzie travel then to Skaro where the Kaleds and Thals have endured aeons of neutron war. Finding themselves with the Kaleds, they meet the scientist Davros, who initially appears benevolent, determined to see both races on Skaro survive the mutations that are

A visualisation of a Gallifrey ruined by war with the Daleks.

destroying their respective gene pools. The truth is that Davros is deliberately incubating the mutant babies, turning them into the spider-like Daleks and encasing them in mobile shells.

The Doctor gets a message to Gallifrey about Davros's plans, but the mad scientist then destroys all the Thals and Kaleds, leaving only himself and his army of Daleks. However, they turn on him and destroy him, finding themselves a new leader – none other than the Master, who planned this all along and used the Doctor and Lizzie to prepare the way. The Doctor destroys the Dalek incubators but the Master escapes with the Dalek army, sending them on a crusade to hunt down his most hated enemy.

The Doctor takes Lizzie back to Earth and they kiss goodbye and then Borusa tells the Doctor he has found Ulysses – as the captain of a sixteenth-century pirate ship, the Cybs as his pirate crew ...

The second draft storyline, dated 27 July, was pretty much the same with a few things altered (the Praetorian Guard became the Chancellery Guard and the Master gained a toadying assistant, Castellan Kelner). The biggest change was the complete removal of the Cybs – here, Ulysses is thrown back into the time stream by a fault in the TARDIS transmat.

A slight rewrite of this was done to include a few of Philip Segal's and Peter Wagg's concerns. The Castellan lost his name and the post-Egypt scenes on Gallifrey became a relayed conversation with the Master. In addition, the Castellan joined the Master on Skaro, and it was set up much earlier that Davros and the Master were in cahoots. The 3 August draft adds

A sketch of a mutated Kaled.

also had some input at this point – and a memo from Tony Greenwood on 15 August conveys the opinions of Alan Yentob and Charles Denton (although not those of a curiously absent Michael Wearing).

Their main concerns are that the Daleks are too spiderish, too given to dispatching people via 'blood and guts etc.', which undermines the 'cold, unemotional efficient killer/exterminator image'.

Image was also of paramount importance regarding Winston Churchill, whom they believe was written as a caricature and could maybe be done away with altogether. They also felt Lizzie wasn't strong enough, becoming a bit of a screamer rather than a trained soldier. There were some comments about the use of the name Ulysses: they felt that it centred too much on real historical figures such as Cheops, possibly suggesting that the Time Lord Ulysses and the Earth historical one were the same person, which they were not meant to be.

The first draft script was written on 24 August and, for the first time, Philip Segal and Peter Wagg were able to see dialogue for the Doctor. They were none to keen on his referring to Ulysses as 'Dad' throughout and made a lot of comments about the Doctor's 'birthright' and the mythology of the scrolls. Leekley also had Ulysses base his regeneration on an image he plucked from Lizzie's mind, that of her own dead father, a Kansas farmer. The most significant change, however, was that the story now ended on a cliffhanger, as Davros caught the Doctor and Lizzie in the incubator room and 'introduced' them to his pet Daleks.

A brief rewrite was issued on 26 August and then Tony Thomopolous of Amblin sent Philip some notes on the script. First, he was concerned that, with Borusa so weak and enfeebled at the beginning, it was going to be very difficult for the audience to accept that he was going to end up the wise one in the series. He also raised the question that, if Ulysses could send the Doctor back to Gallifrey to be raised when he was a baby, why couldn't he go back with him? Thomopolous was also concerned that the Doctor showed no great surprise at Borusa's TARDIS-based resurrection and went on to list various other moments where he found the script confusing.

All of these points concerned the motivation surrounding Time Lords and the question of regenerations (he wondered why a Time Lord called Zorba should be upset that the Master kills him: 'Doesn't he have 12 lives?'). On a general note, he writes, 'I found the script very confusing and a lot to remember.'

The next draft was delivered on 8 September,

a new, if small, twist. Not all the mutants in the incubator room are destroyed – at least one survives, which will remember the Doctor's kindness in trying to save their race.

Another slight rewrite followed, which saw the Daleks learning that the Master controlled Davros, rather than their electing him to be their new leader. And there was an ending in which the Doctor feels saddened at losing Lizzie, to whom he was rather attached. Borusa then jollies him up by telling him he's located Ulysses in the sixteenth-century New Americas …

A few more rewrites followed, generally tidying the story up, cutting back on extraneous scenes and having Borusa send them to Skaro, while 'the Castellan' now becomes plain 'Castellan' – a name rather than a Time Lord rank. The BBC

and most points had been addressed (although the Doctor still called Ulysses 'Dad'). The proper ending had been reinstated, and lot of the running about on Skaro was replaced by a dialogue scene. Similarly, the Egyptian scenes were trimmed to a bare minimum – enough to set up the quest to find Ulysses, but little more. It was this draft that was submitted to the rest of Amblin to see if they wanted to go with it, and to Universal for the same reason. As well as Spielberg's resistance to it, Universal didn't seem too keen, either, and, with the relationship between John Leekley, Peter Wagg and Philip Segal at a bit of a low, it was decided to relieve Leekley of the task.

As a coda to this, it is interesting to note that in February 1995, a copy of the Leekley script found its way to the theatrical movie development offices at Amblin, where two analysts, Marc Haimes and Rick Schwartz, gave it the once over as a potential movie. Haimes noted that 'whilst his television pilot works to capture the feel of the famous British series (with a cult following in America), it doesn't quite manage to appeal to a more mainstream audience. The sophisticated mythologies and esoteric scientific explanations are interesting at first, but soon slow down the progress of the story – never finding the political and philosophical resonance that has brought the *Star Trek* series such successes.' Haimes went on to explain that he thought the characters bland, the transitions between acts confusing, and the whole thing lacking 'the subtlety and wit that was found in the original series'.

Schwartz's comments are much the same – not a patch on the British series, the characters bland, the situations too contrived ... He sums it up as a 'standard sci-fi redux of Greek mythology [which] hits the requisite beats but is wholly undistinguished and routine. NOT RECOMMENDED.'

FAN LIAISON

Before we go into the final stage of the story, there is a small moment that I wanted to talk about that, if nothing else, will tell my side of the whole story as it relates to bringing *Doctor Who* back for the fans.

As many of you know, this franchise has been exploited over the years by its fans, a few of whom have taken a great opportunity to make a small amount of money from *Doctor Who* stories that parallel the main thrust of the franchise. Some exploitation is a good thing: it keeps the franchise alive for people. But sometimes it can be a bad thing. It depends on your motivations.

Over the years a number of fans and curious people have asked me about certain events and rumours or stories that they may have heard. This book gives me a forum to answer some of those questions. In particular, I'd like to share with you a story that at the time seemed important but now seems silly. Nevertheless, I feel it reflects badly on my judgement and it frankly bothers me to this day. I want to preface this small story by saying that I hold no grudge now towards anyone connected with such events.

Jean-Marc Lofficier and his wife and partner, Randy, contacted us in the autumn of 1994 and introduced themselves as the authors of several *Doctor Who* books, such as *The Programme Guide* and *The Universal Databank*. They thought they could be of help in reaching out to the fans and doing any research we might need, including reading the script – at this point, John Leekley's version. Jean-Marc's offer seemed helpful and quite harmless to me at the time.

Jean-Marc did not know that I had secretly been to several conventions and sat in the audience listening to him speak on panels about many things to do with the future of *Doctor Who*, including his thoughts on what Amblin's involvement might mean to the franchise. Most of what I heard Jean-Marc say was very positive and he certainly seemed to have the respect of the fan base, at least in Los Angeles.

I agreed to meet with Jean-Marc and Randy at my office at Amblin. Our first meeting left me with a rather odd impression of both of them. My first mistake was believing that without them I might have trouble being understood by the American fan base. I foolishly agreed to their help but prefaced the whole affair by explaining that I wanted their involvement to be limited at first. I was also concerned about how they would use the presumed association with Amblin.

They asked if they could call themselves 'fan liaisons' for the television movie, and I said yes. We began to strike up a friendship and I put a lot of trust in both of them. I was asked by Jean-Marc to give him copies of the various development materials for his private use. He subsequently used all that source material within a book called *The Nth Doctor*. I felt betrayed. Fortunately, today, I'm less angry than I was back then!

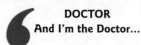
> **DOCTOR**
> And I'm the Doctor...
>
> **JANE**
> Doctor Who?
>
> **DOCTOR**
> Just the Doctor. I'm looking
> for my father, an
> American soldier.
>
> **JANE**
> You've come to the
> right place. Did your father
> have a name, or did he go by
> Doctor Sr.?
>
> **DOCTOR**
> Actually, he "travelled" under
> the name of
> John Smith.
>
> **JANE**
> That wasn't his real name?
>
> **DOCTOR**
> You see, where we
> come from... oh, it's
> not important...
>
> *From the First Draft
> of Dr Who?
> by Robert DeLaurentis,
> 21 December 1994*

• 1994 •

THE DELAURENTIS SCRIPT

I f the John Leekley version of *Doctor Who* was a reinvention of the mythos, the Robert DeLaurentis one was even further removed from the source material. DeLaurentis came aboard at the start of October 1994. After a weekend reading over the Leekley script, he contacted Philip Segal and Tony Thomopolous on 5 October with his opinions on his predecessors' work. 'Great potential,' he enthused, 'but the execution is all too familiar and totally humourless.'

He then broke it up into what he thought was good and bad. 'The concept is fantastic, in the literal sense of the word. Not only is it completely out of the realm of ordinary Network fare, but it represents that unusual opportunity to do something that does not fall into the standard category of television drama. If it isn't a potential antidote to channel surfing, I don't know what is.'

However, he went to say of the script as it stood that he felt it was 'earnest, solemn and derivative. Simply put, it takes itself too seriously. Not only should it be funnier, but more "fun", that is, more of a romp, a wild weekly roller coaster ride. Right now, it's dark and inaccessible, weighed down with unnecessary science fiction baggage. It needs to be a bright, human adventure.' He then punctuated this with 'since criticism is easier to come by than hard solutions, let's get right

to it', and delivered a page on the characters and a three-page analysis of what he saw as the potential errors in the script. It is worth looking at DeLaurentis's suggestions here, as they certainly shape the direction in which he took his scripts as they progressed. However, it might be worth bearing in mind that one of Steven Spielberg's dislikes of Leekley's script was that it veered too close to his and Lucasfilms' *Indiana Jones* concepts – something, that on the surface, DeLaurentis seemed to want to move closer to by disposing of that 'science fiction baggage' and concentrating on 'a bright, human adventure'.

And, if John Leekley fell into the father/son cliché, just wait until you see that other great American 'family drama' obsession creep in with DeLaurentis's idea of an extra sidekick for the Doctor ... DeLaurentis also appears to have had a thing about placing a question mark in the lead character's name (let's overlook the traditional error of calling the Doctor 'Doctor Who', shall we ...?)

CHARACTERS

1 DOCTOR WHO?
He should possess more of everything, particularly LIFE FORCE. He should be more intelligent, quirky, humorous (whimsical and self-depreciating), and most of all HUMAN. Think of Tom Hanks with a Holmsian quality. Make him BRILLIANT and BENT.

POLICE PUBLIC BOX
CALL

POLICE PUBLIC BOX
CALL

POLICE TELEPHONE
FREE
FOR USE OF
PUBLIC
ADVICE AND ASSISTANCE
OBTAINABLE IMMEDIATELY

OFFICERS AND CARS
RESPOND TO
URGENT CALLS

PULL TO OPEN

The interior of the Utah State Capitol Building in Salt Lake City. An early location recce suggested this cavernous space could represent a 'Time Lord temple' or possibly Borusa's home on Gallifrey.

2 BORUSA

Doctor Who's mentor is his Grandfather, Borusa. While appropriately wise and solemn, he's no fun. He's also paternal, which is a conflict with the Doctor's real father. From a series point of view, he doesn't make the environment (of the TARDIS), one that we want to inhabit, or return to on a weekly basis. I suggest we let him die at the end of Act One, and replace him with a comic sidekick.

3 THE MASTER

He should be one of the great villains in the history of TV. Moriarty to the Doctor's Holmes. He needs to be far more insidious, intelligent, and surprising. A master manipulator, he needs extraordinary charm and an unerring instinct for the vulnerability of his enemies, particularly the Doctor.

4 LIZZIE

Simply put, she feels old-fashioned and very familiar. I'd reinvent her as a renegade, a real spitfire. I'd make her less a country bumpkin, more urban and street-smart, with greater confidence and irreverence. She should also be more modern; a feminist before her time, not in the political sense, but pragmatic sense. She enlisted in the army AGAINST the wishes of friends, parents and even a boyfriend, who believed a woman's place is in the kitchen, and not the battlefront. She should have a wonderfully adventurous spirit, and a deep scene of moral righteousness.

5 A NEW CHARACTER

My instinct is that we need a SIDEKICK, someone the Doctor can talk to, who can also enliven the solemn atmosphere of the TARDIS. Dare I suggest a dog? Don't shoot me, but what if the first time we see Lizzie, she's ducking through a blitz in order to save a feisty British Bulldog (WINSTON). She takes him along, over the Doctor's objections. By now you probably have the gun cocked, but not only would we have a 'fun' character in the TARDIS, we'd also get great mileage not of the Doctor trying to understand this unusual species. Before you dismiss the idea completely, consider [the Jim Carrey movie] *The Mask*.

He then goes on to a point-by-point outline of his problems with the structure of the Leekley script: no teaser, so no immediate introduction for *Dr. Who?*; the acts were unbalanced in both length and dramatic strength; too much exposition in Act One, too much Egypt ('familiar and corny') in Acts Three and Four. He also points out that there are a lot of location changes in the pilot and he suggests dropping Egypt completely.

DeLaurentis also had a few thoughts on the basic structure, suggesting that, once Ulysses is lost again, forget the hunt and have Borusa insist on the Doctor's saving Gallifrey by fighting the Daleks (the Davros/Kaled-Thal War strand is dropped completely). He also felt that the ending was a stalemate, with the Master/Doctor plot unresolved, leaving the evil Master still in control of Gallifrey and the Doctor a fugitive, which is unfulfilling after two hours. Similarly, he felt that Lizzie's return to wartime England and the arms of a boyfriend here was wrong – it didn't say much for the Doctor as a hero if the girl leaves him for someone else. He likens it to *Casablanca*, except here we don't even know why she chooses the other man and what he can offer Lizzie that the Doctor can't, and it's she who makes the choice, rather than the hero making the emotional sacrifice – again in *Casablanca*.

DeLaurentis then offered a new story outline, in which a teaser defines the character of the Doctor as we see him defeating danger, but it ends on a cliffhanger.

Act One then sets up Gallifrey, and the struggle between the Master and Borusa, and has the Doctor's apparently dead body brought in, which causes Borusa's seizure. However, the real Doctor is still resolving the events we have seen in the teaser, and then he returns to find Borusa dying, but still able to send him on the mission to find his true father.

Act Two returns to the Blitz, picks up Lizzie and the dog, sets up the romance and gives Lizzie a particular skill that the Doctor will later find useful in his quest.

In Act Three, instead of Egypt, they go to 1994 America, to Lizzie's home (New York, San Francisco or LA), which could give Lizzie some interesting reactions to her own future.

Act Four stays in America as the Master and some Daleks track them down. At the end, the Master captures the Doctor's father (at no point is he called Ulysses), and the Doctor must follow him to Skaro. By now the Doctor/Lizzie romance has kicked in and she refuses to go home.

Acts Five and Six take place on Skaro, and feature the final battle in which the Doctor saves his father and, avoiding the use of force, the Doctor finds a way to defeat the Master, who escapes into the 'great Time Corridor'.

In Act Seven, the Doctor and his father return to Gallifrey and the father becomes leader of the Time Lords. But the Doctor knows he must find the Master, who will spread evil everywhere, and sets off after him. Having peeked into Lizzie's future, he realises she has a pivotal role to play in the resolution of World War II and so realises he must take her home. After dropping her off, he finds Winston still inside the TARDIS, 'as loyal a sidekick as any man, or Doctor, could ever want'.

DeLaurentis expanded these ideas into a full storyline draft, delivered on 7 October. In this we meet the Doctor's (literal) assistant in the teaser, a bumbling science type who whinges and moans a lot. At the end of the teaser we see the Time Corridor open up and threaten to suck them in, but, before it does so, Daleks roll out.

The Master's plan to rule the galaxy is stepped up (he still has an assistant of his own, Casteloan); the Doctor meets Lizzie (handwritten notes on the outline suggest reinserting the idea of the Doctor's being accused of being a German spy); and he learns of a plot to assassinate Hitler. This plot failed and the group were killed bar, one – the Doctor's father.

The TARDIS tracks him to America, 1994, where the Master catches up with them, using Daleks to track them down.

The Doctor and Lizzie locate the father – who has become enmeshed in America because of some (as yet unidentified) project and must stay behind. After a chase through America, they get back to the TARDIS, only to find the father has changed his mind and will take them to Skaro to defeat the Master.

Of course, this is really the Master in disguise – and on Skaro they find the real father has indeed been brought there, as the Master's prisoner.

DeLaurentis suggests here that the father might not actually be terribly pleased to see his son, annoyed that his life on Earth has been disrupted, which would cause the Doctor further emotional distress, and which Lizzie could help him deal with.

Finally a showdown occurs, and the Doctor finds himself making parallels between the lengths he's going to to stop the Master and those his father went to to stop Hitler.

DeLaurentis also suggests the father be killed, a touching deathbed reconciliation scene followed by a regeneration – the regenerated father having changed personality enough to leave his past life behind him and assume control of Gallifrey.

The following Monday in a memo to Philip, DeLaurentis asked the following questions of his own script: Did it need more time travel in the teaser? Was the Master's plan clear enough (and might it be a twist if he implied that the Doctor's father was in fact running the show, the Daleks etc., just to further upset the Doctor)? And could he perhaps be building a time-travelling ship as a secret weapon? Was it essential to have the Master and the Doctor as brothers? And there was a whole load of possible motivations as to why the father can't/won't voluntarily return to Gallifrey – DeLaurentis even suggests leaving the father to go back to America and reintroduce Borusa in time to regenerate and become the Time Lord leader again. He also asks whether the Master could use his new ship to help Nazis win the Second World War?

By the time next version was broken down into the following scenes, most of the Leekley

From the same location visit: the City and County Building at Washington Square, Salt Lake City. Selected as a possible venue for location scenes set in London.

they head into the future to find the Father, the Master 'chases' them through time, and past their destination. They finally lose him, only to land in present day America.

ACT FOUR The Doctor and Lizzie become 'time detectives' as they chart the Father's past in order to find his present whereabouts. They overcome several obstacles, including the Daleks, to discover that the Father has recently died.

ACT FIVE The Doctor and Lizzie find the Father is still alive, and reunite only to have him refuse the mission of leading the Time Lords. Just as the Doctor comes to terms with continuing on alone, his Father has a change of heart, confessing the Master is his eldest son, the Doctor's brother.

ACT SIX The threesome (along with Winston) travel to Skaro, where they initiate a plan to find and sabotage the Master's warship. After a hazardous journey they finally discover the

Paul McGann took time from his busy schedule to meet up with John and Ros Hubbard, who videotaped the actor performing a number of scenes from an early draft of the Leekley script. In these, the Doctor apologies to the apparently dying Borusa, and later meets Lizzie in the blitzed London of the Second World War.

elements had already passed on. All that was left was the death of Borusa, Lizzie's coming from 1944 and the basic search for the father:

TEASER The Doctor, searching for the end of time, falls into a trap set by the Master.

ACT ONE The Master reveals his construction of a giant Time-Travelling Warship capable of making the Daleks an invincible invasionary force. The Doctor escapes to Gallifrey, and joins his grandfather Borusa at his deathbed. Borusa gives the Doctor his mission: find his father and return him to power in time to prevent the Master from ruling the world.

ACT TWO The Doctor tracks his Father to London during World War II, where he's aided by a beautiful young American Intelligence Officer (and her British bulldog, Winston). They find out that the Father led an unsuccessful attempt to assassinate Hitler before being they are discovered by the Master, who has the Doctor jailed for treason.

ACT THREE Lizzie discovers that the Father is a German POW, then helps the Doctor escape. As

Warship only to have the Father morph back into the Master.

ACT SEVEN The Doctor, his Father, Lizzie (and Winston) are held captive on the Warship where they will be forced to witness the initial launch and invasion. The Doctor escapes to confront and outwit the Master, resolving the use-of-force issue. Though the Master (and his Dalek bodyguards) get away, the Warship is destroyed, saving the galaxy.

TAG The Father returns to America to complete his destiny, while the Doctor turns over the Sash of Rassilon to Borusa's widow. The Doctor discovers that Lizzie will soon be a heroine in her own World War and returns her to fulfil that fate. The Doctor assumes his destiny and follows the Master into the Time Corridor ... their 'war' far from over. His sole companion, for now, is Winston.

During October and November, further rewrites and some tightening up took place until the BBC had a chance to look at the latest development. Afterwards, on 12 December, Michael Wearing offered up his comments.

Firstly, he thought the Daleks' role was far too small and that the story was now simply the Doctor/father search. He also worried that the 'somewhat comic research assistant' in the teaser took too much away from the Doctor. 'Does this person die?' he asked. Wearing also wondered how the Doctor escaped from the threat posed in the teaser; he felt that the Master having a morphing ability was too common and something of a cop-out. He felt that the father/son theme was generally overextended to the extent that it was beginning to drag the story down. And, again, the Master's morphing into the father was a bit odd and pointless.

On 17 December, Robert DeLaurentis handed in his first draft of *Dr. Who?* In this, the Doctor has an assistant called Sherman, whom he takes to Skaro, where they are imprisoned by the Master. (Interestingly, the TARDIS still has its chameleon circuit working – its natural state is a pyramid and the Doctor turns it into a sand

dune. It doesn't become 'stuck' as a police box until it reaches blitzed London.)

During Act One Sherman is attacked by ratlike Voxyls and the Doctor has to leave him behind. When he goes to wartime England (Oxford Street, to be precise) he meets Jane McDonald, who agrees to help him after they are chased by the Master and his shape-changing killers, the Daleks ('cloaking device' is used here in the Doctor's speech instead of 'chameleon circuit'). Winston is her pet dog, but is left in England.

In 1995 San Francisco they meet a Professor Anne Baker, who is in her mid-50s and once worked with the Doctor's father on a paper about Einstein's theories. She remembers the Doctor's mother dying in childbirth and his being sent 'to live with grandparents', and thinks the father, calling himself Dr John Smith, went off in a bus painted like the Milky Way to write science fiction, including a book called *Time of my Life*.

Chased by the Master, Castellan and the Daleks, the Doctor and Jane are eventually

reunited with 'Dr John Smith', the father. They return to Skaro, as per the outline, where the Doctor discovers the dead Sherman. The Master kills Castellan and the Doctor blows the warship up. The father returns to Anne on Earth, while the Doctor returns to Gallifrey and gives Varda, Borusa's widow, the Sash of Rassilon, and heads off to fight the Master after leaving Jane in England to fight her war …

A slightly revised version of this was given to Philip Segal and Peter Wagg on 21 December and then a quite major rewrite was delivered on 3 February 1995. In this version the Daleks are gone, replaced by Zenons; Sherman is now a horned alien called Gog (who survives and remains with the Doctor to the end); Borusa is now Pandak (a suggestion of Jean-Marc Lofficier's); and Castellan, who has been turned into a half-Zenon by the Master, kills himself rather than be completely altered.

At this point Robert DeLaurentis's role was finished and, like the Leekley one before it, his *Dr. Who?* was script abandoned and the search was on for yet another writer.

THE DALTENRAYS PROJECT

George Dugdale

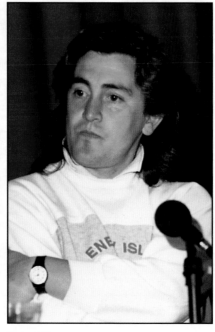

Peter Litten

The Daltenrays project goes back to the summer of 1987, when the group, then under the name Coast to Coast, applied for, and received, the licence to make a theatrical *Doctor Who* movie. Behind this were George Dugdale, Peter Litten and John Humphreys, who formed Daltenrays to get finance for the project. Having done so, they turned to an old writing friend, Mark Ezra, to script, from a storyline by Dugdale and Litten, *Doctor Who – The Movie*.

Feeling that this needed a few changes, they then turned to the established screenwriter Johnny Byrne, who already had a number of *Doctor Who* scripts to his name, as well as a story-editor credit on *Space: 1999*. Over the next few years, he worked on a number of versions of a script he called *Doctor Who – The Timelord*. By the time of its last incarnation, as *Doctor Who – Last of*

the *Time Lords*, in 1991, the Daltenrays team had been joined by Felice Arden and Harold Cellan and they began earnest work in getting up the finances, Arden working particularly hard within the US.

When news had reached them a year earlier that someone from the States was bidding for the show, Arden had made contact with Philip, hoping they could pull together, but it was not possible. As the months passed, so did Daltenrays' initial deadline date – but James Arnold Baker at BBC Enterprises gave them an extension, which would take them to 1994. If they had not begun production by 6 April, the licence would be withdrawn. By now it was clear to the Daltenrays team that the various versions of the Byrne script were not entirely what they were looking for, and Byrne left the team in late 1992, when they joined forces with Lumiere Pictures.

Lumiere immediately went after the *Star Trek* movie writer/director Nicholas Meyer and then, subsequently, the *Star Trek* movie writer Denny Martin Flynn. Going back full circle, Denny Martin Flynn then wrote a script entitled *Doctor Who – The Movie* (it had no relation to the Ezra version) and for quite some time, it seemed as if Daltenrays had found the perfect partners. But Lumiere were worried about one thing: they had heard rumours that the BBC were also offering a licence, albeit for a TV movie, to Amblin. The conflict of two major new *Doctor Who* projects, especially one linked to Steven Spielberg, worried them.

Even though they had talked to Leonard Nimoy about directing, and were considering Pierce Brosnan (an actor Peter Wagg and Philip Segal had already contemplated talking to) as the Doctor, Lumiere began to need reassurances from Daltenrays that the high-profile Amblin project would not happen. It would appear that the BBC were asked what was going on and, as they were presumably entitled to, on 4 March 1994, the BBC confirmed that they were indeed instigating a potential deal with Amblin on a television, not theatrical, project. Letters immediately went back and forth between Daltenrays' solicitors and the BBC's legal department because, once Lumiere had the Amblin rumour confirmed, they pulled out of the Daltenrays project. Daltenrays immediately suggested that the BBC had manoeuvred them into a position that obliged them to tell Lumiere, as business partners, what was going on, and further suggested that the BBC knew this would mean Lumiere's withdrawal.

Hence Daltenrays' contention that the BBC deprived them of recouping their initial £1 million investment by not renewing their licence in April (seven years after they first received it) and, by having effectively forced Lumiere's hand, this meant Daltenrays did not have the opportunity to find further financial backing before that date. At the end of 1994, Universal were contacted by Daltenrays' solicitors, asking for any paperwork they may have that could support their case, anything at all relating to their knowledge of the Daltenrays project. Universal declined, saying that, since they were not making a theatrical movie, they were disinclined to get involved in a fight that legitimately had nothing to do with them.

On 14 February 1997, nearly a year after production began on the *Doctor Who* TV movie, nine months after it had been transmitted, Daltenrays issued a writ against the BBC for damages of £15 million, made up of the initial £1 million costs plus a proposed loss of £14 million from sales of three films, merchandise and so on. As of writing this book, the case had still not been heard in court (although a date set for October 1998 passed without event) and the situation remains unresolved.

I did have several meetings with the Daltenrays guys back in late 1989, while I was still at Columbia Pictures Television. They seemed to be very nice people. I always found it so interesting that they never tried to join forces with me later on, once they knew what I was doing at Amblin. Frankly, I would have tried if the shoe had been on the other foot. Things might have turned out very differently indeed.

But let's go back for a moment to April 1994. It was about this time that I had my meeting with Leonard Nimoy. A very strange meeting indeed. The BBC legal department had contacted me in January of that year, to advise me that Lumiere and the Daltenrays production company were pressuring the BBC to extend their feature-rights option because they had a director in place and were ready to start filming their feature version of *Doctor Who*, after a number of false starts and previous licence extensions. I was not sure what would result from all of this but it was going to be the BBC's position that the film-rights option had expired (and indeed it had) because no filming had taken place by an allotted time, and therefore that there could not be any further extensions.

Leonard gladly had a meeting with me to discuss directing our TV movie. I concluded after the meeting that he was not the right person for the job. Why? Frankly, I was worried about his health. At the time I met him, he appeared to be very tired. I had also learnt from various sources that he had a tendency to suggest

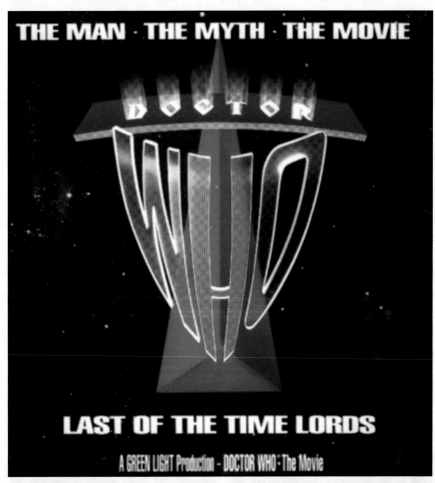

THE MAN · THE MYTH · THE MOVIE

DOCTOR WHO

LAST OF THE TIME LORDS

A GREEN LIGHT Production · DOCTOR WHO · The Movie

 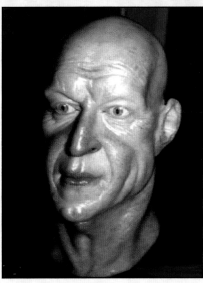

Daltenrays took time to promote their ultimately abandoned film, with a promotional poster and these character busts, which went on display at the launch party for a Doctor Who exhibition the Museum of the Moving Image in London in 1993.

rewrites. Because of our very small window of opportunity, that fact alone scared me off.

Nevertheless, meeting Leonard was an absolute thrill and a distinct pleasure and, under the right circumstances, I would be honoured

to work with him in the future. I think it's also important to point out that the whole Daltenrays/Lumiere affair was very disturbing and rather sad to me. Secretly, I would rather have been involved with a theatrical movie of *Doctor Who*: it could have been quite wonderful.

• 1995 •

MISSION TO THE UNKNOWN

Before discussing the extraordinary series of events that led us into and through 1995, let me take you just a little way back to the spring of 1994 and a significant meeting that was so remarkable that I will never forget it.

I had received a call from Tom Thayer, who at that time was president of Universal Television. He told me that he had just had lunch with Trevor Walton, who was the head of Fox Network's made-for-television movie division. Tom went on to explain that Trevor was British and, when he had mentioned *Doctor Who* to him, Trevor got very excited. Tom suggested that I give Trevor a call and go and see him. The second I hung up with Tom I called Trevor Walton's office and arranged for Peter Wagg and myself to pay him a visit.

Several days later, Peter Wagg and I found ourselves in Walton's outer office wondering just how we should pitch this whole thing to him. To add insult to injury, as excited as I was, I was also worried. The movie department at the network was a completely separate road from the series department. I sat in my chair waiting for Walton and drifting off into my own dimension. How was I going to persuade the BBC to make this a television movie. And if I did, how could I persuade Fox to follow it up with a series?

Trevor came into the hall and greeted us and the meeting began. The whole thing took about ten minutes. Nine minutes of 'How are you?' and 'What part of England are you from?' and one minute of 'Let's do this'.

Peter and I looked at each other and could hardly believe this day had come around yet again. We thanked Trevor for his time, got up and left his office. As we strolled down the long hallway at the studio with big smiles on our faces the joy was overwhelming. So much so that at one point I remember Peter jumping on my back and I found myself giving him a piggy-back ride all the way down the stairs.

The next day, I was on the phone to Tony Greenwood giving him the good news. By this time, I had decided to be honest with Tony about the situation and ask for his help in strategising how to formally present this whole thing to the board of directors at the BBC and get their blessing to proceed.

Clearly now all the rules had changed, as had the wave of enthusiasm at the Beeb. I must add, though, that through all of this, apart from Tony, I continued to have one long-standing supporter at the BBC – Alan Yentob. I will never forget how much effort Alan put into supporting me and the project. For that, I will be eternally grateful. Through all the false starts and silly press reports, Alan never faltered.

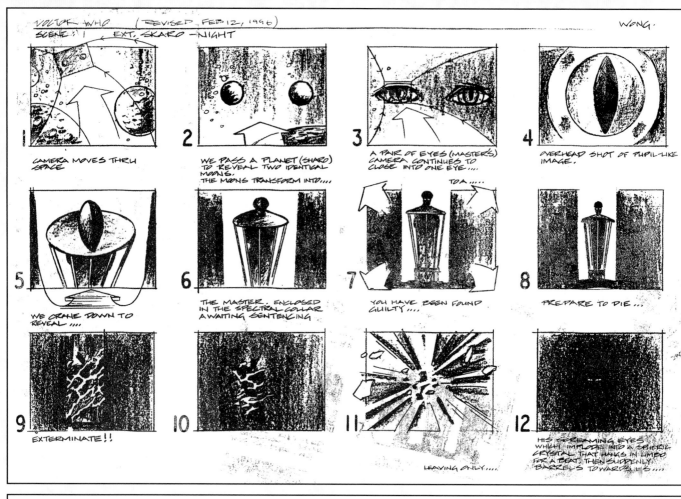

DOCTOR WHO (REVISED FEB 12, 1990)   WONG.
SCENE: 1   EXT. SKARO - NIGHT

1. CAMERA MOVES THRU SPACE

2. WE PASS A PLANET (SKARO) TO REVEAL TWO IDENTICAL MOONS. THE MOONS TRANSFORM INTO....

3. A PAIR OF EYES (MASTER'S) CAMERA CONTINUES TO CLOSE INTO ONE EYE..... TO A.....

4. OVERHEAD SHOT OF PUPIL-LIKE IMAGE.

5. WE CRANE DOWN TO REVEAL....

6. THE MASTER. ENCLOSED IN THE SPECTRAL COLLAR AWAITING SENTENCING

7. YOU HAVE BEEN FOUND GUILTY....

8. PREPARE TO DIE ...

9. EXTERMINATE!!

10.

11. LEAVING ONLY.....

12. HIS SCREAMING EYES WHICH IMPLODE INTO A SPHERE CRYSTAL THAT HANGS IN LIMBO FOR A BEAT, THEN SUDDENLY BARRELS TOWARDS US.....

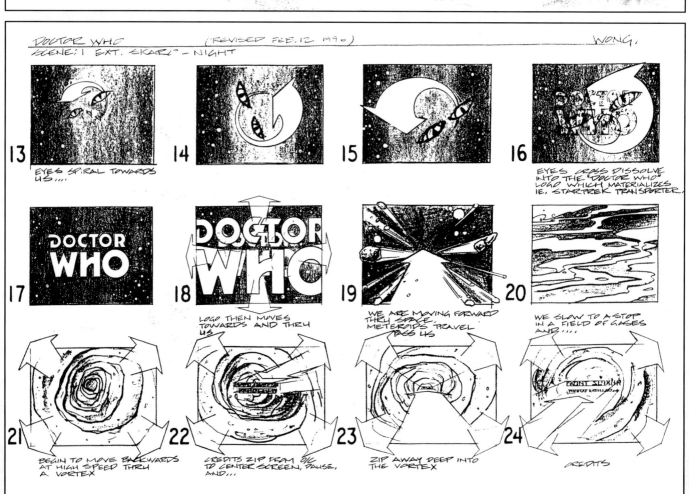

DOCTOR WHO (REVISED FEB. 12 1990)   WONG.
SCENE: 1 EXT. SKARO - NIGHT

13. EYES SPIRAL TOWARDS US.....

14.

15.

16. EYES CROSS DISSOLVE INTO THE "DOCTOR WHO" LOGO WHICH MATERIALIZES IE. STARTREK TRANSPORTER.

17. DOCTOR WHO

18. DOCTOR WHO
LOGO THEN MOVES TOWARDS AND THRU US

19. WE ARE MOVING FORWARD THRU SPACE, METEROIDS TRAVEL PASS US

20. WE SLOW TO A STOP IN A FIELD OF GASES AND.....

21. BEGIN TO MOVE BACKWARDS AT HIGH SPEED THRU A VORTEX

22. CREDITS ZIP FROM O/C TO CENTER SCREEN, PAUSE, AND....

23. ZIP AWAY DEEP INTO THE VORTEX

24. CREDITS

Tony came back to me several days later and explained that two factions were building inside the BBC. Remember, I had two entities to deal with: BBC1 and BBC Enterprises, the latter by now slowly metamorphosing into BBC Worldwide. Each entity had its own politics and bureaucracy and it now appeared that one, namely Worldwide, might be losing interest in the project.

Some time in the autumn of 1994 Worldwide's leadership changed for what must have been the third or fourth time since I had begun my campaign for *Doctor Who*. This time a woman by the name of Juliet Grimm was given a position that essentially took Tony's power base away – Director, Co-Productions and Business Development.

I was devastated. Tony was very smart about the whole situation and instinctively knew how to manage things. It had become obvious by June of 1994 that, by being in a partnership with Fox, all we were going to be able to do was make a film for television. Simply put, if the film's Nielson numbers (the name given to the US ratings) were strong, we would have a shot at being on Fox Network's autumn schedule as a series. If not … well, there was never a guarantee, even a promise, that we would go beyond the Movie of the Week.

Anyway, at this point, all systems appeared to be go. Then came the latest, and biggest, fly in the ointment. Juliet Grimm called me and pointed out that we didn't have a budget and there was no concrete schedule. On top of all of that, she felt her partner, BBC1, was not paying enough for the rights to broadcast the film. I'm on the floor grasping for smelling salts at this point. I started to get annoyed with her. 'Why are you making this my problem?' I asked. She explained that she wanted to caution anyone against thinking we could move forward to production unless some serious issued had been worked out. I backed off.

'Fine I said, I'll keep plugging away here and we should hook up in the next few weeks and see where we are.' She seemed to be happy with the plan and we left it at that.

By late June we were in meetings with Fox about who should write the film, although we still had Universal's choice of John Leekley on board, and had yet to work through to Robert DeLaurentis. Once they were out of the picture, I was being barraged with résumés and requests from people who wanted to write the pilot or be involved with the production. They'd come from writers both in the UK and the States. All the names were listed and presented to Fox.

But Trevor Walton, the vice president in charge of movies at Fox, had his own plans. During a meeting with him, he asked us to read some work of Matthew Jacobs. At this point, I had not heard of Matthew so Peter Wagg and I went off, did some research, read some of his material and arranged a meeting.

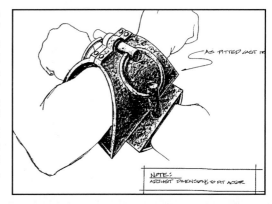

Matthew was delightful. Our first impressions were quite memorable. Matthew had all the qualities we needed in a writer. His energy and his childlike qualities were all part of his charm. He also explained to us how his father had been an actor and had played Doc Holliday in the Hartnell-era story entitled *The Gunfighters*. Matthew recalled clearly actually being on that set, hiding under the bar in some scenes. He went on to explain that his father was very distant from him and his family due to severe personal problems that I will not go into.

Needless to say, as he grew up, Matthew never really had the kind of relationship with his father that most of us hope for. It came to pass in later life that Matthew did finally settle his differences with his father but, tragically, that happened on the man's death bed. At least they had a chance to make peace and say their goodbyes.

All this emotion and life experience made the case for Matthew to write our version of *Doctor Who*, and so, shortly after that meeting, he was engaged. I should point out that, prior to engaging Matthew, we had to discuss his hire with the BBC, but they were in agreement with Fox, which thankfully avoided any potential trouble. It's also important to remember that there were several meetings in London that took place prior to the start of the TV Movie. I remark on those meetings only because it's important to remember certain players from the BBC who stayed with the project through to its completion. Jo Wright was in on all these sessions and spoke for the BBC and took an executive producer's credit on the film. She reported to Michael Wearing, who in turn reported to Alan Yentob.

Saying goodbye is never easy and right before we were, once again, about to begin the story creation process, Peter came to me and announced that after giving it all some serious thought he wanted to leave right away for London. He missed his kids terribly – they were growing too fast and he didn't want to miss another second. We hugged,

Above: Never actually seen on screen, a set of elaborate manacles were designed and constructed for the Master to wear in the opening sequence.

Left: Detailed storyboards were created for the pre-credits sequence – showing the 'death' of the Master – and the main titles.

wrong: Fox has a pretty broad audience, but it's their core audience that dictates ratings. This may help you understand why the movie did not get a high rating.

The ultimate conclusion was that the script would centre on a story that brought the audience to the centre of the *Doctor Who* mythology. It would introduce a new Doctor and not feature creatures that were too 'out there' – which meant losing our plans for revamped Daleks and Cybermen. This obviously explains why we featured the Master and why the Dalek opening sequence was cut so much it ultimately made no sense to anyone. The original intention was to create a small tease opening that would feature a self-contained little adventure, leading us into the main story. I chose the Daleks because of the awareness factor, but, in retrospect, I think that was a mistake.

The Cloister Room, seen in early stages of construction above, was a four-walled, free-standing set which stood in the centre of the its studio space. Special lighting effects were created using 'stained glass' panels and lights shining into the room from the 'outside'.

cried a little, and said goodbye. I learnt several months later that he had accepted a job running the production end of a very successful international company, where he remains today.

Devising the story was not easy. Fox had serious concerns about using monsters that might confuse the broad American audience. Their other concern dealt with the network's own demographics (the analysed composite make-up of the viewers who watched Fox Network – each network is different and they rely on the demographics to help them plan their own schedule). In the case of Fox, the demographics are urban, black, young males and females and senior citizens. Don't get me

Designing new Daleks was no easy task and, besides, there are so many other creatures that we could have chosen that would not require a royalty payment to someone. As many of you will know, Terry Nation first introduced the Daleks when he was involved as a writer on the original series. His deal struck with the BBC back in 1963 gave him all rights to the Daleks. We were forced to pay Terry $20,000 dollars to use them in the show and, as it happened, Universal and Fox made me shorten the Dalek introduction to cut the budget.

In the earliest draft of the story, Matthew wanted to focus on the Chang Lee character and his relationship with his grandfather. We had Chang Lee living in an old water tower, in an alley behind his grandfather's store. Lee would witness the extortion of his grandfather by a gang that the young man may have been associated with.

All of this was whittled down in the movie. Chang Lee's character never gets fleshed out but does still work effectively, in my opinion. We also battled with the key elements of our story. After all, saving the world is just about all you can really do with an Earth-bound story and, although that may seem a clichéd approach, with such a restriction you cannot create a small story because there is no real event to hook viewers and make them stay. It all sounded so tired to me, but time was running out for us and multiple choices were frankly becoming a luxury.

This problem of lack of time was because this was a critical window for Fox – they needed quickly to see and approve a script and allocate funds for *Doctor Who's* production, or pass and allocate the funds to something else. Then, from BBC's perspective, we were changing the rules of engagement. The deal originally called for the production of a pilot for a series. We were now attempting to produce a television movie that we wanted Fox Network to recognise as a 'back-door' pilot (a term coined for the production of films that have series potential but do not come with a definite confirmation). The end result was basically the story produced with some minor variations.

While all the story meetings were happening, I was frantically trying to lock in on our lead actor. I had several meetings with potential actors while on trips to London. The actual events that led to the decision to go with Paul McGann are the most interesting to me, so I will share those with you.

Way back, when I was proposing a resurrection of *Doctor Who*, I had discussed the idea of asking Michael Crawford to play the Doctor. The truth is, he was my first choice. I discussed the idea with his agent at the time, Mort Viner over at ICM, and even went so far as to meet with Michael backstage at the Ahmanson Theater in Los Angeles while he was performing *The Phantom of the Opera*. The problem was that, at the time, he had been doing *Phantom* for so long that he was physically and mentally exhausted. So the man I saw in *Barnum* and fell in love with years before really didn't want to hear about an action role: he just wanted to sleep. (Michael eventually took a $40 million contract to go to Las Vegas for three years and do a show called *EFX*.)

It was not long after my meeting with Crawford that I found myself on a plane bound for London sitting next to David Putnam, as I mentioned earlier. We got talking and before I knew it, the conversation turned to *Doctor Who*. Surprise, surprise: here was another fan with fond memories of our show. As you may recall, it was he who suggested we look at Liam Cunningham. I did get to see the dailies (or rushes) and eventually even met with Liam in London and again in Los Angeles.

He was great, very vibrant. He reminded me of Tom Baker. He went on the list. I knew he would be a tough sell to both the BBC and Fox simply because he had no recognisable experience. However, we did make a 'reading deal' with him and presented him to the network. (A reading deal is a prenegotiated set of terms for an actor so he or she can be offered to the network as a candidate. If they say yes, because the deal's already drawn up, all we need to do is exercise it.) They passed. We talked about a lot of bigger names. I think Peter and I discussed Roger Daltry and David Bowie over lunch once.

The TARDIS in the studio recreation of its alleyway landing site. Note the cheeky UK Tourist Board poster behind.

A storyboard illustration for the regeneration sequence.

There was so much speculation at the time on the Internet about who we were discussing. Obviously it was all rumours and none of it true but I loved the gossip, because I believe that any publicity is good publicity. Someone once said to me, 'You better start worrying when they don't talk about you.'

Anyway, back to Paul McGann.

At this point we were having problems with John Leekley's script and had probably just begun talking to Bob DeLaurentis as well as battling with casting problems. (This last problem is made all the worse without a usable script, of course.) On top of this we were trying to get the whole thing designed.

It was recommended to me one day that I watch a film called *Dealers* with a young up-and-coming cast: Paul McGann and Rebecca DeMornay. This was the first time I had ever really seen Paul act and I was very impressed. You have to remember that at this time, Paul was considered a film star, not a television personality. This difference obviously made him quite interesting to Trevor Walton at Fox, who did claim to know of him. (Frankly, I have my doubts about that, but it was nice of him to say he did.)

It was also a name that the BBC loved, especially Jo Wright, as Paul had made a couple of high-profile dramas for them over the years. I was in Los Angeles at the time I received Paul's film to look at, so I picked up the phone and called Peter Wagg in London and asked him to do me a favour and meet Paul for me. Peter obliged and called me with the results.

'He's a smasher,' Peter said. 'I love him. You should definitely meet this guy.' I asked our London casting agents, John and Ros Hubbard, to put Paul on tape for me. All we had at this point was Leekley's script and a not very impressive set of ideas from DeLaurentis, so I asked them to pull some scenes from Leekley's script and give them to Paul McGann to read. The tape eventually found its way back to me and I was very impressed with what I saw.

At the time, Paul was represented in the UK by a lovely woman by the name of Marina Martin. Peter Wagg knew her very well and was instrumental in opening a dialogue between Marina and me. Funnily enough, Marina had a partner at the time, Janet Fielding, who was negotiating to buy the Marina Martin agency from her, and subsequently did so. So, by the time Paul was cast as the Doctor, he was managed by a former *Doctor Who* assistant. (Fielding, for those who've forgotten, played Tegan Jovanka with the fourth and fifth Doctors.)

Very bizarre! There is more to Paul's story but it comes in a little later.

Now, one of the things to remember is that knowing you have a green light and can get started is not always as simple as it sounds with US networks – unless they really have some burning desire to do something, or create their own artificial deadline to produce a programme because a competing network has a similar idea. In the case of *Doctor Who*, it was really nothing more than my overwhelming passion for the project and Trevor Walton's desire to see it make a comeback. I say all this so as to keep in perspective the shambles that occurred when we were actually in the writing process of the film. To most it was just another piece of business – just another television movie to crank out and get into the distribution pipeline. To me, and, of course, to the fans, it was more than that. But instilling that level of enthusiasm and excitement in other people was impossible. Don't get me wrong: the crew did rise to the occasion, but of course that was a little later in the process.

In was in the early part of September 1995 that I got a call from Bill Hamm, vice president at Universal, asking me to meet him and his boss, Tom Thayer. I knew Bill Hamm quite well: we had worked together on other projects, and personally I liked him and thought he was pretty smart.

However, Bill omitted to tell me the real reason for that meeting before I got there, so I was rather surprised to discover I was going to be given a boss. Simply put, Universal was not going to allow me to be the only executive producer on the picture – they wanted 'their' man on the job, someone they thought they could trust. That someone was a very dear man by the name of Alex Beaton.

We were introduced in Tom's office and the meeting went very well. I had come so far with the project that I was determined to hang on to as much creative power as I could.

My initial instincts were to scream and complain bitterly, which I did, both to Fox and to the BBC, and it was only after assurances from both organisations that I would control the entire creative process that I agreed to the partnership with Beaton. I must say, looking back, it was very kind of them to give such assurances because, the truth is, a film like this is really too big a job for one person anyway.

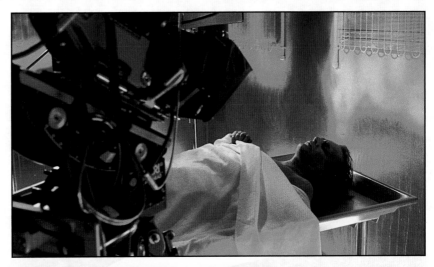

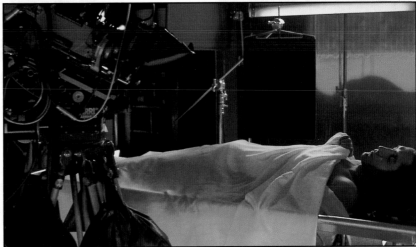

So Alex and I became firm friends. Ultimately, we understood each other: if I was honest with him, he said he would stay out of my way, and, to his credit, he was a man of his word.

Later that September I left Amblin as it was changing into Dreamworks. I took an overall deal developing programmes for Paramount and moved into offices on the Paramount lot, working through Lakeshore Productions. As a thank-you from Steven Spielberg, I was allowed to take *Doctor Who* with me, but the challenge of mounting *Doctor Who* while developing other shows was a daunting task. Alex spearheaded preproduction from his office on the Universal lot, where all meetings on *Doctor Who* took place from now on, and in many ways Alex became a new Peter Wagg to me, someone to bounce ideas off and talk through problems with.

We started by offering the job of casting director to Beth Hymson. Beth had been working with Alex on the *Hercules* series and I agreed to meet her.

We connected right away and have remained good friends today. Beth started making lists of actors for us to play the Doctor as well as the Master. While this was happening, we

A computer-driven motion control camera ensured exactly the same 'pass' was made over both Sylvester McCoy (top) and Paul McGann (bottom), enabling the two sequences to be seemlessly melded for the regeneration.

engaged our line producer, Peter Ware. He in turn arranged for the creation of a Vancouver production office right away. Deciding to shoot the movie in Vancouver was a decision that the studio made immediately. I have no doubt in my mind that it was the right decision. I am also sure that, if the story had been set in a location that Vancouver could not replicate, we would have moved it to one that it could.

The one thing I never had a problem with was the studio's sense of production. The

The Jules Verne approach was something I had thought about a lot. It was obvious to me then, as it is now, that this feel works perfectly for the Doctor. When you embrace the past and show a futuristic world or environment, the blend looks and feels timeless. We had two major sets to design and build, and they were to be housed at what was once the old Aaron Spelling Studios in Burnaby, a town about forty-five minutes' drive from downtown Vancouver, where we were all housed. The Burnaby studios were also the headquarters for the production offices, which made us totally self-contained. Every aspect of the production was set up in Burnaby: construction mill, iron works, props, costumes, transportation, accounting, production design, model shop and all the producers' offices.

The TARDIS control room during construction.

Top: The beams to support the console and time rotor are prepared.

Bottom: Decorators set to work painting the detail for the barely-seen dooway area.

machine always worked quite well. My concerns always stemmed from the executives who were not in production-orientated jobs. We had different ideas about the concept of the production.

At this point in the gearing-up process we hired our production designer, Richard Hudolin. Richard is wonderful – what a talent! He was unassuming and never a complainer – a real team player with a very special sense of design.

He understood what I wanted out of the production; we spoke over the phone many times and he would, after every phone call, fax me sketches of his progress. I detailed for him my feeling about the history of the project and the feel of the main character.

We discussed the need to make the production feel timeless and not dated. I urged him to avoid the over-hi-tech, futuristic look of any aspect of the show: the interiors of the TARDIS were to mimic the feel of the Victorian era; I wanted no supercomputers or overly designed panels and buttons; I asked for plain, old-fashioned knobs and switches. Every aspect of the TARDIS was to feel dated and antique.

I was very impressed at the level of enthusiasm, even passion, for our project that all the crew showed. Every single member knew who the Doctor was and, if they didn't, they pretended they did. We created a sort of inner sanctum where everyone pulled together – it was quite special. Construction on the TARDIS interior and Cloister Room sets began in late September 1995, long before we had a shooting script. Yes, as strange as it may seem, very rarely is a script shootable or ready before you actually shoot the film.

In fact, it's not uncommon to working on a script while you're shooting the picture. Such was the case with this one. While we were working on the script with the network, and prepping our production headquarters in Vancouver, we began the search for a director. The approvals process of any film in television and features can be very frustrating. You never have any real idea of what the network is looking for. Most times the studio does not like the choices that the network makes: the former always feels like it's completely misunderstood by the latter. Studio executives will tell you that network executives have no production experience and therefore can't make sound judgments when it comes to hiring the director and other key players.

For the network it's all about what they can promote to their advertisers and whom they like artistically. To the studio, it's all about control: control of the budget, control of the creative elements and control of the personnel. It has always fascinated me how one marries the other, but it happens.

Alex and I compiled a list of directors we thought would be good and then submitted that list to the studio for their additions or subtractions. Checking out a director is a very strange thing. You end up calling other people who worked with the director either at a studio or a network or a production company and you try to take their word for the work ethic of the director. Did he or she fall down on the job? How fast can they shoot? How did they get along with actors? That sort of thing. You then narrow down the choices and look at the director's individual showreels – usually a hodgepodge of films or clips from the work they are most proud of – and from all of that you make a decision. Having used that basic strategy and come up with several choices, we whittled them down to three and checked interest and availability. Once we had achieved that, we decided who were our first, second and third choices. With all that information we marched into the

network, put on a brave face and stood ready to defend our decision. In this case, we didn't have to. Trevor heard the first name on the list, Geoff Sax, and said, 'Fine, hire him'.

Alex and I looked at each other, smiled and left. That was the shortest meeting in network history – all of about one minute. That gives you an idea of the arbitrary nature of it all.

If the decision to hire an actor to play the Doctor had been as easy as hiring the director, we could have saved the studio about $100,000 dollars. As it was, the acting choice was not made until less than two weeks before we were ready to shoot. We actually made a deal with Sylvester McCoy before we made the deal with Paul McGann. The casting of the film was complicated by the difference in vision between the three pairs made up of me and Universal, Universal and Fox, and Fox and BBC. Imagine being stuck in the middle of that!

The first problem was that the BBC would not make concessions on the Doctor – and indeed why should they? Contractually, they were to decide who got that role. The deal we made with the BBC had no bearing on the one we

A possessed Grace is ready to take charge ... Director Geoffrey Sax directs Paul McGann and Daphne Ashbrook.

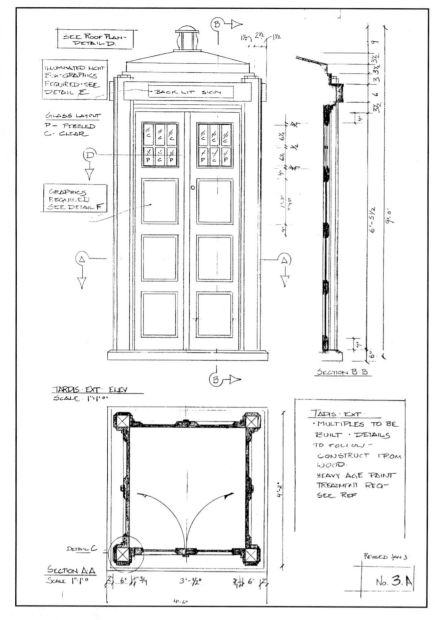

TARDIS EXT ELEV
SCALE 1"=1'.0"

SECTION B.B

SECTION A.A
SCALE 1".1'.0

TARDIS EXT
· MULTIPLES TO BE
BUILT · DETAILS
TO FOLLOW –
CONSTRUCT FROM
WOOD.
HEAVY AGE POINT
TREATMENT REQ–
SEE REF

REVISED JAN 3

No. 3.A

The plans for the TARDIS police box exterior – one of British television's most enduring icons.

Opposite: Storyboards for the scene where the 'morphant' Master locates a new body. The CGI snake created for this sequence would provoke a few raised eyebrows at the BBC.

made with the network. In other words, Fox had to inherit the contract Universal had made with BBC.

If Fox could not agree to any of the terms we had negotiated with BBC, there would have been no film. The only thing we had going for us was that Trevor Walton of Fox was British. If it had not been for that fact, I believe we might not have gotten this project off the ground. In fact, in my opinion, he was the only reason we did get this project off the ground!

September was dragging into October and we did not have a cast. Construction continued and so did our search for actors. By mid-October Geoff Sax had joined us in Los Angeles. Geoff was British too. Seeing a pattern here? When Geoff arrived we focused on what we thought would be the least of our problems: finding the Doctor's female companion. The plan was always to cast the Master and the female companion out of Los

Angeles. The Doctor we had presumed would come from Britain. Everyone else would be cast locally in Vancouver. This is done on most television films and series, in order to take advantage of certain tax credits one can get when shooting in Canada. Geoff and I had our first real casting session in early October.

One particular day, later on in the casting process, we were scheduled to meet several actresses Beth Hymson had identified to play the female companion. Beth informed me that at the end of the session, she would like to bring in a possible Grace candidate. The session went quite well, but our 12 o'clock meeting had not arrived and it was now 12.10. We agreed to wait around until 12.30 to see if this Daphne Ashbrook would show.

Well, as if on cue, she came running in, unprepared and slightly out of it. We both laughed and knew we had a winner. I get a lot of criticism for casting Daphne, but I will defend the decision until the end. Remember, we needed someone who had a certain quirkiness – after all, you would have to be slightly odd to hang out with a man who claims he's from the Gallifrey and flies around the universe in blue police box.

Beth also knew of someone she thought we might want to see for the Doctor, if our plans for Paul McGann fell through. So it was that later in the day a young actor by the name of Harry Van Gorkum strolled in. British, of slender build, with fairly long hair, slightly protruding eyes. Very interesting. He read several scenes and both Geoff and I thought he had potential. Now, Geoff agreed with me that our choice at this point was Paul McGann, but we needed a second choice, in order to make it look like we were really trying to cover a lot of ground, really giving Fox what they wanted. Now please understand: I truly do believe Harry was and is talented, but he was not really right for the role. However, we needed to underscore the need to hire Paul. At this point it was a political move against Fox. I'll never forget the day I called Jo Wright at the BBC and tried to tell her we had an alternate for the role of the Doctor in case Fox did not approve Paul.

'Who is it?' she asked. 'Harry Van Gorkum,' I replied. 'Harry who?' she said. Well those immortal words lived on: Harry Who? Geoff and I never lived that one down. Can you imagine, here we are at the eleventh hour desperately trying to cast this thing and all we could think about was Harry Who?

When we did finally get into principal photography, I had a sweatshirt made for Geoff with those immortal words 'Harry

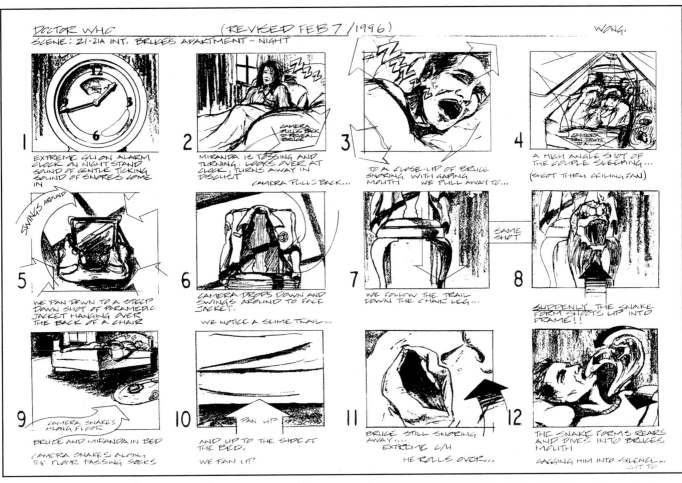

DOCTOR WHO   (REVISED FEB 7 /1996)   WONG.
SCENE: 21-21A INT. BRUCE'S APARTMENT - NIGHT

1. EXTREME C/U ON ALARM CLOCK ON NIGHT STAND. SOUND OF GENTLE TICKING. SOUND OF SNORES COME IN

2. MIRANDA IS TOSSING AND TURNING. LOOKS OVER AT CLOCK, TURNS AWAY IN DISGUST. CAMERA PULLS BACK...

3. TO A CLOSE-UP OF BRUCE SNORING WITH GAPING MOUTH. WE PULL AWAY TO...

4. A HIGH ANGLE SHOT OF THE COUPLE SLEEPING... (SHOOT THRU CEILING FAN)

5. WE PAN DOWN TO A STEEP DOWN SHOT OF PARAMEDIC JACKET HANGING OVER THE BACK OF A CHAIR

6. CAMERA DROPS DOWN AND SWINGS AROUND TO FACE JACKET. WE NOTICE A SLIME TRAIL...

7. WE FOLLOW THE TRAIL DOWN THE CHAIR LEG... SAME SHOT

8. SUDDENLY THE SNAKE FORM SHOOTS UP INTO FRAME!!

9. CAMERA SNAKES ALONG FLOOR. BRUCE AND MIRANDA IN BED. CAMERA SNAKES ALONG THE FLOOR PASSING SOCKS

10. PAN UP. AND UP TO THE SIDE OF THE BED, WE FAN UP

11. BRUCE STILL SNORING AWAY.... EXTREME C/U. HE ROLLS OVER...

12. THE SNAKE FORM REARS AND DIVES INTO BRUCE'S MOUTH. GAGGING HIM INTO SILENCE... CUT TO

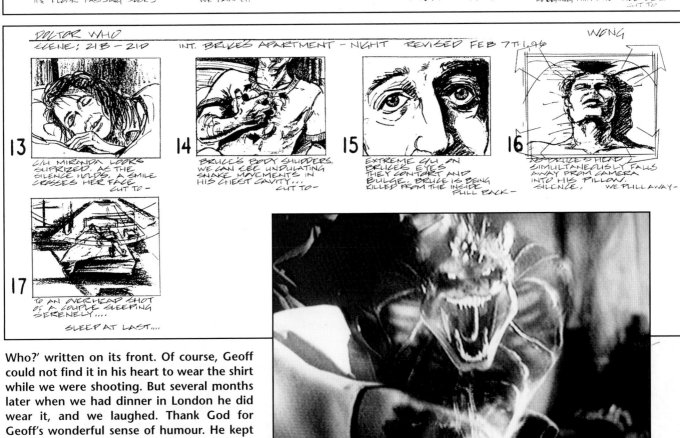

DOCTOR WHO   WONG
SCENE: 21B - 21D   INT. BRUCE'S APARTMENT - NIGHT   REVISED FEB 7TH, 96

13. C/U MIRANDA LOOKS SURPRISED. AS THE SILENCE HOLDS, A SMILE CROSSES HER FACE. CUT TO -

14. BRUCE'S BODY SHUDDERS, WE CAN SEE UNDULATING SNAKE MOVEMENTS IN HIS CHEST CAVITY.... CUT TO-

15. EXTREME C/U ON BRUCE'S EYES. THEY CONTORT AND BULGE. BRUCE IS BEING KILLED FROM THE INSIDE. PULL BACK-

16. BRUCE'S HEAD SIMULTANEOUSLY FALLS AWAY FROM CAMERA INTO HIS PILLOW. SILENCE. WE PULL AWAY-

17. TO AN OVERHEAD SHOT OF A COUPLE SLEEPING SERENELY.... SLEEP AT LAST....

Who?' written on its front. Of course, Geoff could not find it in his heart to wear the shirt while we were shooting. But several months later when we had dinner in London he did wear it, and we laughed. Thank God for Geoff's wonderful sense of humour. He kept me laughing through the whole process.

I now want to publicly apologise to Harry. A real champ and a very talented man, who for one brief moment might have thought he

Richard Hudolin, the production designer, inspects castings based on his sketch of a bust of Time Lord Rassilon. These would be used as torch holders in the TARDIS, and would also top the mirrored columns around the Eye of Harmony.

idea Fox would pull an eleventh-hour rug from under our feet. I could not conceive of anyone else playing the Doctor at this point. But Fox insisted we keep looking. Why?

Well looking back on it I think I know the answer. This television film was about to become the most expensive two hours of TV Fox had ever produced. I now believe Trevor Walton was feeling the pressure from his top brass to put 'names' into the film so they could promote it. Fox had never heard of Paul McGann and they were sure their audience hadn't either.

We finally got over this hurdle by promising Fox that we would put a 'name' into the role of the Master. They finally acquiesced and allowed us to make the offer to Paul.

was going to make history. Sorry, Harry. At this point, Daphne was signed and on board. Things felt like they were falling into place. After the casting session that had gotten us Daphne, Geoff and I were planing to catch a plane that evening to Vancouver to catch up with the frantic build-up and scouting that still had to be done. Imagine: we were into December, building sets, still looking for locations, still waiting on the script and still trying to resolve casting issues. I was now feeling the pressure, as was everyone else.

About an hour before we got on the plane, I received word that Paul McGann wanted to have a conversation with me. I was not surprised, because, with confidence several weeks earlier, I had promised Paul the role. Now this was a secret and a mistake. I really did want Paul, but, when I called Marina Martin, his representation, to advise them that he was going to get an offer, I had no

Too late. We shouldn't have made Paul wait as long as we had. Universal were now in the position of having to pony up more money and they were not happy.

After a day or two of politicking, the offer was made and the deal closed with Paul. We finally had a Doctor. By this time, everyone was going full steam ahead in Vancouver, and we were now making all decisions and deals from our base camp in Burnaby – all we needed now was the Master. While we continued our search for this character, local casting was picking up the rest of the actors, including Chang Lee.

Very early on in the casting process, I had asked Universal to make an offer to Christopher Lloyd to play the Master. Fox approved of the choice, but Universal thought that Lloyd was asking for too much money, so they kept stalling. By the time

Universal were ready to make an offer to Christopher Lloyd he had taken another project. Needless to say, I was very upset and so was Fox.

So Beth Hymson started making lists for us. We finally settled on Eric Roberts. However, when Universal went to make Eric's deal, they discovered that the cost of hiring him was going to be greater than the deal they had refused to make with Christopher Lloyd. This was about the time Geoff Sax got the shot fired over his bow.

Originally, when Geoff signed on to direct *Doctor Who*, Alex Beaton negotiated his deal on behalf of the studio and told Geoff he had 30 days to shoot the film. To put this in perspective, most television movies are shot in 18 to 25 days, depending on the complexity of the film. Telling Geoff he had 30 days seemed like a vacation. Granted, it is a very complex script but a studio has never given a director 30 days to make a television film. This would have been a first.

Except that now the schedule was about to change. As always, the first thing you do when you're trying to make ends meet and cut the budget is reduce the number of days a director has to make the film. On an average shooting day, the cost of production is approximately $50,000 to $65,000. When Alex wanted to cut the budget, I was not consulted and Alex was the kind of line producer who just got in your face and barked out an order. The magical thing about Alex was that he did it with a smile. Geoff was furious and had every right to be – cutting the number of days meant more than just time to Geoff. Alex had negotiated an 'on-time, on-budget' bonus incentive for him. Cutting the number of days was going to make it impossible for Geoff to hit his contracted target and thus would deprive him of money he could have made under his deal. Yeah, a real morale booster if ever I've seen one!

I must say, this kind of behaviour is sadly quite common in the studio system, but Geoff was a real gentlemen about the whole thing. However, he did raise a red flag. 'I'm not sure this film can be made in twenty-five days,' he said. Alex Beaton was more confident. He just smiled and patted Geoff on the back. 'You'll do it.'

Of course, Geoff did not make the 25 days allotted. How could he? We actually completed the principal photography in 29 days. Still, not bad in my book. So, we had a cast and a crew as we headed into Christmas. The TARDIS set was moving along, as was the Cloister Room set. The Burnaby Studios were a beehive of activity.

The next fire that had to be put out was a call I received from Universal business affairs telling me that we would have to find another piece of music to use for the main titles. What? We only learnt at this late stage of the game that the BBC did not actually own the rights to the *Doctor Who* main title theme. The composer Ron Grainer was a freelancer back in the 1960s and his deal was with Warner/Chappel music, who now had to be approached.

I was beside myself: 'We can't use another piece of music,' I said. 'Why don't we find out how much Warner/Chappel would charge us to use it?' After all, who else would want use it? The word came back that Warner/Chappel wanted $25,000 for the right to use the music in our film. Universal said no. That was their pattern – always say no and maybe the price will drop. Of course, that way, you also run the risk of backing yourself into a tight corner and can end up having to spend even more to complete your film.

I called the BBC and persuaded them to tell Universal that they would pick up the cost of the music, although at this point, I knew that both Universal and the BBC were beginning to spend far more than they had agreed to or had budgeted for. The music problem was the start of a rather dangerous situation, because, invariably, what happens next is that the studio will call the network and say, if you really want this film, you'll have to come up with more money.

At this late stage in the game, if a network loses interest or decides that life's too short, they will pull the plug. So it was *very* dangerous. In the case of this *Doctor Who*, earlier in the year Tom Thayer had

One of the TARDIS models built for the visual effects sequences.

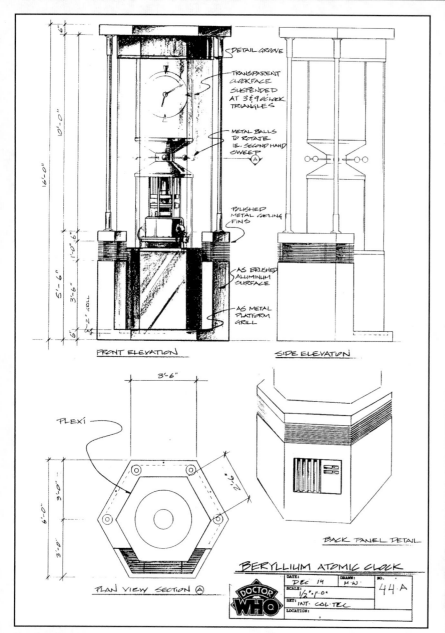

FRONT ELEVATION

SIDE ELEVATION

DETAIL GROOVE

TRANSPARENT CLOCKFACE SUSPENDED AT 3 & 9 O'CLOCK TRIANGLES

METAL BALLS TO ROTATE IE. SECOND HAND SWEEP Ⓐ

POLISHED METAL COOLING FINS

AS BRUSHED ALUMINIUM SURFACE

AS METAL PLATFORM GRILL

FLEXI

PLAN VIEW SECTION Ⓐ

BACK PANEL DETAIL

BERYLLIUM ATOMIC CLOCK

DATE: DEC 14	DRAWN: M·W	NO.
SCALE: 1/2"·1'·0"		44·A
SET: INT·COL·TEC		
LOCATION:		

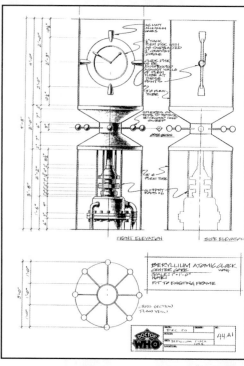

FRONT ELEVATION   SIDE ELEVATION

BERYLLIUM ATOMIC CLOCK
CENTER GUIDE WONG
SCALE: 1"·1'·0"
NOTE:
FIT TO EXISTING FRAME

CROSS SECTION PLAN VIEW

DATE: DEC 20	DRAWN:	NO.
	BERYLLIUM FIBER CORE	44·A1
LOCATION:		

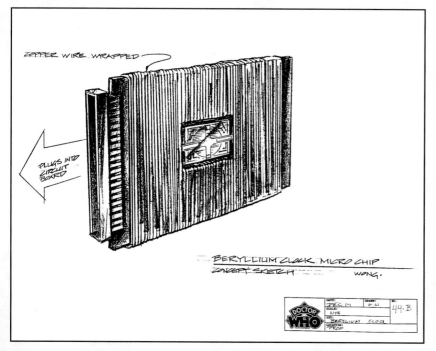

ZIPPER WIRE WRAPPED

PLUGS INTO CIRCUIT BOARD

BERYLLIUM CLOCK MICRO CHIP
CONCEPT SKETCH   WONG.

DATE: DEC 14	DRAWN: M·W	NO.
SCALE: NTS		44·B
SET: PROP		
LOCATION: BERYLLIUM CLOCK		

persuaded Fox to recognise this project as a so-called 'back-door' pilot, as I mentioned earlier. However, spending the kind of money that Fox had already committed to the project meant that other departments would have less to spend this year, namely the series division. OK, it forces that division to take a serious look at the project as a contender, but the truth is, it is very rare for 'back-door' pilots to ever make it into series form.

Soon after the Christmas break, everyone returned to Burnaby to resume pre-production. In less then a week, our actors were going to arrive and start rehearsals. During the Eric Roberts contract negotiations we had to agree to certain perks for the actor. A perk package is not uncommon for actors of his calibre. The rule of thumb is never agree to things that had not been given by producers on previous jobs. It is also expected that agents will inevitably try to get much more.

Eric's requests were pretty standard: access to a gym, chin-up bar in the room, certain food requests and his own make-up artist. Paul's only request was to have his family brought to the location to visit him. He was always concerned about his wife and loves his kids. We did have a problem in the beginning with untrue press reports of a so-called affair Paul allegedly had with a co-star on a picture he had made the year before. Several of the British papers intended to use his having been named the eighth Doctor to banner a nasty headline or two. When Paul arrived, there was a week before his wife and children were due to fly in and I had two serious problems to deal with.

First, the picture Paul had just completed had him playing an SAS officer. So Paul arrived with a crew cut. I was really angry – no one had warned us. The first time I'd met Paul he'd had long hair and it suited his face. It was the one feature of his I thought we could take advantage of. Now I see him standing in front of me and he's practically bald!

Paul's first comment was rather typical of actors who want to try to keep the peace: 'I think it would be great if this Doctor had short hair – we can work with it.' 'No!' I said. 'Never! This Doctor will have long hair.'

So what was going to be the best way to get it? We called the hair stylist on the picture and asked her to join us in my suite at the hotel. It was late in the evening and everyone was tired. Present at the meeting were Peter Ware, the line producer, myself, Geoff Sax, our hair stylist Julie McHaffire, and Paul. Julie recommended going with a special kind of wig made of individual strands of hand-sewn human hair that would be pasted to Paul's head. I said to go with that, but price was an issue. It was going to cost us $5,000 to make just one of the pieces, and we needed at least two. Eventually we all agreed and sent Julie off to produce the wigs.

She had about a week in which to do it. There would be no time to make changes if it didn't work. If it came to us too long, the only thing we'd be able to do would be to cut it. If it was too short, we were stuck. The wig arrived in time and it did fit, and, although it did have to be trimmed, I think the end result was pretty good. There is one scene shot towards the end of the picture, however, when the Doctor is saying goodbye to Grace, in which I thought it looked very fake.

The second problem we encountered came to me in the form of a phone call from our unit publicist. She explained that Paul was refusing to meet with the British press at this time. She was not clear why and I agreed to sit down with Paul and find out what was wrong. He explained that several of the tabloids had run stories earlier in the year claiming he had been unfaithful to his wife. He was very upset and therefore saw no reason to meet with them now. I completely understood. I asked him if we could just exclude those papers that had been unkind or unfair. He agreed.

My problem was that a plane had just left the UK with an arsenal of reporters and we were not sure who they were. In that group of reporters was going to be an unlucky soul or two who would be denied access to the set and Paul. For obvious reasons, I cannot divulge which reporters or papers, but they were rags.

Opposite: Concept sketches by Michael Wong for the Beryllium Clock housing, the clock itself, and the vital chip the Doctor 'borrows'. The prop was assembled at Burnaby studios.

Below: Shooting a scene in the ruined hospital ward.

FINAL CASTING

Beth Hymson arranged a number of auditions in Los Angeles for the three main parts. With Paul McGann still not confirmed because Fox were concerned about not having a 'name' lead, Beth put together a lengthy list for everyone to talk through on 11 December at a meeting. As it turned out, very few of these people actually auditioned and a majority of the list – not, therefore, reproduced here – was a regurgitation of the Hubbards' list from 1994.

However there were some newcomers and a few returning names. 'NTG', by the way, is shorthand for, presumably, 'Not The Guy'. Again, the comments in brackets are as per the notes beside each name – but bear in mind that this was intended to keep the Fox executives sweet and not necessarily an indication of the direction Philip or Geoffrey was really wanting to go in:

Paul McGann (to meet Trevor Walton in London 19th Dec), Harry van Gorkum (seen 6th Dec – 2 p.m. 'quite good/street!!', liked, callback 11th – 3 p.m. 'could do it, BBC???', screen test 15th), Peter Capaldi (trying to arrange meet with Trevor Walton 19th Dec), Adrian Dunbar (trying to arrange meet with TW 19th), Anthony Higgins (tta meeting TW 19th), Anthony Head (seen 4th 11am – NTG), Martin Kemp (seen tape – NTG), David Hunt (seen 11th – 2.15 p.m. 'heavy!!' 'Age?' NTG), Colin Firth (poss interest), Sebastian Roche (seen in London and on 11th Dec – 2.30 p.m. 'odd – but not as strong as Paul'), Jason Connery (taped 1st Dec), Bruce Payne (asked to meet Philip 12th, seen 13th), Roger Rees, James Wilby, Paul Reese, Jonathan Morris, John Gordon Sinclair, Christopher Villiers (seen tape – NTG), Alistair MacDougal (seen 8th Dec NTG), Arnold Vosloo (due on 6th but ill – seen 11th – 2.00 p.m. 'no' NTG), Simon Clark (seen 5th NTG), Julian Stone (seen tape NTG), Robert Reynold (seen tape NTG), Marcus Gilbert (seen 6th – 2.15 p.m. 'no' NTG),

Greg Cutwell (seen tape NTG), Paul Rhys (seen tape NTG), Michael Cumpstey (seen tape NTG), Mark Lindsay Chapman (seen 6th – 2.30 p.m. 'not right. Good fun though'), Simon Templeman (seen 6th – 3.00 p.m. 'no'), Stuart Finley McLennan (seen 11th – 2.30 p.m. 'no'), Daniel Gerroll (seen 11th – 2.45 p.m. 'no'), Anthony Higgins (seen tape 19th), Clive Owen, Nigel Havers (seen tape NTG), Kendrick Hughes (seen 5th NTG), Simon Clarke (seen 5th NTG), John Gegenhuber (seen 5th NTG) Thomas Arklie (seen 5th NTG), Ingo Rademacher (seen 8th NTG), Peter Lavin (seen 8th NTG), Brian Murray (seen 8th NTG), Douglas Weston (seen tape NTG), Tony Coleman (seen tape NTG) and Scott Houston (unable to audition – sick)

A further list was appended to this one, of people either not available or not interested for whatever reason: Peter Weller, Michael Crawford, Julian Sands, Anthony LaPaplia, Kevin Smith, Steven Waddington, Alistair Duncan, Jared Harris, Gary Stretch, Martin Donovan, Lloyd Owen, Nathaniel Parker and Patrick Fitzgerald.

Eager to get in on the act, even though they wanted McGann, the BBC forwarded a new list of possible on 3 January: Jonathan Cake, James Purefoy, William Masson, John Hannah, Greg Wise, John Michie, Clive Owen, Jason Isaacs, James Frayn, Sam West, Alfred Molina, Michael Sheen, Alan Davies, Craig Ferguson and Simon Shepherd.

Meanwhile, Beth Hymson also had her hands full with trying to cast Grace Holloway (or Wilson, as the part still was then). A majority of these people were seen between 4 and 12 December 1995. Again, comments in brackets are those made by the people who sat in on the auditions at this time. It won't surprise you that 'NTL' means 'Not The Lady'.

Isabel Glasser (tape viewed NTL), Leslie Hope (tape viewed NTL), Dana Wheeler Nicholson, Pam Gidley (tape viewed NTL – not interested anyway), Andrea Parker (seen Dec 4th 1115am 'possible. Great attitude. Didn't adjust very well' – liked, callback 12th 2 p.m.), Daphne Ashbrook (seen 6th – 2.45 'yes. Can do it.', liked, call back 12th 2.15 p.m. – circled suggesting she was the one), Lysette Anthony (viewing tape 14th – NTL too expensive), Marcia Gay Hardin (viewing tape 14th. Liked a lot. Possibly too old. Expensive), Wendy Makkena (too expensive), Cecil Hoffman, Farrah Forke, Mary Paige Keller (liked tape), Bobbi Phillips, Kate Vernon, Ally Walker, Sam Jenkins, Jamie Gertz (too expensive), Jennifer Rubin, Christine Harnos (seen 4th – 11.45am), Michelle Renee Thomas, Dana Wheeler Nicholson (viewing tape 15th), Paige French (tried to get tape but sick ultimately not available anyway), Mia Sara (too expensive), Nia Peeples (too expensive), Lindsay Frost (too expensive), Stacy Haiduk (waiting for tape – Philip loved it. Very possibly the one), Jessica Steen (seen 4th – 1130am, liked a lot), Yancy Butler (too expensive), Erika Eleniak (not available), Chelsea Field (too expensive), Kelly Rutherford (tape liked – not available), Helen Slater (not interested in series), Kathleen York (too expensive), Catherine Mary Stewart, Kristen Alfonso (too expensive), Megan Gallagher, Susan Diol, Finn Carter (seen 11th – 3.30 'age!! could do it'), Marie Marshall (seen 11th – 3.30 p.m.), Jessica Stern (seen 4th, liked but will not do 7 eps out of 13), Susanna Thompson (seen 11th – 3.30 p.m.), Kathe Mazur (seen 4th 11.15am), Susan Walters (seen 4th 11am), Molly Hagen (seen 4th 11.45am – liked, called back 12th – 2.15 p.m. emphatic no), Adelaide Miller (seen 6th – 2 p.m. 'nice good attitude', liked callback 12th – 2 p.m. 'energy'), Sydney Walsh (seen 11th – 3.45 p.m. 'OK', callback 12th – 2.30 p.m.), Cindy Katz (seen 11th – 4.15 p.m. 'no'), Clare Carey (seen 11th – 4.15 p.m. 'age! Not a healer'), Mimi Craven (seen 11th – 4.30 p.m.), Romy Walthal (4th 11am – seen 11th – 4.00 p.m.), Wendy Kilbourne (seen 11th – 4.30 p.m.), Carol Huston (seen 11th – 4.45 p.m.), Lisa Waltz (seen 6th – 2.30 p.m. 'no'), Diane Delascio (seen 6th – 2.15 p.m.), Fay Masterson (seen 5th – not the lady), Frankie Thorn (seen 5th – NTL), Janet Gunn (seen 8th – NTL), LaReine Chabut (seen 8th NTL), Christine Ashe (seen 8th NTL), Katherine Kousi (seen 8th – NTL), Barbara Tyson (seen 8th NTL), Hellena Schmeid (seen 8th NTL), Gretchen

German (seen 8th NTL), Lisa Howard (Seen 8th NTL), Lisa Chess (seen 8th NTL), Cali Timmons (seen 8th NTL), Goria Payne (seen 8th NTL), Jo Champa (seen 11th NTL), Kim Raver, Jenna Stern, Julia Campbell (tape viewed NTL), Perrey Reeves (tape viewed NTL)

Again, a number of actors were considered but let it be known that this wasn't their thing, or they would not be available:

Beth Toussaint, Carrie Ann Moss, Kelly Lynch, Julianne Phillips, Carolyn Goodall, Nancy Everhard, Lisa Rienna, Andrea Roth (originally due 4th 12.15 but then seen 2 p.m. 6th), Liza Snyder (possibly seen 6th 2.45), Colleen Flynn (tape seen – liked a lot), Jessica Tuck, Tracy Griffith, Maria Bello, Judith Hoag (too expensive), Leslie Hope

Finally, with the realisation that a 'name' was needed for the Master, and fast, Beth put together a wish list for that role.

Rip Torn (too expensive), Sting (offered but passed due to recording/personal commitments), Christopher Lloyd (too expensive), Richard Dean Anderson, Roger Daltry, James Woods (doubtful), Richard Crenna, Peter Coyote, Ron Silver, Keith Carridine, Charles Dance (too expensive), Patrick Bergin, Brian Cox, Jeffrey DeMunn. JT Walsh, Peter MacNichol, Miquel Ferrer, Christopher Lee, Michael McKean, Randy Quaid, Leonard Nimoy ('gettable' according to agent as 'looking to act again'), Charles Dutton (interested), Reuban Blades, Terry Kinney, Stephen Lang, Steven McHattie, Terry O'Quinn, Jonathan Banks, Robert Englund, Ted Levine, Robert Davi, Clancy Brown, Charles Martin Smith, Rex Linn, Steven Tobolowsky, Bill Sadler, Larry Drake, Tom Noonan, Lance Henrikson, Bruno Kirby, Saun Rubnik, Ron Rifkin, Matt Frewer, Arliss Howard, Fisher Stevens, Martin Sheen, Sam Elliott, Michael York, Tim Curry (does not like Dr Who), Joe Morton, Michael Biehn (not available), Tome Sizemore (not available), A Martinez, Phil Casnoff, Harry Hamlin (Not available), Peter Gallagher (doubtful), Oliver Platt, Tim Hutton, Dermot Mulroney (not interested in TV), Judd Nelson ('something Judd would really respond to' according to his agent), David Keith (not available), Corbin Bernsen, John Corbett, Michael Ontkean, Matt Dillon (not interested), Gregory Hines, Ray Liotta (not interested

Daphne Ashbrook's rather scatty audition won Philip Segal over totally.

in TV), Michael O'Keefe (not available – doing Roseanne), Ernie Hudson, Alan Rosenberg (not available), Daniel Stern (not interested in TV), Steve Buscimi (not available), Judge Reinhold (not available), Jim Belushi (interest doubtful), Eric Bogosian (not available) Eric Roberts (probably available as movie Porkchop is on/off), Peter Scolari, Henry Winkler, Mario van Peebles (not available), Michael Jetter, Peter Weller (not available), Kyle MacLachlan (too expensive), Tom Waits, Rick Moranis, Malcolm McDowell, Chevy Chase (not interested), Chris Issak, Mick Jagger, Howie Long, Art Garfunkel, Tom Selleck (Geoff Sax has contacted him – will not happen), Kyle MacLachlan (awaiting response of offer), Damon Wayans, Malcolm McDowell (awaiting outcome of a movie offer), Rutger Hauer ('major Who fan' – too expensive)

Among those definitely not interested or available were:

Keenan Ivory Wayans, Scott Glenn, Phil Collins, Matt Craven, Patrick Stewart, Howie Long, Dennis Hopper, Dan Ackroyd, Bill Murray, Robert Duvall, John Lithgow, Matt Craven, Louis Gossett, Jay O Saunders, Eric Stoltz, Dana Carvey, Mario van Peebles, Mandy Patinkin, Jonathan Pryce, Scott Bakula, Peter Riegert, Tom Berenger, Griffin Dunne, F Murray Abraham, John Heard, Armand Assante, William Hurt, Jon Voight, Frank Langella, David Bowie, Richard Dreyfus, Ben Kingsley, John Malkovich, Gary Busey, Timothy Dalton, Gabriel Byrne, David Clennon, Tom Hulce, Kevin Spacey, Jeff Goldblum, Edward James Olmos, Daniel Baldwin, Robert Patrick, Richard Grieco (Philip not keen), Jeff Fahey, Brent Spiner, Michael Dorn (prob not avail due to Deep Space 9), Jonathan Frakes (N/A due to directing DS9 Jan 17 – Feb 27)

Incidentally, Rutgar Hauer's name cropped up as a potential Doctor/villain right back at the start of the Daltenrays project in 1987. One suspects that 'major Doctor Who fan' is just another example of hyperbole from an actor's agent, since Hauer himself said in an interview for the British film magazine Empire in October 1998 that he was not even aware of Doctor Who and had no idea what a Dalek was.

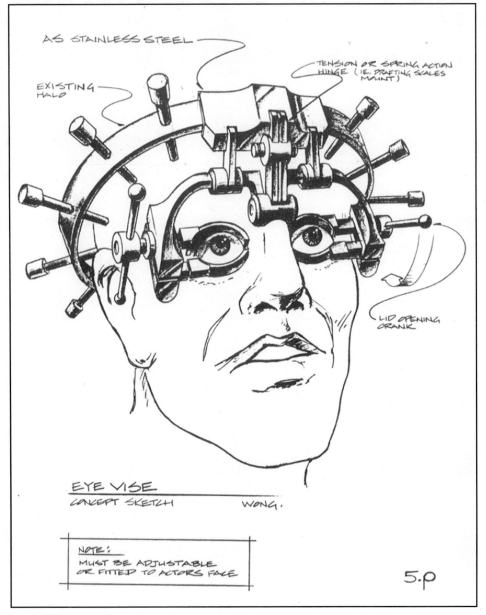

AS STAINLESS STEEL

EXISTING HALO

TENSION OR SPRING ACTION HINGE (I.E. DRAFTING SCALES MOUNT)

LID OPENING CRANK

EYE VISE
CONCEPT SKETCH   WONG.

NOTE:
MUST BE ADJUSTABLE
OR FITTED TO ACTORS FACE

5.p

The design for the device used by the Master to hold the Doctor's eyes open. It owes more than a small debt to Kubrick's film of *A Clockwork Orange*.

I always found Paul to be charming and completely cooperative. Helping to keep him happy and focused was part of my job.

If 1994 had been a headache, 1995 was a positive nightmare. With the green light being given to enter preproduction, and a new script needing to be found, Matthew Jacobs was brought on board as writer, and Peter Wagg and Philip Segal continued their hunt for a cast. Concerned by the now growing press reports about who had been offered various roles (no one had this time round), Philip asked Peter Wagg to contact representatives of Alan Rickman, probably the most oft-quoted 'new Doctor/new Master' in the British tabloids. Although recognising him as one of the finest actors around, neither man was keen on involving Rickman, nor did they want false stories getting out that they had made, then retracted, an offer – or any other permutation of that particular rumour.

In July, Peter Wagg duly contacted Rickman, who very nicely assured them he was categorically not interested in either role. Peter also got back in touch with Marina Martin, who was the agent representing both their possible Doctors – Liam Cunningham and the number-one option, Paul McGann. If required, both actors were still up for it, all things being equal.

July 1995 also saw the long-awaited deal come into effect, signed by all parties: BBC Television, BBC Worldwide (as they now were), Amblin and Universal. Philip was beginning to get interest from potential crew from around the world. Musicians including Tony Banks of Genesis, Dave Greenslade, Simon May, Mike Moran, David Hughes and John Murphy were all showing interest in the project. John Bloomfield, the Oscar-winning costume designer of *Waterworld*, *The Last Emperor* and *Robin Hood – Prince of Thieves*, was interested (he'd designed a number of BBC *Doctor Who* stories during the '70s), while agents representing Jack Coleman, Patrick Bergen, Amanda Pays, Kim Cattrall, Stephanie Zimbalist, Joel Grey and John Hurt were calling to find out what parts their clients could be considered for.

As the move to Vancouver, and thus preproduction proper, loomed larger, the BBC were still concerned about the influence of Fox. In particular, Alan Yentob was worried about names such as Sting being bandied around, believing that, while he might do a one-off, no way was he going to go with a series, and a series was the BBC1 controller's main aim. Incidentally, due to an oversight, it may have been the case that neither Universal nor Fox had informed the BBC of the current status of the show as only a movie – they were too far down the line to have the BBC back out now, even if they could. Besides which, everyone still hoped it could get picked up as a series later.

Philip, meanwhile, had faced the two major upheavals for him by the middle of September. He had left Amblin and joined Lakeshore Television, taking the whole project with him under the auspices of working directly with Alex Beaton at Universal, and Peter Wagg had returned home to Britain for the foreseeable future, officially severing his connection with the show, but always staying in touch to add as much support to Philip as he could.

By early October, Fox (who still had not actually signed their commitment) had confirmed a transmission date of mid-May 1996 for their *Doctor Who* two-hour Movie of the Week, amid the traditional Sweeps period, when US networks make their major pitches to advertisers.

With Fox and the Beeb still negotiating over casting and Philip stuck in the middle unable to proceed further, he and Tony Greenwood were reduced to sending subtext-laden faxes to each other, communicating the truth as they understood it but veiled enough to keep anyone else who saw them in the dark. Trying to keep their respective studios happy was a task neither of them relished. With the disputes still going on, Philip briefly flirted with the idea of bringing Paramount in on the deal as well, especially as Lakeshore's offices were on their Melrose Avenue lot.

The budget had been set at $5 million – Fox looking after $2.5 million and the BBC $300,000, leaving the remaining $2.2 to be split between BBC Worldwide and Universal. Universal were getting edgy about this amount, inspiring Lakeshore to talk to Paramount. Nothing came of this, which disappointed Philip: having come to know the Paramount executives, he would have found appealing the prospect of moving the project over to them even at this stage, and leaving Universal out completely.

Only three weeks before starting in Vancouver on 27 November, Universal were still querying the state of property ownership. Universal was a studio used to making things it subsequently owned, lock, stock and barrel. Going into production on a television movie whose rights actually belonged to someone else entirely (the BBC) did not make them comfortable. Certainly they were up for a hefty percentage of anything this particular version of *Doctor Who*

made, but they seemed uncomfortable with the fact that the BBC could still exploit the previous thirty-odd years of the show.

Philip suggested telling Universal they had 24 hours to decide, or everyone else would go elsewhere (Universal's investment so far would probably be non-regainable), and actually instructed his attorneys to contact Jim Brock at Universal, asking whether they were to sever Philip's service contract with the company. This was just ten days before the production was due to start and no one was feeling particularly positive about it. As well as this, the only confirmed casting was Sylvester McCoy's, reprising the part of the seventh Doctor, and even he was having trouble fitting it into his schedule, since he was simultaneously preparing for a theatre role.

Fox signed up their part of the package and money towards the end of November, giving the final green light to commence production, but there was still a small contractual problem to sort out – the BBC's contract was still with Amblin rather than just Universal. This had to be corrected before production could begin. Jim Brock at Universal quickly sorted it all out and, for the first time since 1989, everyone seemed reasonably calm and content. With the director Geoffrey Sax heading for Vancouver, his new wife Karina as his PA at his side, things were looking even better.

Right on schedule, 27 November 1995, number 8651 Eastlake Drive, Burnaby, British Columbia, became the first official *Doctor Who* production office since John Nathan-Turner had taken the *Doctor Who* sign down from his third-floor office door at Union House in West London's Shepherd's Bush. Now the fun could really begin …

Michael Wong's storyboards for the final fight scene were done once filming had begun on the TARDIS set, and the team were clear on what was, and what was not, possible to choreograph.

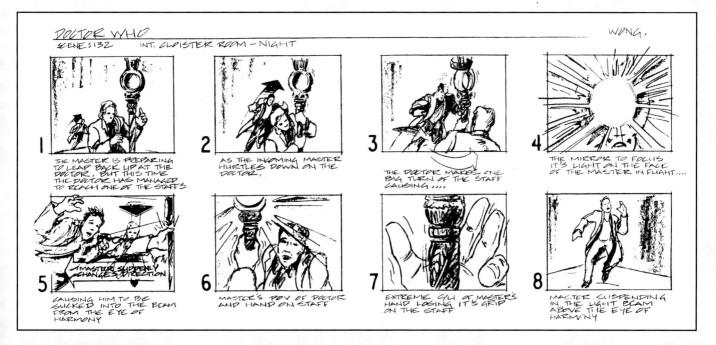

Above: Eric Roberts as the Master, trying to survive in the decaying body of Bruce the paramedic.

Opposite: Daphne Ashbrook and Paul McGann on set.

• 1995 •
THE JACOBS SCRIPT

Once Matthew Jacobs had been agreed as the new writer by all parties, they called him to a meeting on 5 May 1995 to outline what they were looking for. Their brief was to move away from all the Leekley/DeLaurentis concepts and start again – the only hangover from any of this was the fact he has a human mother, an idea Philip Segal had instigated right from the word go (although none of the Ulysses/Borusa back story was carried over either).

This was the first time it had been decided that this new *Doctor Who* would be linked to the past – with regenerations and other TV ephemera attached to the concepts. Both Leekley and DeLaurentis had come from the direction of reinvention, whereas Jacobs was given the opportunity to rebuild from the existing show rather than re-create one from scratch. The notes Matthew had to work from were as follows:

The story should be small and personal; it should unfold and blossom. He is thrown out into the world, not unlike *Starman*. When he regenerates, his head is scrambled – he doesn't know where he is or who he is (what his real powers are). He must always go through a period of knowing or finding out about himself.

Prior to the regeneration process he retreats to

the planet Earth, as it is a safe haven; there he recharges his batteries – perhaps one of the reasons he does this is that his mother was an Earthling and it feels safe and comfortable to him. He has a great love of the human race, which also may be rooted in his mother.

Unlike *The Terminator* or *Quantum Leap*, he never worries about his effect on the Time Line. He has much more to do with chaos. He is an anarchic character that begs to be underestimated.

As a hero, he is less a Kurt Russell, serious heavy type. He is mischievous; a Puck of the Time Lord world.

It is his humorous side that appeals to people, not the athletic, not the handsome. He is a hero, but doesn't parallel a typical hero. He is closest to the William Hartnell character.

There should be a triangular relationship between the Doctor and the people he meets. This should be the crux of the drama. Will they go with him? Part of that triangle is the audience. They are the real innocents.

One of the things to avoid is giving too much information. There are too many rules of Time and Space for the viewer to get lost in. There should be very simple guidelines.

His process of regeneration and remembering who he is will imply his world (of the Time Lords)

and bring us the info in digestible pieces rather than in large expositional chunks. This would lend to a more organic way of revealing, by having his past surface as part of his new experiences.

We need to come up with a new Dalek. A new antagonist. We would expect this anyway from the original. Here's who he is: here's his world. What new adventures is he to embark on.

We should think about the genius of the Daleks. Why they originally came up with them for the show and where we are now, in the 90s, and create our on version of the Daleks. Need to start fresh, and layer in. Whatever, this alien life force is in pursuit of him.

Trevor is nervous about going to the tired conveniences of World War II. Things we've seen before. We shouldn't be history hopping. If he is to arrive in today's world, then it is important for us to see something of the fantastic, something about his amazing world. Triggering this world might be his being an alien or his discovery he's meddled in someone's business.

We need to bear in mind that what he's there for is of much larger implications. His essence is that he's come to this time, this space to fix something. What is a Doctor? He's someone who heals, who fixes things. He is unaware of his

powers. We only have a hint of what the future will bring.

The TARDIS could be the fantastic element we're looking for. It tells us we're dealing with an alien and something of his personality.

The Doctor is between 30 and 45. He has a certain lunacy coupled with an Alan Rickman charisma – not an on-the-nose leading man. He has an insatiable curiosity – he loves the journey more than the getting there.

His genius quality means he has the sense of someone who deals in the world of quantum physics yet can't figure out how to give change back from a dollar. We should be too cautious of his knowing everything. There should be room for him to learn.

Matthew Jacobs received those notes from Philip on 8 May and by 19 May had delivered a highly detailed five-page document outlining some of his initial thoughts. These ideas including going back to the earlier idea of using the Master as Philip's 'new Daleks' for the story.

Logline/Theme
Only when Doctor Who knows who he is will he be able to save us all. Only if you know yourself can you save yourself.

Once Roberts understood what Segal and Sax were trying to achieve with the TV Movie, he threw himself wholeheatedly into his role – and clearly enjoyed dressing for the occasion.

POLICE PUBLIC CALL BOX

POLICE TELEPHONE
FREE
FOR USE OF
PUBLIC

PULL TO OP

Bowing out with great dignity, Sylvester McCoy as the Seventh Doctor on location in a cold and damp Vancouver winter.

Backstory and some general thoughts

The Master and the Doctor go back a long way. The Master is also a Time Lord, but he is the personification of pure evil and is on his twelfth, last and most repulsive regeneration. Now fearing the end, the Master is hoping to achieve total immortality by harnessing the very rare life/death force of the plane Earth. In harnessing this (maybe through use of the Doctor's TARDIS) he will resurrect all that is dead and create a new life force, a life force strong enough to make him the most powerful being in the universe. The fact is that, by doing this, the Master will bring about a spiritual and physical destruction for the Doctor's mother-world – literally transforming it into Hell on Earth – is merely a gratifying by-product of becoming what will be, to all intents and purposes, God.

The plan is to tell this primal conflict as a very exciting and fantastically intimate TV movie about a great man trying to discover 'who', 'what' and 'why' he is! It is a story which we live through the very people who have to help the Doctor rediscover his fantastic battle spirit and ultimately help him win.

Our story starts just after the Master has succeeded in stowing away on the TARDIS and is forcing it to land on Earth, present day (San Francisco or New Orleans – the jury's still out on this). In doing this the Master has mortally wounded the Doctor … or has he?

(Here is an extremely roughly drawn outline of the movie broken down into seven acts as requested. Everything is open territory in my mind as I am still exploring the characters and what their exact journeys could be. If it seems front heavy, that's because I've only had a few days with it.)

ACT ONE Opening credits: oblique images of the TARDIS travelling through time and space, almost incomprehensible, but full of promise for the science-fiction scale that the piece will reach.

1. The TARDIS arrives in some apt surrounding, the Doctor (still Sylvester McCoy) bursts out, slamming the door shut behind him to keep back whatever evil force he's been fighting with. Then he turns and either he realises that he has been mortally wounded or he finds that he is standing straight in the path on an oncoming juggernaut! Either way, the Doctor is down and out for the count. In that moment, a worm-thin strand of DNA slithers out through the keyhole of the TARDIS, grows into a sinister snake and slides off into the nearest sewer. Though we don't know it yet, this snake is the Master.

2. Jack (16), a tough street-kid, finds the Doctor and rifles through his pockets. Jack is a modern day Huck Finn, on the run from a horrifyingly lost childhood. He has nothing to lose. He is just placing the TARDIS key in his pocket when he realises the old guy is still alive. Thinking that this man is wealthy, he decides to take him to casualty.

3. The snake/Master finds its host in a terrifying little sequence where we realise very clearly that the Doctor has brought something very dangerous with him.

4. The Doctor is swept into the ER. Hearing his hearts, they conclude that he is fibrillating and they prepare him for immediate surgery. Jack

In earlier drafts of Michael Jacobs' script, the amnesiac new Doctor fled the hospital only to see an apparition of his human mother.

8. Kelly tells Jack; he twists his disappointment into feigned grief and tries to bluff his way but Kelly sees through him and she realises the boy has no idea who the stranger is. Jack cleverly makes it back on to the street, still in possession of the Doctor's keys etc. All in all, not a bad night's work.

9. We follow the Doctor's body as it is put on ice, slammed into the cold, dark chamber, 'John Doe' on his toe. Then it happens – we literally see him regenerating. Glowing from within his very body … in a fantastic sequence we see the new Doctor being born.

(From here on in, VERY ROUGH only, in very broad strokes.)

ACT TWO 10. The Doctor escapes from the morgue, terrifying the attendant. The Doctor wanders the streets; he literally has no idea who he is.

11. Kelly finds out that the body has gone; she realises she is on to something big, so rather than raise a hue and cry she keeps it quiet, fearing that people might think she's gone insane if she says what is really on her mind.

12. The next day. The host body for the Master starts the day by murdering his wife, then sets out to the hospital to try and track the Doctor down.

13. At the hospital the Master asks questions and is told that a John Doe died the previous night. We see that the Doctor in his new incarnation is also hanging around the hospital. Both Time Lords should pass each other, maybe even talk to each other without realising who the other is … Maybe the Master asks to see the doctor who declared the John Doe dead, and he meets with Kelly and he seems pleased when she insists that the John Doe is in the deep freeze.

As the Master goes, Doctor Who sees Kelly, he recognises her immediately – this is the first thing he recognises … He goes after her, but of course she doesn't know who he is. He's going to have to wait until the end of he shift. As he waits, other things come back to him and maybe he even assumes the identity of a visiting doctor and literally calls himself 'Dr Who'. Why not?

14. Meanwhile Jack has gone back to the TARDIS. He tries to open it and can't at first. Then, taking out the Doctor's gloves maybe, he succeeds. He steps inside … it's massive, incredible, transcendental, etc. The kid starts to explore, having no idea of the danger he's in.

15. The Doctor waits until the shift comes out at dusk and follows Kelly to her car. Then he identifies himself to her by repeating what she said privately to him before he went under. She takes him back to her place.

claims to be a friend, assuming the Doctor's wealthy and that there will be something in this for him if he survives, so he waits … They page the surgeon; she's at the opera.

5. Dr Grace's bleeper goes off just as Puccini's Turandot is about to guess the name of the stranger. Kelly Grace (30+) is a surgeon and one of the best. Everything has to be proved, quantified and tested before she will make a move. Turandot is a pretty apt opera for her to be watching.

6. The Doctor comes round momentarily just as he's about to be given the anaesthetic. He sees Kelly; she whispers a few private words of encouragement to him (maybe from the opera?). He tries to stop her, but he's already going under.

7. The operation. Kelly gets inside him (hi-tech journeying down arteries with micro-thin tube, but of course getting lost). She is too late: the Doctor dies on the table, but, as they close him up, she realises something is seriously wrong. He has two hearts. She keeps quiet about it. The Doctor's sent down to the morgue.

ACT THREE In this act we explore the relationship between the Doctor and Kelly Grace as he searches to find out who he is and she tries to work out what he is.

We learn that Kelly's special area is nanomechanics. She has found in the Doctor everything she never dreamt could be possible – the secret of regenerating cells. With his help she will find a cure for all the terrible ills of mankind. In his quest, the Doctor finds the TARDIS and Jack – who is now inside of it and maybe has been watching his own life being replayed before him. Now the Doctor knows who he is, if only he could remember why he is here and what he was doing.

Meanwhile, the Master is preparing with his neighbours for Halloween. He literally raises someone from the dead ... we recognise the person he has raised from the dead. It is Jack's father ... On Halloween it will happen. What, we do not know yet...

ACT FOUR The Doctor remembers everything only when he realises how much he loves humans. But already it's too late. 'Oh God! If I'm here, the Master's here and it's already too late!' On Halloween, Earth will literally become a living Hell and the Master will become its God!! Halloween: exploiting Jack's father, the Master manages to take possession of the TARDIS and trap Jack, the Doctor and Kelly in a horrible/terrible situation (TBD). Now we know that the Master is unleashing hoardes of the dead through the TARDIS and why (see backstory for details)!!

ACT FIVE Only with the help of Kelly and Jack does the Doctor manage to escape the terrible trap (TBD). And then, in the midst of the Halloween celebration, they make it to the TARDIS and the Doctor comes up with a clever plot to lure the Master back into oblivion! But will it work? Jack achieves some resolution with his ghost father.

ACT SIX Halloween in full swing, and now the dead are pouring out of the TARDIS and playing havoc with the night's celebrations. It's as if the TARDIS is being twisted into a gateway that should never have been opened.

The Master has almost triumphed when the Doctor's plot is put into action, and, exploiting the Master's major weakness, he and Kelly manage to lure both him and the living dead back into the TARDIS and take off to a different dimension. Only problem is Jack and Kelly are with the Doctor too.

ACT SEVEN Big face-off between the Master and the Doctor. In a truly sci-fi setting (TBD), the Doctor vanquishes the Master. Maybe Jack is killed in the process and it is the Doctor and Kelly who literally bring the boy back to life.

Finally the Doctor returns them to Earth – a world that has no idea what kind of danger it was in the previous night. Jack decides to stay, having been given literally a second chance at life. But Dr Kelly Grace, at the last moment, decides to go with the Doctor.

This is the first day of the Doctor's new life; she's going to be part of it, even though he has absolutely no idea where their next adventure will be.

On 27 June Matthew Jacobs handed over a 'rough screenplay in progress notes' document to Philip. This followed but developed the earlier notes, and fleshed out more bits in a point-by-point way.

The opening credits were the same. Act One saw the Doctor arrive in Chinatown, San Francisco, mortally wounded, and rush out of the TARDIS before he collapses. The DNA snake appears as before. Jack is lighting a candle in a temple to his late father 'kind of like Harvey Kietel in the church at the start of *Mean Streets*', according to Matthew. He heads into the street and meets some of his mates and in a back alley finds the Doctor, steals his stuff as before and, realising he's alive, calls 911.

Philip's notes on this suggest it is important we know how and why the Doctor is wounded. He also suggests that maybe the DNA slime should detach itself from the Doctor rather than come out through the TARDIS key hole. He also suggests that Jack should hear the TARDIS arrive and investigate, thus finding the Doctor.

Matthew goes on to reiterate the 'Master finding his new body' scene as before, adding that it should be akin to a 'snoring Bruce Willis gets a mouthful and Demi sleeps peacefully at last...'

A fight to the death in the Cloister Room.

Due to complications with both the latex skin effect and his green contact lenses, it was decided to fit the Master out with leathers and dark glasses to emphasise his malevolent nature.

From what we learn, his father was an alien, his mother a human from a different era and from a different place – as we are brought crashing back into San Francisco… Tortured, the Doctor yells into the night, "Who am I?"'

In this version Kelly tries to find the missing John Doe, even tries calling the cops, but the administrator of the hospital stops her – it would look bad to have lost a corpse. She resigns.

As before, New Year's Eve dawns with the Master murdering his wife and then heading to the hospital to find the Doctor. As per before, the two Time Lords pass each other in the hospital, but this time the Master recognises it is the Doctor but loses him in the crowd.

Jack is trying to sell the Doctor's things to a pawn broker. The Master watches him and, after he leaves, ransacks the pawnbroker's store, trying to find the TARDIS key. But Jack kept that one item, so the Master heads off to find him.

As before, the Doctor goes with Kelly to her condo (in this version, she packs her boyfriend's things up and chucks them out). She dubs him Doctor Who as he can't remember who he is (Philip says no to this idea, by the way) and, as they discuss his two hearts, Kelly wonders if he has two of everything. They share their first kiss and his memory returns as he recalls liking humans so much.

This time Jack and the Master enter the TARDIS and he promises to bring Jack's father back if the boy will help him capture the Doctor tonight, before the New Year.

The Doctor is remembering more – the TARDIS in Chinatown and Jack. They see the pawnbroker's shop on TV, the storekeeper saying his attacker was looking for a key – the one to the TARDIS, realises the Doctor, and he understands what the Master is going to do – turn Earth into a living Hell.

Kelly isn't sure about the Doctor, but goes along with his plan and then meets Jack, who leads them into a trap inside the TARDIS. Both Jack's father and someone from Kelly's past materialise and the Doctor realises the TARDIS shouldn't be doing this.

They leave the TARDIS and go back into what they think is Chinatown – Kelly and Jack are getting on spikily – and see Jack's father again. Jack makes up with his father, who then disappears and Jack joins the Doctor's side.

Then they realise they are still inside the TARDIS – the Master is manipulating it, creating false realities, and at the stroke of midnight the Master will become the master of

The hospital sequences are petty much the same as before, although Matthew adds in the sequence of Kelly arguing with her boyfriend over the phone. The words Kelly whispers are 'Il suo nome e amor' from *Turandot* – 'His name is love.'

The operation scenes are pretty much as per before, and in the morgue the attendant, 'a local university student', talks about getting ready for the New Year's Eve party.

After regenerating, the Doctor takes the now fainted attendant's costume (Philip notes it could be either H.G. Wells or Sherlock Holmes) and wanders the streets, aware this must be Earth. He stops outside 'an Edwardian boarding house. In the hallway is a mannequin wearing a period costume. For a moment the mannequin becomes real. We realise the Doctor is literally seeing his mother. A British woman (we will be defining something new for the Doctor). This takes us right inside the man.

everything. (Matthew notes for the first time that maybe it could be New Year's Eve 1999). As all over the world people will reflect on their beloved dead, the Master will be able to bring them back to life, using the TARDIS as a gateway 'to everything that has ever been'.

The Doctor tries to bait the Master: 'Why simply be resurrected as an immortal when you can be so much more?' he asks. It is Kelly and Jack's presence that is stopping the Master's scheme starting – Matthew describes their being there as akin the the famous Dutch boy with his finger in the burst dike. The Doctor exploits the Master's vanity and makes him believe that they could work together, to create an even bigger evil than the Master dreamt up.

Matthew says he is tempted to take the TARDIS to Gallifrey for their final confrontation, although in reality it'll still be inside the TARDIS. He also says as they move through the universe we might see Daleks, Cybermen, etc.

The Doctor goes too far; the Master sees through the ruse but it is too late. They fight. Jack is killed but the Doctor refuses to believe that the Master's evil is stronger than his good and the Master is defeated, while Kelly brings Jack back to life – for her the dead are no longer just the dead – grey areas do exist even in mortality.

The Doctor returns the TARDIS to Earth just before the Master started his plan at midnight, obliterating the Master, and the world is as normal. In this version, Jack stays on Earth and Kelly wants to go with the Doctor, but he talks her out of it, saying she could do so much more good as a doctor on Earth.

Using these revisions, Matthew then wrote and delivered his first draft screenplay on 18 July. This obviously expands in all areas, but the most significant changes are that Jack becomes Chang Lee, and his Uncle Sam, with whom he lives, is in trouble with the local gangs who are extorting money from him. Sam wants nothing to do with Lee because he is a member of a street gang.

For the first time, we learn that the Master's victim is a thugish fireman called Bruce, although we never really meet him except asleep in bed, when he is killed and his body taken over.

We meet Curtis, Wheeler and Salinger at the hospital, and at the opera we meet Brian and his surgeon girlfriend Dr Grace Wilson, who is called back to the ER to work on the Doctor. Dr Swift is introduced as the hospital administrator; Bill and Ted are the student porters in the morgue – the Doctor talks briefly to Bill in the morgue after his regeneration and in this version it is an Abraham Lincoln

costume he takes. The scene where the Doctor sees his mother still occurs, although not in a shop. This time, the Doctor stands at a busy road which turns into a street of horses and carriages. On the other side of these he sees his mother, who sees him, referring to him as 'my little boy – he's so handsome'. The Doctor starts to cross towards her and is almost run down by a bus as he breaks out of his reverie. He eventually goes to a park and sees his face reflected in an ornamental pond. He asks, 'Who am I?'

The next morning, Chang Lee is asleep with the stolen Doctor's things, beside him a photo of Jimmy Lee, his dead father. Bruce/Master kills Miranda his wife as before, using a gun. Grace and Swift argue – he cuts the 'double-exposure' X-rays up and she resigns.

The Master tracks the Doctor to the hospital via smell, and he asks Curtis to help him locate the Doctor and she tells him to take a seat. He sits beside the Doctor and the two talk before Grace arrives and explains to the Master how her John Doe died. He says he has regenerated and then realises he was talking to the Doctor, who has fled. The Master gives chase, sniffing him out.

Grace is getting her things and tells Salinger she's quit. Lee is trying to show his Uncle Sam the Doctor's things, including the sonic screwdriver. He tries to sell them to Sam, claiming they were given to him by his father, but Sam doesn't believe him.

After Lee has gone, the Master arrives, demanding the TARDIS key, and telepathically destroys the shop. He apparently kills Sam in anger before leaving, passing the hiding Chang Lee, who takes the key towards the TARDIS.

The relationship between Lee and the Master was well realised due to the good working partnership between Yee Jee Tso and Eric Roberts.

Above: With the Doctor chained up by the Master, it falls to Grace Holloway (formally Kelly Grace and Grace Wilson) to save the day. And the next millennium.

Opposte: The newly regenerated Doctor inside the morgue.

The Doctor goes with Grace to her condo, while Lee is followed into the TARDIS by the Master. Lee is alarmed by the Master, not least because his body is decaying, but the Master tells him of a strange dimension called the Eye of Harmony – accessed via a sort of silver well deep in the TARDIS – and Lee sees his Father reflected in it.

At Grace's condo, the Doctor spots a fake Matisse on the wall and says he was with Puccini when he died before finishing *Turandot*. They talk on the balcony overlooking San Francisco Bay, discussing the millennium and Grace's dreams of finding a way to hold back death.

They go to a dime store, where two brothers are fighting. The Doctor buys some jelly babies – unaware that the storekeeper has been replaced by the Master, and they return to Grace's condo. On TV they see the report of Sam Lee's Trading Co. being attacked, and the Doctor hears the word 'keys' being used and remembers the TARDIS. As his memories come back, he realises the significance of New Year's Eve, the Master's plan, quoting the song *Auld Lang Syne*, about old acquaintances not being forgotten on this particular night.

Trying to get to the TARDIS, they are caught up in traffic on the Golden Gate Bridge and the Doctor and Grace steal a cop's motorbike, although they stop at a library for the Doctor to tell a young librarian called Gareth about his future. Eventually they get to Chinatown and find Rose Alley, where the TARDIS is. Opening the TARDIS door, a motorcycle cop zooms in, unable to stop, but quickly zooms out again, and the two enter the TARDIS themselves.

Back at the hospital, Curtis and Wheeler recognise Grace Wilson and the Doctor on the TV as they are wanted by the police. The Doctor and Grace are in the Cloister Room – the Eye of Harmony has been opened and the other dimension is breaching into the Cloister Room. In a far corner, Chang Lee is sitting at a pool, laughing. The Doctor retrieves his things from Lee, who makes him look into the pool, and we see things from the Doctor's past. The Doctor is alarmed that Lee opened the Eye and exposed the pool, and he explains that under the pool is 'a kind of mirror world, made from the energy of a black hole, harnessed by my ancestors from the dawn of time. Beneath the surface all dimensions and times can be reached. In short, it runs the TARDIS – or the TARDIS runs in it, depending on how you view the universe.'

As the Doctor uses his sonic screwdriver trying to operate the cover for the Eye, Lee sees his father reflected in the pool, and Grace her grandmother, who originally inspired her to pursue a medical career. As they both reach out to touch their returning loved one, a furious wind strikes up. Grace's grandmother tries to crush her; Lee's father accuses the boy of dishonouring him.

The Master is reverting back bit by bit to his reptilian form as his body decays. He morphs his arms into lassos, capturing Lee and Grace's relatives and swallowing them whole, increasing his own body mass.

Outside, as New Year approaches, white light beams out of the TARDIS. The Master holds the Doctor and bleeds the energy of the pool into his now almost totally reptilian form, and outside everyone sings, 'Should auld acquaintance...' Grace tries to distract the Master, but it is the Doctor who succeeds by upping the ante, suggesting that he should completely drain the Eye of Harmony – all or nothing. Either the universe will be obliterated or the Master will become as one with it, complete mastery over all creation.

Agreeing, the Master drags the Doctor and the others into the heart of the pool, through it and into the Eye of Harmony's dimension. There, silhouettes of the dead are waiting for them – it is a beautiful serene place and the Master wants none of it. He tries to reject it but instead it rejects him, rejects his evil, as the Eye brings out both the best and the worst in people. The Master fights back, throwing lightning about and killing Chang Lee. The only way the Doctor can defeat the Master is by being honest about his own inner self, but that terrifies him.

Via the kiss of life, Grace brings back Lee, while the Doctor uses the power of the Eye to bring back his mother and thus embrace his past, his origins. The Master tries to do the same thing but all that happens is a terrible darkness descends and obliterates him. The Doctor leads Lee and Grace out through the Eye and back to the real world, which is partying to greet the new millennium. Lee and Grace stay in San Francisco, while the Doctor departs.

A second version of the script with slight amendments – most notably to the beginning and end scenes, adding the morphant snake biting the Doctor to injure him and lessening the Master's final metamorphosis – arrived on 28 July, while a character list was put together, noting which ones could be eliminated if necessary for budgetary reasons: these were Ted from the morgue, the TV newscaster, the radio newscaster and the TV reporter. Interestingly enough, the suggestion appeared to be that Bruce the fireman was a non-speaking role to be played by someone other than the actor playing the Master. Although vastly different from the televised version, it is interesting that all the characters from that version are already here plus many more: Brian, Turandot, Sam Lee, First Investor, Doctor's mother, Doctor as a

child, two brothers in shop, Lee's Father and Grace's grandmother.

By 8 August, the BBC's reception to this script was cool. Jo Wright, also representing Alan Yentob's and Michael Wearing's opinions, felt that there was too much chasing between the Doctor and the Master, going nowhere. Philip agreed with this point, saying they were working on trimming it. She felt concerned that, for an alien traveller through time and space, there was too much emphasis on Earth, particularly with the Doctor's mother. The BBC also didn't like the snake biting the Doctor and crawling into Bruce's snoring mouth, suggesting this was teetering on camp. Philip and Peter Wagg didn't agree with this, nor the request to lose the Chinatown stuff, which the Beeb felt was clichéd. The BBC also felt the stuff in the hospital was too long and ended up reading like a script for *ER* – Philip said they'd look at trimming it back – but they did like the scenes in the morgue.

The BBC added that they considered the scene in the dime store was overdoing the 'chase' elements. Philip said they'd look at that again. The BBC also objected to the Doctor pulling the surgical probe out of his chest, feeling it wasn't what *Doctor Who* is about. However, as it was one of Philip's favourite ideas, it ultimately stayed in. The next three points Philip and Peter agreed with: the speed with which the Doctor gets his memory back was too fast; the Doctor discussing 'love' with his younger self in the Eye and the ending lacked any real emotion; and they wanted more out of the Grace-Doctor relationship.

Ten days later, Matthew Jacobs delivered a revised script. A few changes are worth noting, apart from generally more character development for the major characters. The Master no

longer wrecks Sam Lee's store; instead he reads his mind, revealing that he killed Chang Lee's father and wishes the boy were dead too, leaving Sam Lee badly shaken. He catches up with Chang Lee outside the TARDIS and, after a slight confusion, they enter the TARDIS together and the Master hypnotises him into believing in him. The Master, when Lee opens the Eye, now realises the Doctor is half-human, via the retinal print, and it is through this that he can use the Eye to capture the rush of emotion at midnight that'll reshape the universe in his image. At Grace's condo, Brian has taken everything except a pair of shoes, which the Doctor finds and puts on. The dime store becomes a toy store and on the TV Sam Lee confesses to Jimmy Lee's murder and it is the words 'key evidence' that remind him of the TARDIS. There is a lot more explanation of what the other-dimensional world of lost souls is, and how the Master is going to drain it through the Eye into this universe and thus start the universe all over again. And one nice touch: when the Master telepathically becomes aware that the Doctor has returned to the TARDIS, he mutters, 'He's back … and it's about time!'

Once they're in the thrall of the Master and the pool, there is no appearance by Jimmy Lee or Grace's grandmother. Instead, the Doctor's retinal print is used to focus the Master's bringing through of the dead from 'the other side', until Grace punches the Master. He kills Lee and Grace but, as he and the Doctor fight, the Master is sucked into the Eye and down into the other dimension, which has grown dark, and obliterated. The Eye of Harmony then sends out a bright light which brings Grace and Lee back to life. In the TARDIS console room, the TARDIS belches and the Doctor mutters about 'indigestion' and drops Grace and Lee off, promising to come to them soon. Together, they head for a party while the TARDIS dematerialises.

Matthew then spent a month on further revisions, and dropped the whole Eye of Harmony/Living Dead threat, replacing it with the Master harnessing the power of something he termed the Millennium Star, which is passing overhead on New Year's Eve 1999. With this, he will severely damaged Earth and appoint himself as a false Messiah and rule. The Millennium star was described as:

an intergalactic roving force field that gives out a massive light so bright it can be seen like a glowing star moving through both the day and night sky … Every thousand years this shining force field loops around Earth for a few days and moves on. 2000 years ago the three wise men followed its path to discover the Christ child. 1,000 years ago it marked the start of the Crusade. And now it's due back … The Master is bringing the TARDIS and the Doctor to Earth to

Chang Lee finds his destiny within the gothic vaults of the Cloister Room.

meet it. Here, he will open the Eye of Harmony, creating another force field as a beacon.

The TARDIS' presence on Earth at the exact point the Millennium Star approaches will act as a magnet to keep the star in orbit long enough for the Master to exact his plan. The two will be drawn together ... As they come closer and closer all the laws of relativity will be progressively broken until finally the entire thrust of the Universe's existence will be thrown into reverse, the slate will be cleaned and the Master will rule. Unfortunately for the Master he needs the Doctor's humanity to carry out his plan and act as an Adam and Eve to sire a master race over which he can rule ...

How does the Doctor fit into this? The Doctor's half-human heritage controls the access to the full power of the Eye of Harmony – the only power strong enough to harness the Millennium Star/force field and bring it to Earth. Also, the Doctor is a rival Time Lord and has always foiled the Master's plans in the past. The Doctor has four lives left and the Master is about to die. The Master wants to live for ever and get rid of the Doctor. What is the Master's way into Chang Lee and Grace. And what do they want? Chang Lee seeks justice in an unjust world. The false Messiah offers it to him. He believes the Master until he sees the Master being unjust. Grace wants to be able to hold back death ... The Master promises

her this secret but, when she realises she had the secret all along, the Master loses control over her.

Basically the Master seduces them both into believing that he is the Messiah, but all along we know he is the False Messiah ...

On Monday 18 September, Matthew delivered the new script. The story began the same, although when the dying Doctor asks a crazy man nearby if he saw 'it' (meaning the morphant snake), Crazy Man assumes he means the Millennium Star which shines in the sky. Less infirm than in previous scripts, the Doctor tells the Crazy Man it's really a force field and wonders if he can find an antidote to the Master's bite before succumbing to unconsciousness. Lee is introduced as a pickpocket until he finds the Doctor and gets him some help.

The rest follows pretty much as before, bar the odd reference to the Star, and the Doctor telling everyone in the hospital to 'beware the False Messiah'. After he has regenerated, we see him walking around the hospital at night and learn it is the Walker General for the first time. Although he ventures outside and nearly gets hit by a bus, there is no scene with him seeing his mother at all.

The Master, after shooting Miranda, knows to

The Doctor frantically fits the Beryllium Chip to the TARDIS.

The Master uses Grace's human retina to access the Eye of Harmony and power the transference of his life force to the Doctor's body.

the TARDIS. Unaware of this until the lights go out, the Doctor emerges from under the console and heads for the Cloister Room. There, the Master is hypnotising Grace, sending her into a dreamworld where she is a little girl with her grandmother. The real Grace, thinking she is playing, begins to climb on to a small platform hovering above the open Eye.

When the Doctor arrives in the Cloister Room, led by Lee, he falls into the Master's trap and, in trying to rescue Grace, finds himself on a similar floating platform, the light from the Eye more powerful than ever. He daren't look into it, because he knows his retinal print will be the final key to releasing the force field that will draw the Millennium Star to Earth. The Master, on another platform (as is Lee), taunts the Doctor about his half-human heritage and, although he initially denies it, the Master uses part of the Eye to reveal the truth to the Doctor. He briefly sees his mother.

As midnight occurs, the four platforms join over the Eye, forming an iris, and Lee and Grace force the Doctor to look down into the light and the world ends, breaking Lee and Grace's spell. The pre-programmed TARDIS activates and, as in the previous script, the Master and Doctor fight, Lee and Grace dying as before. The Master drops into the Eye and is consumed; the world reverts and the Doctor bids farewell to Lee and Grace.

go to Walker General because he has seen the sign for it through his telepathic link with the Doctor. Arriving, he has the talk with Curtis (removing a dead fingernail in the process) and then sees a sick patient who looks like Sylvester McCoy's Doctor, pulls off his drip feed and pushes the gurney he is strapped to out of the hospital and into the path of an incoming ambulance, before calmly walking back into Walker General.

He then meets Grace, reading her mind about her desire to hold back death, and influences her. Next, he goes to the TARDIS and finds Chang Lee, recruiting him to his 'cause'. As the earlier script (bar changes to dialogue to reflect the new thrust of the story), the Master and Lee explore the TARDIS, while Grace takes the Doctor to her condo (Brian is/was now her fiancé). However, there are a couple of new scenes of the Doctor discussing his weight loss and a shower scene in which water behaves strangely, resulting in him walking around her condo naked. This time the word 'key' comes from the co-anchor on TV discussing the 'key' ways to get around San Francisco.

After the chase through the City, they arrive at the TARDIS. Grace is unimpressed with its 'low-tech' look. When they are tying to jump-start the TARDIS, Grace is grabbed by Lee and the Master imitates Grace's voice while sabotaging

This version of the script didn't seem to impress the BBC either – they were 'disappointed to see that the structure has hardly changed', suggesting that there was still too much chasing around, that Lee was a directionless character and that the opening Act with the Crazy Man was unbelievable – especially as the Doctor has been bitten by a snake.

They then went on to question something that had niggled them from the start – the whole snake/morphant idea. Smaller queries concerned why the Master tells Lee his plans; that the idea of the morgue guys being called Bill and Ted was dated; and why the Doctor leaves the hospital then returns. The BBC also wondered if it was worth considering whether a new writer should be employed to shake it up and give the Master a coherent character.

As Fox had now given the production a green light and preproducton was due to commence in just two months, Philip replied that, while he would love the luxury of time and money to keep rewriting scripts and maybe even hiring new writers, there simply wasn't the time. He pointed out that both Fox and Universal had approved it.

At the same time Matthew Jacobs was in the UK, so he arranged a meeting with the BBC, and on 9 October he sent Philip Segal a set of revision notes after two quite creative days of talks with them. These involved starting the story with the Master requesting his remains to be taken back to Gallifrey by the Doctor and then escaping, in the snake-morphant form, within the TARDIS.

The Doctor arrives on Earth but is killed by something directly related to Lee. The snake then hides in the ambulance driven by Bruce (a fireman no longer, and now a proper role). The Doctor is taken to the hospital; the Master enters Bruce; the operation and failure; Lee steals the Doctor's things – all as before. The Doctor regenerates and goes out into the rain to ponder his identity, also as before.

Matthew noted that the BBC didn't like the Master killing Miranda, so he proposed toning it down – maybe having it happen off screen. Matthew also found alternate justifications for Lee's involvement with the Master, settling on financial reward rather than the boy wanting justice or revenge or some other nebulous conceptual thing. The scene with Grace resigning, the Master at the hospital killing the lookalike, Grace meeting the Master, his heading to Chinatown, all as before. He follows Lee into the TARDIS as before; they discuss the Millennium Star as before; the Eye opens, triggering the Doctor's memories; the Master sees the Doctor is half-human and through the Eye sees that the Doctor is at Grace's place – he now knows where they are.

The Master drives to Grace's and picks them up but gets caught in traffic and the Doctor and Grace head for the TARDIS under their own steam, via a hi-tech establishment that deals with the world's most accurate clock. Back at the TARDIS the Master oozes a bit of himself inside Lee – he now occupies two bodies. Gareth is now working at the hi-tech facility. The Doctor tampers with the clock and dashes to the TARDIS, where Grace is possessed by the Master as Lee was. It is she who forces the Doctor to look into the Eye, and she almost kisses the Master as they succeed in opening it. The final act was pretty much as it was before.

The next script was delivered on 14 November. This followed the outline Matthew had suggested – with the Doctor searching for a Beryllium Atomic Clock at KAL-TECH, and the opening scene set on Skaro, featuring the Daleks placing the Master on trial and exterminating him.

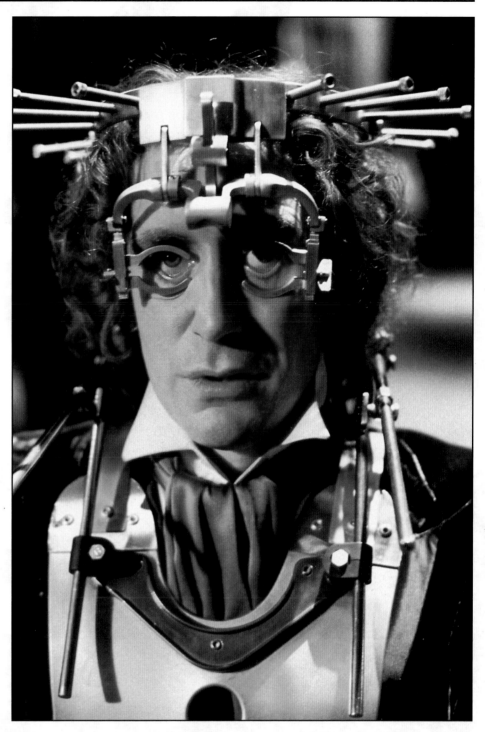

This script was better received by the BBC, who obviously felt that discussing it in person with the writer had been a good move. A BBC script editor, Craig Dickson, was brought in to give the script the once-over, and subsequently Matthew revised the script again after further conversations with Jo Wright, dropping the Millennium Star and concentrating on the Master's struggle to take over the Doctor's body before Bruce's gives out.

On 29 December, Matthew's latest version was prepared as the shooting script and, although it went through fourteen minor variants during the actual shooting (the last one was 15 February 1996), *Doctor Who* finally began principal shooting on 15 January.

A prisoner of the Master, all the Doctor can do is hope that Grace can operate the TARDIS and cut off the Master's power.

• 1996 •

ANATOMY OF A MOVIE

From top: Director Geoffrey Sax and actors Sylvester McCoy, Daphne Ashbrook and Yee Jee Tso take us through the final televised version of *Doctor Who*.

Opposite: Battling to save *Doctor Who* from certain death.

TEASER We pan across Skaro and its two moons, which become a pair of eyes. These belong to the Master, who is on trial. His captors, the Daleks, exterminate him.

Geoffrey Sax *That was an actor called Gordon Tipple as the Master, not a CGI effect – he was actually there, although we eventually cut his voice-over and replaced it with Paul McGann's. I had to learn a lot about CGI doing this – most stuff I do is straight drama that doesn't require those sort of effects, so I was learning something new as a result of this, which is good. It's always good to find you come up against something you haven't done before.*

ACT ONE The old Doctor is taking the Master's remains back to Skaro but the snakelike remnants escape their box and enter the TARDIS console, causing a malfunction that sends the TARDIS off course.

Geoffrey Sax *I didn't watch any old programmes before starting, not even Sylvester's. I'd seen them at the time and I wanted to reflect what I remembered rather than sitting down and researching them. I wanted it to come from my perceptions or what I remembered growing up with* Doctor Who. *I did read up a bit, though, to refresh myself on the mythology.*

Sylvester McCoy *I thought that as this was their movie, and they asked me over, which was really nice of them, whatever they wanted, I'd do it, just*

enjoy myself and not worry. I did suggest I use the umbrella, and they said no. But they wanted the hat, which I thought was great, because I went to the original Doctor Who *audition for John Nathan-Turner wearing my hat, and that was why I got the job … it was great that I got shot wearing it at the end. It went with me from the beginning to the end of my journey through* Doctor Who.

Geoffrey Sax *I originally wanted* Swing on a Star *to be playing in the TARDIS but they couldn't afford the copyright, so we got this library piece, which had the word 'time' in it – a motif I was very keen on throughout the film, with the clocks everywhere, sounds of chimes and bells et cetera. That goo was on the set but I think added a bit later via CGI. We used the same goo later oozing out of the keyhole.*

In Chinatown, San Francisco, a group of Chinese boys are being chased into Rose Alley by a rival gang and a gun fight starts.

Geoffrey Sax *We did film in Vancouver's Chinatown, but the stuff in the alley was heavily dressed up. The gates we put up, as well as all the cans, neon signs and everything. And we added that nice English Tourist Board poster, which no one really notices – the design department thought that might be fun.*

It was very cold that night when we shot it – the steam of their breath is real. Poor Sylvester had to lie in the wet for a long time. I did the edits for

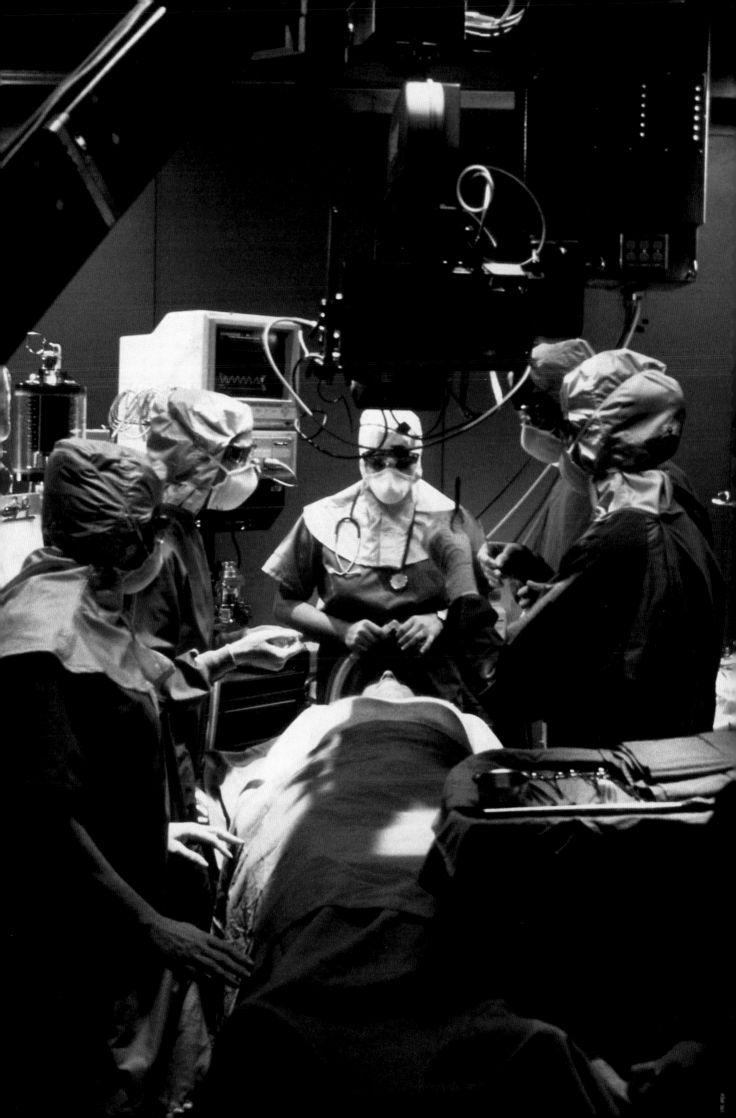

the BBC Video version, taking out the gunfight, because of Dunblane, the shooting there. Sadly it means the scene really doesn't make sense now – you miss the bit of the gang being shot up, which is why there's feathers and everything in the air. This was a decision made by the British Board of Film Classification, and not BBC Video's fault.

On the first day we went into Chinatown, I saw the apartment I wanted to use, where the old people were cooking. Now, on a British film, everything has to be worked out months beforehand and if you suddenly say, 'Hey what about doing such and such?' they all throw up their hands and say you can't because it wasn't budgeted for. Peter Ware [the line producer] and his Vancouver crew were far more relaxed and amenable. I saw this room and said that to get the shot I wanted would need a crane – so I could be upstairs, pull back out through the window and down on to the street to follow Chang Lee's gang all in one shot. I thought they'd all say no, but Peter thought it was a great opening shot and, because he could see the artistic integrity of doing such a move, he and the design crew discussed and said they would do it. That kind of cooperation typified this particular shoot. Everyone loved the project and pulled together to make it work, despite the lack of preparation time we'd been given. I joined the crew late – about five weeks before we started shooting, because of all the delays – and this meant I had almost no preparation time. Usually you get a couple of months – I had a couple of weeks.

Of his gang, only Chang Lee survives – and it looks as if his time is up until the TARDIS materialises in front of him. The door opens and the Doctor steps out – and the surprised gunmen shoot him down before escaping.

Yee Jee Tso *Originally Chang Lee had gone through this tragedy with his father being dead – his uncle blew up his store – so I guess he was a poor guy trying to find a way out. A lot of the character background got cut – to keep it all would have needed a four-hour movie – and there were all these reasons why he carried a gun and everything. Even though it wasn't there any more, I still knew it and it made the character more real to me.*

The injured Doctor is attended by Lee, who fails to spot the Master's morphant form oozing out through the TARDIS keyhole and forming into a puddle.

Geoffrey Sax *We shot the puddle to get the reflection of the neons, then brushed it away, shot the floor without it and then merged the two in a CGI effect.*

A short while later, Lee accompanies the injured Doctor in an ambulance. The paramedic, Bruce, gets Lee to fill in the forms, and Lee says the man's name is John Smith, as he notes the date as 30 December 1999. The ambulance pulls up at Walker General Hospital and the Doctor is taken to the ER. While in the ambulance, the Master's morphant form takes on a snakelike appearance, hiding inside Bruce's jacket.

Geoffrey Sax *The front of the hospital, the ambulance park, is actually the back of the buildings by the alley in Chinatown. We did all the ambulance interiors in the studio, using an air bladder to move the jacket as the snake goes in. The hospital itself was partially a working one and so we worked in a closed wing, which we dressed, borrowing stuff from the working part of the place. There were X-ray machines there that were disused, so we used them. We had a medical adviser on set checking what we said and did for accuracy. Now and again, they would try and stop us and say, 'Oh, Grace couldn't hold a phone once she's been masked-up', but I had to remind them that this was a drama and the rules needed to be bent a little.*

In the trauma room, the resident, Salinger, and two nurses, Curtis and Wheeler, are examining the X-rays. No matter how many they do, a double-exposure shows up. Or perhaps the patient really does have two hearts. They remove the bullets but the patient's heart it fibrillating badly and they need to perform surgery. The surgeon on call is Grace Holloway, currently at the opera watching *Madame Butterfly* with her boyfriend, Brian.

Geoffrey Sax *This was just a few chairs on the stage – the budget wouldn't allow us to use the proper aria, so again it's a library stock version, precleared for use in movies.*

Daphne Ashbrook *I was basically sent this script by my agent probably three or four weeks prior to me getting the job. And then quickly I was whisked off to Vancouver to shoot, so I didn't have a lot of prep time. At my first audition the scene that they had chosen for me to read didn't end up being in the final script at all, and it was a very heavy scene, very dramatic. It was when I think I've killed the Doctor and it delves back into my childhood and my father.*

So the tongue-in-cheek aspects of it I wasn't completely aware of until I was actually rehearsing with Paul McGann and with the director and stuff. I mean, I'm sure it was in the script, and I'm sure I picked it up, but I didn't realise how far they were going to take it.

Because I really had no idea what kind of project this was, it wasn't until I was working with everybody that it started to really come to life, and I realised, 'Oh, okay, now I understand.' Even the heavier stuff was filled with tongue-in-cheek and dry humour, which British guys are famous for, and I love!

Opposite top: Lee's gang believe they have safely seen off the opposition. The phrase 'it's behind you' seems strangely appropriate now...

Opposite bottom: The resultant gang shoot out leaves Lee's two friends dead and the Seventh Doctor injured, watched over by a concerned Lee and a rather more stoic Coldstream Guard.

Below: George Clooney never had to face this! Doctor Grace Holloway tries to get to grips with the Doctor's alien physiognomy. Either that, or he really is a donkey!

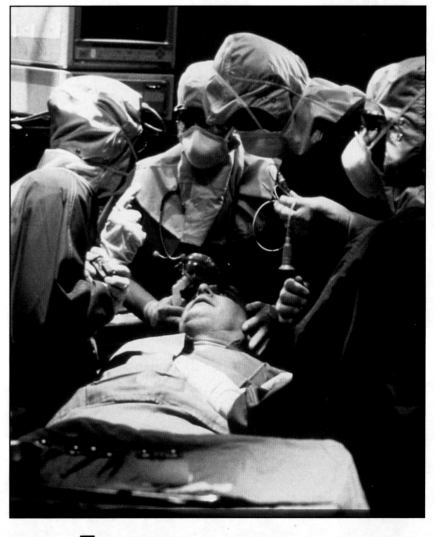

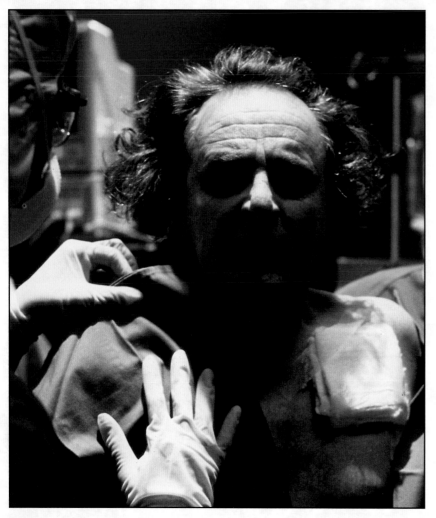

Traumas brought on by age, radiation poisoning, deadly viruses and even a fall from a great height have triggered previous regenerations. The Seventh Doctor bowed out in fine style, making a dignified exit on a surgeon's table, under the care of a group of doctors who had never seen a man with two hearts before. Can we really blame them?

Her bleeper goes off and she heads to work, although Brian angrily phones her there and threatens to leave. Grace prepares to operate, playing the rest of *Madame Butterfly* from a CD while she works.

Daphne Ashbrook *That was not an easy sequence to shoot at all. It was tough to breathe with these masks on and I also had that gown on underneath everything, which wasn't easy to breathe in either. It got very hot in there, and there were a lot of strange things we didn't know anything about.*

We didn't get to be prepped on what heart surgery was all about, so we were learning as we went. But it was also very quick, rapid-fire kind of dialogue delivery, and millions of different angles – it was a very long couple of days in there. One of the nurses was really a nurse – she might have had one line. She was basically just standing and helping us – you know, passing things. Actually, you know, what I think she was doing was looking at the machines – that's what her thing was: she was the anaesthetist. So she was really our technical adviser, and was actually in the scene. Thank God for her. Otherwise we wouldn't have known anything.

So I went to her and asked her everything. I wouldn't say something if I didn't know what it

was, to some degree anyway. I gathered as much information as I could from her, especially about protocol, like what we were actually doing at the time, [asking:] 'Is this the way it would be done? Am I holding this correctly? What does this do? What happens when a person starts to fibrillate?' All of this technical stuff this lady was able to give us, and she was great, too. But there was some of it we had to fudge, too, because she'd say, 'Wait, wait, you wouldn't do it that way' – and by that time Geoff Sax was saying, like, 'Too bad! That's the way we're doing it.' But there was a large attempt to make it as accurate as possible …

The Doctor awakens, warning them about the Master, and says he needs to find a Beryllium Atomic Clock. Assuming he is delirious, Grace has him anaesthetised but the operation goes wrong and, when she inserts her micro-surgery probe into his arteries, he has a seizure and dies – right in front of the hospital's administrator, Dr Swift, who is showing some potential investors around.

Geoffrey Sax *Again, there's a bit here that the BBFC insisted was edited from the BBC Video. They thought, when the Doctor woke up, it was too scary for the children. I don't know why. They also cut the bits when Grace loses the probe inside him. Later on I had to cut the two neck-breaking scenes (or noise, in the case of Bruce's wife). During the dub I chose to raise the volume of the opera just as Grace loses the Doctor, to reinforce it as the last thing he hears and so remembers it later, and even hums it as he walks through the deserted hospital.*

Sylvester McCoy *After years of changing in the BBC gents' toilet, to suddenly go over there and have to change in a big, big caravan, with my own lorry driver – it was wonderful. It was grand. I loved it. And they kept calling me Sir. 'This way, Sir.' And I'd say, 'No, no, no, I'm not Sir, please no, please don't.' I enjoyed all that immensely. British actors are different from American actors: we tend to be more used to sharing. American actors, necessarily because of the nature of working in film, work very much internally, and with themselves, and their relationship is more with the camera than with the fellow actor, whereas British actors are much more sharing. And because of that Paul and I are used to that thing of going off and sharing with the other actors, sharing with the crew on the set.*

The Canadians and the Americans who worked on this in Vancouver weren't used to that. The actual last scene one night – it was done at three o'clock in the morning in a freezing morning in Vancouver – they shot me and I fell in this iced puddle, had to lie there dead for a bit. Well, while we were rehearsing it, the wardrobe ladies and the make-up ladies ran up to the producer and said, 'Please, please, could he not just stand up and say, "You missed"?' Because they didn't want to lose a British actor from the cast.

Later, in her office, Grace angrily realises the X-rays were not double-exposures: the mysterious 'John Doe' really did have two hearts. Wheeler brings in Lee, who, Grace realises, doesn't know 'Mr Smith' at all, but, before she can learn more, he runs off with the Doctor's possessions.

Geoffrey Sax *Yee Jee hadn't done a great deal, but I thought he was very good. Very natural.*

Bruce the ambulance man is asleep, snoring loudly, much to the annoyance of his wife Miranda. Unseen by either of them, the Master's snake form emerges from Bruce's gear and jumps into his open mouth choking him to death and taking over his body. Miranda merely thinks she can finally get some sleep.

Geoffrey Sax *All the San Francisco location shots are library stock – no one went near the place. The bedroom was a set – it gave us the chance to move around and control the effects scenes. It was storyboarded so we could work out how the jacket arm would move, and I wanted to use a crane to get the height and the movement. Eric said it would be nice if there was a part for his wife [Eliza Roberts] and I thought it was a good idea, because she's a very good actress – so this one seemed ideal.*

In the morgue, Bill and Ted prepare the Doctor's body but, once in the freezer, the Doctor regenerates and escapes, much to Bill's terror. The new Doctor stumbles through the corridors, wondering who he is.

Geoffrey Sax *The guy playing the mortuary attendant was a real find – very good in the audition. I wanted to get someone who could be a real pain in the arse so, when he gets his comeuppance, it's justified.*

The whole morgue was a set – we built it all in the swimming-pool area of the hospital, deep down, where they used to have the therapy pools.

I wanted to link the Doctor coming alive with the big guy watching something on TV. Matthew [Jacobs] wrote that he was watching television and I said, 'Why don't we have him watching Frankenstein?' And, as it was a Universal movie, we had no clearance problems at all. I really wanted to mirror the shots of the fingers moving etc.

The regeneration was all done by motion control – we did it twice, the pan up and everything, with each actor. It took a long time. It was very handy that Sylvester could twist his face around like that, because it gave the effects people something to latch on to and distort further.

Paul's breath was done via a hose pipe – that set wasn't that cold at all. The door he pushes down

was actually metal – two props guys behind it were hitting it with mallets.

The Christ motif wasn't there originally. We didn't even see it, to be honest. It wasn't until Fox saw the director's cut and said 'It's Christ' that we started to see it – quite honestly, there was no intended connection at all. I can see it now: the shroud, the bit where he falls to the floor and asks, 'Who am I?', the metal contraption at the end, looking like a crown of thorns. But we never thought that back then, none of us. Very strange. The mirrors was my idea – I just thought it was a good way for him to see himself. Some people have read into it that there's the same amount of reflections in this shot as there are Doctors or companions or something but it's all nonsense. I just said to put some mirrors there and they did.

ACT TWO The following morning, while Grace sleeps in her office and the Doctor, in a stolen Bill Hickcock costume, relaxes in reception, Chang Lee examines his stolen goods.

At Bruce's, Miranda awakens to find her husband is no longer entirely human – and he kills her, deciding to find the Doctor and take over his body.

Grace and Bill discuss the apparent theft of the Doctor's body and she later tells Curtis. Swift arrives and in Grace's office destroys the evidence of the X-rays. Grace angrily resigns. She then meets the Doctor, but fails to recognise him until, in her car, he tugs the lost microsurgery probe from inside his chest.

Geoffrey Sax *The guy doing the administrator was a local Vancouver actor – very solid, very good. The talent pools in a place like Vancouver are very reliable. He's the kind of talent you need on a tight shoot like this. Solid as a rock, comes in, gives a great performance with no fuss.*

Curtis meanwhile is greeted by Bruce/the Master, who is looking for the Doctor's body and, on learning it has vanished, decides to track down Chang Lee.

Yee Jee Tso *I'd heard rumours about Eric Roberts but, to be totally honest, he was the nicest guy to work with. I learned a lot from him – and he was willing to take the time out to teach me. We got along great. There was a theme running through Chang Lee and the Master – a sort of father/son thing. As Chang Lee was an orphan with no father figure, he was very vulnerable and easily influenced – he wanted that role filled. Eric and I thought that, not only was this a powerful basis for their relationship, it was an even more powerful basis for his reaction to the Master's eventual betrayal. When Chang Lee is upset at being lied to, it's not just the lie: it's the shock that his vulnerability had been so easily preyed upon.*

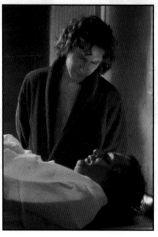

While two doctors argue over their patient, two Doctors have to be patient while their regeneration sequence is prepared.

At Grace's condo, she and the Doctor explore the bizarre physiology he has and slowly she begins to believe what he says might have more than a grain of truth in it ...

Geoffrey Sax *I first met Paul here in England, at Christmas. Phil was very, very keen on him, and I was, too. The studio were nervous: he wasn't known there and they wanted to see other choices, like Harry Van Gorkum, but in the end they saw Paul's tapes and said yes to him. Phil fought very hard to get Paul.*

He's got marvellous eyes – a terribly good actor, perfect for this part. In the director's cut I used a different version of the lift scene because Paul was very quiet and I thought I'd show the studio a take where he was louder – and they needed the cut done quickly. The studio were very good: they didn't interfere with the cut at all; but in the end I opted to change it because I thought it was too much, too loud. They were very good – most networks will see a director's cut, then say thank you and goodbye, leaving it with their editors to finalise the thing. You've done your bit. But on Doctor Who *they were very good to me and I stayed to the very end, which meant I had the opportunity to develop things better and, as here, change the take to a different one.*

Fox were very good to work with – Trevor Walton was very talented, very sharp. Lots of ideas, all of them good. As a network, they're very good at being enthusiastic and encouraging.

The very first morning of the shoot, we did these scenes of them coming to the condo and talking inside. We spent the weekend before rehearsing at the apartment – we wanted the chemistry to be right so we rehearsed this particular stuff a lot to get Daphne and Paul used to each other, to get to really know each other.

Yee Jee Tso *I had heard of Paul McGann – my ex-girlfriend's brother was a fan of* Withnail And I, *so I sat and watched that and thought, Oh, so that's Paul McGann. Wow. Such a great actor.*

Daphne Ashbrook *I knew who Paul McGann was because I'd seen* Withnail And I, *but that was only because I had a British friend who said I had to see it.*

I was completely unaware of what I was letting myself in for. It was like standing in line for an amusement ride, but not knowing what the ride was, and then suddenly getting on it, you know, and it's a wild roller coaster. It was a lot of fun. A whole lot of fun ...

While the Doctor comes to grips with some primitive surgical appliances, Grace begins to think there may be something in his story after all. And perhaps she needs to make sure the man she signed off as dead doesn't try to sue for malpractice.

In the TARDIS, Lee meets the Master, who convinces him that it is really his TARDIS and the Doctor stole it from him, along with his rightful body. The Master persuades Lee to help him fight the Doctor.

Geoffrey Sax *We had Lee going round the outside of the TARDIS because we thought the new American audience might not get the idea that this was all inside a police box. We take the TARDIS for granted in Britain, but we were aware that this was something the new audience might not have got yet. You have to visually tell that side of the story.*

ACT THREE Grace and the Doctor go for a walk in the park and bits of his memory return. Delightedly, he kisses her, and she is equally delighted, but for different reasons …

Geoffrey Sax *I knew we'd get criticisms for the kiss.*

Yee Jee Tso *The fact that they brought* Doctor Who *back and still wanted to move it on in a new direction, with the kiss and the half-human thing, was brilliant. It was essential not to just bring it back the same – why bother? – so instead they added a potential new lease of life.*

Daphne Ashbrook *Paul's such a good actor, and he's just a delight to work with. He's a professional. He respects everybody's attitude, and he's very funny, which makes those long hours much nicer. We did lots of night shoots and he was so wonderful … It could have been a nightmare, but he was a delight, and I have nothing but good things to say about him.*

In the TARDIS, the Master and Lee are exploring, once Lee has been bribed with gold dust.

Geoffrey Sax *All the scenes with Eric and Yee Jee were rehearsed the weekend before. If you're doing scenes with comic touches in them, you need to rehearse it to find the right moments. If you just try and do it on the day, with seventy-five crew watching you, you don't get those nice touches, but by rehearsing you can find the exact moment.*

It's unusual to get that amount of time – in Vancouver, under Canadian union rules, you can only shoot five days a week. But the actors aren't on that deal, and the LA-based staff like me and Phil weren't on that deal, so we went into the sets and rehearsed. The actors wanted to do it – they enjoy it.

Glen MacPherson [the director of photography] kindly worked with me on his days off and therefore we could do a shot list as we watched them rehearse. This meant you could actually get more shot on the working days because you'd already storyboarded out your shot lists for the

day and didn't keep the crew waiting while you worked out the angles and areas you were shooting from. The whole thing is much more efficient.

I think the TARDIS interiors worked well on the big screen: they had a filmic look which I wanted and I'm pleased came across.

They enter the Cloister Room and the Master uses Lee's human eye to open the Eye of Harmony.

Geoffrey Sax *The camera going into the Cloister Room for the first time was also motion control again, but note the stuff at the top. Around the ceiling is all CGI but the join is hard to spot. We also added in the bats. I was rather hoping for a flock, but I suppose the CGI budget could only support two!*

Lee sees the old Doctor, the new one and the Doctor's retinal print, and the Master realises the Doctor is half human.

Geoffrey Sax *We were hoping to get all the Doctors in the bit where Lee sees Sylvester in the Eye, but we couldn't get copyright clearance on the images.*

Through the Doctor's current point of view they also see Grace, and Lee recognises her.

Geoffrey Sax *The Sausalito sign was added to establish it looking like San Francisco.*

In the park, the Doctor realises what the Master is doing, but Grace is convinced he is mad and runs back to the condo to call for an ambulance. It dawns on the Doctor that, with the Eye open, the Earth will start to alter

Contrary to industry tittletattle, Geoffrey Sax and Yee Jee Tso both found working alongside Eric Roberts to be a blast.

CLOISTER ROOM
CONCEPT SKETCH   WONG.

EYE OF HARMONY
CONCEPT SKETCH   WONG.

Richard Hudolin's TARDIS interiors played an important part in the choreography of the climactic battle between good and evil around the Eye of Harmony.

RASSILON (DETAIL 513)
CONCEPT SKETCH   WONG.

molecularly until it is sucked through the Eye, destroying everything. He shows Grace this is starting by walking through solid glass, but she still isn't convinced.

Geoffrey Sax *The scene at the condo picture window where the world went loopy was a very tricky thing to do, but we costed it out. We wanted something special. We did the scenes outside the door, the stuff inside, and then took all the glass out just for the bit when he stands there. They did a 3D version of his hand in CGI to push through the CGI glass – we later added the reflection of Grace distorting via CGI as well. It was very tricky to set up but well worth it.*

Twenty minutes later he observes he is losing weight, while on television a news anchor observes strange tidal movements in the bay. The story changes to one about a new atomic clock being started tonight that will measure time accurately in the future. The Doctor realises he needs to get that clock – or the chip controlling it – to accurately pilot the TARDIS out of time to stop the Master.

The Master, as Bruce, then arrives and the Doctor demands to be taken to the Institute of Technological Advancement and Research (ITAR).

Geoffrey Sax *We did the TV footage way before the shoot stated because we needed the video footage for the first day. We did it about a week after Christmas – we went along to the local Vancouver station and filmed in their news studio and the two ladies are the real Vancouver news anchors.*

ACT FOUR Delayed by an accident on the way to the Institute, the Doctor recognises the Master, who spits venom at Grace. Fleeing from the ambulance, they hijack a police motorcycle and race to ITAR, but the Master and Lee have got there first.

Geoffrey Sax *This was done over one night and the chase over the next couple of nights. If we were going to do something to hold them up, I wanted something special. In the script I think it's a road blockage, but I thought it needed something different. What I wanted was an upturned circus truck and we could have giraffes and things running amok. This is why we have planning meetings – so that everyone can look at the director like he's mad.*

Eyebrows shot up, jaws dropped, but the design department actually looked into it. It was Peter Ware who finally said, 'Well, I can get you some chickens!' So I said, 'Can I have five hundred, because half of them'll bugger off on the night anyway?' Therefore we ended up with chickens. It was great fun, and I did that chicken noise as the camera pans past the one in the foreground, because chickens don't act on cue!

Over there, they don't really know jelly babies, so I told the actor playing the policeman to bite its head off, because it would really say something about his character! We had to lose the bit where the other drivers yell at the policeman to give the Doctor the keys to his bike. The studio thought it was too arch, not funny. I was disappointed, I thought it was good, but it's probably very British humour and Fox couldn't see it.

The close-ups on the bike were done with a bike mounted on a trailer. The inside of the ambulance cab was done in the studio and the second unit shot all the stunt work. Patrick Lussier edited this together – he's the most amazing editor I've ever worked with, and the fastest. He does all the Wes Craven movies, like Scream. He did the first edit of this and I didn't ask for a single change – it was perfect. He cuts action very well indeed.

Daphne Ashbrook I did one sort-of stunt, on the back of the motorcycle. We were doing the dialogue – but we were connected to a piece of truck or something. It wasn't like Paul was actually driving free-form on the motorcycle when I was on it. That sequence of shots was done right before the sun was about to come up and we had been waiting around all night to do it, so we were exhausted. Then we saw the light in the sky start to change and it was very frightening – we had to get a lot of stuff done and not mess it up, and every time we had to do it again, another take, we'd have to go right back and turn around and drive back. So that was an interesting night shoot, to try and squeeze that in right before the sun's about to rise.

ACT FIVE At ITAR, Grace gets the Doctor in, despite a sardonic guard trying to stop them. They meet Professor Wagg, who has developed the clock and, by stealing his pass, the Doctor and Grace gain access to the clock, where the Time Lord steals the necessary Beryllium chip. They encounter another guard, Gareth, whose future the Doctor knows, and then see the Master and Lee, who have disposed of some other guards.

Geoffrey Sax The director's cut of the ITAR stuff was a bit different because structurally we had to get the film down to a certain length and so we had to lose a few nice scenes. But people thought we'd lost a bit of ... soul. So we then added the security guard back in to the give the Doctor some more obstructions, otherwise it looked like he and Grace got into the event far too easily. That then is why we took out the bit where the Master faces off with the other security guards – something had to go. This was such a huge room to light – logistically it was difficult to do all the shots needed in the time.

There was more script I would have kept in, more Doctorish stuff, if I'd had the time. But, by the time it was all lit, we had to get a move on. We had about two days trying to get feature-film

values – but on a feature film we'd have had two weeks there. Maybe if I'd had more prep time we could have found a location that was more manageable, easier to shoot in. It's always a toss-up: you want it to look impressive, but you had so much to get through in such a small amount of time. On top of all these bits, there's the countdown-to-New-Year scenes as well.

We did the scene of the Doctor and Grace finding the ladder and hose pipe back in the studio because we could control it better – did it the same day we did the bits with Eric Roberts and his wife. I asked Matthew to rewrite the scene so they could use the hose pipe to lower themselves down, because I thought it might be fun, visually.

The Master gives chase and again the Doctor and Grace escape on their bike, this time heading back to the TARDIS, where they avoid being caught by a motorcycle cop.

Geoffrey Sax That was a lock-off shot – we took the TARDIS away, the motorcyclist drove forward,

'And it has to be finished when exactly?' The art team came up trumps despite having a very short preproduction period – for short, read almost nonexistent – but despite that, everyone's love of the project showed via the stunning visuals that accompanied the performances.

Above: Seeing the light – the actors' stand-ins Rita Whicker, Ronin and Dale Reynolds help Geoffrey Sax and Glen MacPherson prepare their shots before filming begins.

Opposite top: 'You just can't get the staff these days' – the real Grace Holloway blindly tries to help the Doctor stop the Master.

Opposite bottom: Fred Perron, Eric Roberts and Charles Andre try to find an amicable solution to the question of who gets the water bottle next.

turned around, drove away, and we put the TARDIS back in and mixed it together in the studio.

Inside, Grace helps the Doctor set a sort of alarm clock that will tell the TARDIS when to dematerialise, but the TARDIS lacks the power to go back in time. They decide to use the Eye's power to jump-start the TARDIS but, before the Doctor can complete the circuitry necessary, Grace knocks him unconscious – a result of the Master's venom, she is now possessed by him.

Geoffrey Sax *The contact lenses hurt her eyes – we thought we weren't going to be able to use her for one day as they had scratched her eyes, but Daphne insisted on carrying on.*

Daphne Ashbrook *I've never worked on a set that was that amazing. As a matter of fact, most of the sets were amazing in the show. And I have to say that part of it was because of the people that were involved. That set really takes the prize, because the detail was amazing, and it was just beautiful and packed with history. They just really had a lot of fun, and they did it beautifully. It was comfortable, too – you could find a great chair to sit on. Oh, except for the smoke. It was very smokey because of the look that they were going for, and that got to be a drag. But it was so beautiful.*

ACT SIX The Doctor awakens in the Cloister Room, by the open Eye. He is strapped to a gurney, and tries to convince Lee that the Master has lied to him. The Master appears, now in full Time Lord regalia, and has Grace attach a surgical device to his head that will force his eyes to stay open.

Geoffrey Sax *When we knew we had Eric, we sent him the script and he said yes. Once he was aboard, we did some rewrites. I said to Matthew that Eric was so versatile an actor we could change a few bits to suit him, add a lot more humour because he could play it. Matthew did them and we gave them to Eric on the day he arrived. He later phoned me and said it was ridiculous – he didn't understand because it was completely different to the dialogue he'd seen before.*

I said we still had the original stuff, but we thought he could to do this version – I said that if he wanted to view the first week's rushes and liked what he saw, he'd get the spirit of what we were trying to do and agree with the changes. If he didn't, then fine, we'd revert back to the original. I understood it's unfair to give him these changes late, so he had the option to say no. I knew once he'd seen it, he'd come round to our way of thinking. He saw it and immediately called me and said he understood (bear in mind he wasn't very familiar with Doctor Who*); he got it* *and agreed to do it. From that moment on I think he'd have turned somersaults if we'd asked, he was so accommodating, so willing to try anything.*

The other thing about Eric was that the set was incredibly hot and heavy and he was wearing both costumes in it – either the dark rubber one or the Time Lord one. He was so very, very hot but never complained, not once. Eric was a complete team player – I'd heard he could be very difficult but I think he just thoroughly enjoyed the movie and he felt comfortable doing what he did.

At Walker General and at ITAR the New Year countdown begins. The Doctor is now hung upright on a balcony overlooking the Eye. Lee and the Master are positioning the reflector staffs so that the Eye's energy will become beams of light – one to the Doctor, another to the Master on the opposite balcony, with the Eye sucking the life energy from the Doctor and boosting it into the Master, giving him the Doctor's life energy. As Lee prepares to activate the Eye again, the Doctor tricks the Master into confessing that he has indeed lied to Lee. The Master merely kills Lee and uses Grace to open the Eye, returning her to normality but temporarily blinding her.

Yee Jee Tso *Originally I was to have been thrown across the room, hit the wall and fall dead. I even got rigged up in the harness, but in the end there wasn't the time to go the whole way. Shame.*

As the Eye's energy begins to bleed his life away, the Doctor tells Grace to get back to the console room and finish his work – get the power to their jury-rigged alarm clock.

Geoffrey Sax *We rehearsed all this beforehand with the stunt people as well as Eric, Daphne, Yee Jee and Paul. This whole climax was a nightmare to coordinate and I was very grateful that everyone was willing to rehearse it. That device really was keeping Paul's eyes open, by the way. This was another case of Peter Ware and the crew accommodating me.*

When we got into the studio and saw the sets, Phil Segal and I looked at the scripts – and this is why Phil is such a good, creative producer – and wondered what we were going to do, as it just said, 'The Doctor and the Master fight'. I said we should use the balconies and on the spot Phil looked at the staffs around the Eye of Harmony thing and suggested putting mirrors on them, and using them to illuminate the face of the Doctor and the Master, and making that the way the energy went between them. He could see how to stage the entire scene from a given set, which was great. He blocked out the basic ideas on paper and then he went away and let me get on with it.

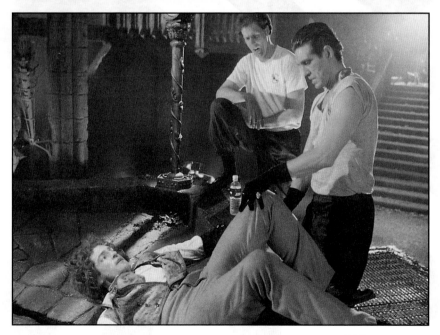

All over San Francisco, the New Year countdown continues. In the TARDIS Cloister Room the Doctor realises it may all be over ...

ACT SEVEN Grace tries desperately to finish the Doctor's work while in the Cloister Room the Master, immobile under the force of the Eye's energies, begins to feel alive again, while the Doctor weakens. Grace succeeds, and the TARDIS dematerialises, cutting off the power the Master needs and taking it into temporal orbit – out of time completely, just as the world is destroyed in a blinding flash of light.

Geoffrey Sax *That was done in post-production, taking the stock shots of San Francisco, CGI-ing in the lightning and blotting out the neon signs as it strikes the buildings.*

Grace dashes back to the Cloister Room to free the Doctor – although he is safe and the Master has lost, the Master has gained enough strength to attack and kill her.

Daphne Ashbrook *Eric was a sweetie. He was somewhat intimidating, probably because of the role he was playing. I don't think you can really completely keep all the energies that characters like the Master have outside, not completely. He was a big scary guy, and he came in after we'd already been shooting, so he was sort of an outsider and, yeah, he was a little intimidating. I mean, I didn't get to spend much social time with him at all. I was working with Paul the rest of the time, so when Eric wasn't working I was. So my experience with Eric was mostly when we were on the set doing our thing. I wasn't frightened of him, and he was lovely to be around, but he could be a bit intimidating, you know?*

The Master then turns on the Doctor, almost bestial in his rage, and the two fight around the Eye until the Doctor uses the light beams from a reflector staff to deflect the Master into the centrifugal force of the Eye. Unwilling to take the Doctor's helping hand, the Master is obliterated in the vast surge of power, which then stops.

Geoffrey Sax *This was done on the very last night – Patrick Lussier used every shot I took to make this move so well. Eric was on wires but the cutting is so fast, you don't linger on anything long enough to think about it. I'm very pleased with the look of that fight.*

The Doctor carries the dead bodies of Grace and Lee and the last vestiges of power from the Eye heals their injuries, bringing them back to life before the Eye closes for good.

Geoffrey Sax *This sequence had to be very well storyboarded early on because of the light. You see the light reflected on his coat from the effect that hasn't been added yet – so we had to know what the effect was going to look like so we could*

get the lighting right in the studio. You can do a lot with light on the set and it helps bring the effects to life later.

In the console room, the Doctor takes the TARDIS out of its temporal orbit and heads back to Earth on New Year's Eve, a few minutes before midnight. Lee runs off, but not before the Doctor has warned him to be far away from the city next Christmas – and he then, with a farewell kiss, leaves Grace behind as well.

Daphne Ashbrook *Daphne thinks that Grace is an idiot ... I mean, how often do you get to hop on a spaceship and experience all those amazing things? Yeah, so Daphne was disappointed, but I guess I understood Grace's point of view. It was just the way they wanted to finish the story and so that's the way it had to be.*

Geoffrey Sax *This scene was a nightmare to do because it kept raining. Then it stopped. Then it started again. I suggested doing it under umbrellas, but, when we did the wide shot, it had stopped, so we didn't bother. When we went into the close-ups, it was pouring down. Now, unless you backlight a scene, rain doesn't show up on film, but look at their hair, especially Daphne's, which gets frizzier as it gets wetter, and Paul's wig looks very flat. Both of their hair changes from shot to shot as we either dried it or it got soaked again – there was nothing we could do.*

We tried to match that on the one studio shot – that final kiss was done in the studio against a green screen so we could matte in the fireworks. By the time they were saying goodbye, it was really coming down – and it didn't stop for the next ten hours, by which time, we'd stopped shooting. It was the wettest night I've ever known in all my years of shooting.

Daphne Ashbrook *I had been to Vancouver before, about ten years earlier. I was shooting a Movie of the Week, and it was way back when Vancouver was not at all what it is today – I mean, they call it Hollywood II, because there's so much work being done up there. It's a huge industry now. When I first went there, you know, we were the only ones shooting in town, and it was kind of an aberration, as far as American shoots went.*

I love Vancouver very much. I just adore it. I wouldn't mind relocating there if I needed to. When we were there, we actually had a lot of bad weather: we had snow in the city and, according to all the locals, this was not a normal occurrence. It did kind of create a little bit of havoc with our shooting schedule, though, because we shot in the rain. It was very damp that night. I think it was our last night at the location shoot too, so we really didn't have much time and we were doing the last kiss scene, with the rain coming down. It was crazy. But I was

Roughly sketched visuals for the 'vortex' that would claim the Master after he falls into the Eye of Harmony.

An early design concept for the TARDIS Cloister Room ceiling. Note the tiny seal of Rassilon embedded into the lattice-work – the art team were keen to feature identifying marks like this as much as possible.

dressed for it – luckily I got to wear a big coat at the end.

Actually I really love that weather: being born in Long Beach and raised in San Diego and living in LA for the last fifteen years, it's just a desert! I'm living in a desert! I hate the desert! So whenever I get the chance to get wet I'm very happy.

Happy in his TARDIS, the Doctor returns to a life of wandering through time and space …

Geoffrey Sax It's a shame the Americans didn't go for this, you know. It would have made such a good series.

Daphne Ashbrook I would have loved it to have carried into a series! Absolutely. I mean, it's perfect for me! I have to say I am a big science-fiction fan and have been for years. I mean, if you're going to do a series, then this is the kind of series you want to do – because it's limitless. Your imagination can't even begin to dream of what you could possibly get to do as an actor.

I did an episode of Star Trek: Deep Space Nine and I played a type of character that there's no way I will ever play again. In most series situations it can get quite restrictive if you're playing the same person who has the same lines and the same situations over and over again for years at a time. That's a drag, you know? But with these science-fiction shows you know there is no limit and you can just go anywhere and have anything happen to you, and, as an actress, that's a real joy.

There are things that I got to do in this that I'll never get to do again – being possessed and all that stuff. But I'd also love to work on this show again because Paul McGann was wonderful to

work with, and I'd have loved to work with him some more.

Yee Jee Tso I'd love to have done the series. I knew Doctor Who when I was a kid – I watched it doing my homework if it was on – and I was so happy to be a part of the new version. Everyone involved had asked to be on it – all the crew knew what they were doing. It was an unusual feeling, everyone pulled together and gave their absolute best because they were in love with the script, the show, everything. It's rare to find that in TV, I find.

Sylvester McCoy I don't think it was perfect, but it didn't bomb. Especially in Britain, it did incredibly well. And in America it got great critical acclaim. The sad thing was it was badly scheduled, so it didn't get as good an audience as perhaps it might have done if it hadn't had such strong opposition.

One of the rather nice things about the film was that Philip Segal kept dropping in little bits that the American fans, or people new to it, wouldn't quite know what it was, but would see it and think, that's interesting: jelly babies – oh, that bit's nice.

I thought that was good. Phil put that in, because he did it for the Doctor Who fans who had, in a sense, helped keep it going, keep it alive, and I think that was a little kind of reward to them, from him. When it first came out the response seemed to be very, very enthusiastic in conventions that I've been to, but now, because nothing has happened with it, I think people are now looking at it as a failure with hindsight. It's like, 'Oh it didn't work, so it must be bad,' which isn't fair or true. It's just there's a different critical approach now.

• 1996 •

THE FINAL PHASE

An innovative press pack was created for the US Directors' Guild screening of the movie. In a specially designed TARDIS tin could be found a video of the film, a selection of photographs, a spiral-bound set of press notes and a small bag of imported jelly babies!

Opposite: Shades of black – two regenerated Time Lords who don't see eye to eye.

As 1995 ended and 1996 began, faxes and phone calls between Lakeshore's Los Angeles base and the Burnaby office were buzzing around like bees on a honey pot. Relentlessly, fax paper was placed in machines, spewed out and replaced every few hours.

With BBC Worldwide gearing up for what they saw as their biggest merchandising opportunity for years, the press and publicity people were everywhere. Amid all this Juliet Grimm was trying to hold the BBC Worldwide flag up for the production; Jo Wright was poring over rewrite after rewrite at BBC Television; and Philip Segal was bashing his head against a brick wall at still not having a Doctor whom all parties could agree on.

Over the Christmas holiday, Trevor Walton of Fox had returned to the UK to see his family, and arranged to meet up with Paul McGann at the Atheneum Hotel in Piccadilly, London. With Jo Wright, Walton spent much of Christmas Eve convincing the actor that not only did he, Jo and Philip want him, but the part was written perfectly for him. At the end of their meeting, McGann confirmed that all deals being equal, and providing the American Fox executives were convinced, he would be delighted to become the eighth Doctor.

So while Fox wanted to do a screen test with

Harry van Gorkum, Philip wanted them to go with Paul McGann and the BBC just wanted an answer. In the midst of this, production difficulties were still arising. Tests had been done for the CGI 'morphant snake' that contained the essence of the Master, but Philip was not convinced. Hensons, the world-renowned animatronic experts, were talking about helping out, maybe supplying a fully operable, motion-controlled snake.

Penny Mills at BBC Video was hoping to do a 'Making Of …' video (this fell through because of the additional payments required by participants, as it was not in anyone's contract to do this sort of thing for no fee). Meanwhile, Philip wanted a similarly themed book, written by an old mate from his *seaQuest DSV* days, Louis Chunovik, to be arranged (this author notes, by the way – with some satisfaction – that that deal fell through), and noises were being made about BBC Children's Publishing doing a tie-in novelisation and script book.

Meanwhile, back to those subtext-laden faxes: Philip sent Juliet one stating unequivocally that: 'Geoff and yours truly have fallen in love with Harry Van Gorkum … Geoff and I worked with him for several hours today and after the session, Geoff and I looked at each other and in stereo exclaimed 'He is the Doctor!' … At the end of the day, either Paul or Harry would be fantastic but we can now say … Harry is our first choice.' The sign-off line to Juliet, 'Look forward to discussing this mess with you later',

tells the truer story. As Juliet was very much aware, Fox did not know who Paul McGann was. Quite why they felt that Van Gorkum, even more of an unknown and another Brit (albeit one resident in LA), would satisfy their viewers is unclear, but the message to Juliet was obvious. This was even more political wrangling with Fox and poor Harry Van Gorkum was the Judas goat caught in the middle.

But, after much toing and froing between Philip, Fox and the BBC, on Wednesday, 10 January 1996, the world received confirmation. Thirty-six-year-old Paul McGann was indeed to be the eighth Doctor – although the star himself was already on an aeroplane to Vancouver, having done a secret photocall on the 7th outside the permanent TARDIS prop at Longleat's *Doctor Who* exhibition.

Doctor Who, the brand-new television movie, was going to work after all: production was steaming ahead, enthusiasm was high everywhere and everyone involved hoped this would somehow or other spin off into a new series of the world's most popular time traveller. All it required was good viewing figures Stateside …

Days before the shoot now, and things were beginning to heat up and take shape. Our sets were nearing completion. The entire crew was on board; there were daily scouts to

possible exterior locations; and we were still working on the script.

At this point Jo Wright had arrived from the UK to be with the production for its first week. I was happy to see her in one sense and not in others. I knew that by her being with us we could try to get all the script notes put to bed. It's far easier working on these things in person than it is over a long distance.

Our primary concern was the story itself. We still had spots that lacked focus and the main jeopardy of the story still felt rather false. The truth is, we had painted ourselves into a bit of a corner. End-of-the-world threats are rather over the top and phoney. We know the end of the world can't come, therefore the world must be saved. All that's left to do is make the adventure fun, and that was my main concern.

Jo is a very logical thinker in my opinion, and I always felt she wanted to cling on to that logic too long. *Doctor Who* is obviously pure fantasy and does have a certain humour and lightness of touch to it. It was my goal to hold on to that special lightness as much as possible. I must confess, the story ended as a bit of a disappointment to me personally. I really wanted to take the Doctor into space and have a real adventure with him.

Deep down inside, I had pangs over the

Richard Hudolin gazes at the new TARDIS console and wonders if he can get it to actually fly.

A detailed model of the TARDIS control room set. Only about a third of the vast set is actually seen clearly in the finished programme.

Leekley script. Hard as it is for me to admit, that was my favourite. John knew exactly what to do. In Matthew's defence, he was given certain parameters that he had to work in. Leekley was not. Matthew was forced to ground the story on Earth, as well as build a certain amount of introductory material into the story for those American viewers whom the network assumed would not know our universe.

There were several occasions when I found out Jo had met with the writer without me, to discuss changes she wanted. Although, in Jo's defence, I knew she was representing the BBC, things are done a little differently in the US. We have more respect for producers than British television networks do. The executive producer in America has creative control of the product. In the UK, the executive producers work for the network and are simply executives.

This clash in culture took its toll on my relationship with Jo. We butted heads many times. The biggest blow to my ego came when I heard through Universal business affairs that Jo was going to be taking an executive producer's credit on this film. I was really angry. Seven years of trying to put this whole thing together and slowly people were taking credit for things in ways that, in my opinion, took the credit away from me.

I completely understood the ramifications of this move. Even Alex Beaton was angry. He and I had agreed to share the executive producers' credit, even though we would be on separate cards and mine would be the last one you saw. Alex and I got together to fight this move. In retrospect I made a judgment error – even though Jo and I talk today and remain friends, I know this incident hurt our

relationship. The end result of all this was that Alex and I got credit as the execs in the opening titles of the film and Jo's credit runs in the end sequence.

Talking of the title sequence, there was also that to deal with while we were hammering out the script. At first, the studio wanted only plain credits to run at the front of the film. I knew this was a mistake. For obvious reasons, I felt that live action would help fill in some of the blanks and bring the audience into the film.

Creating a main title sequence became the work of Northwest Imaging, our CGI team. They combined the live action of a miniature version of the TARDIS with a CGI space field to create the effects you see at the beginning of the film. To accomplish this we first had our prop department build a scale version of the TARDIS out of wood, then had that model shipped down to Los Angeles, to a company called VFX. They mounted the model on a 'control' arm that allowed the model to slowly spin as it moved towards the camera, against a blue screen.

As this move was made, a high-speed camera captured the image on film so it could be played back in real time. Hence the term 'motion control'. Using a blue screen allowed us to remove the blue background in post-production and replace it with the starfield and gaseous clouds you see pass the TARDIS. The end result is quite effective.

I remember watching this young Polish artist come to the model/prop shop every day and build that small replica of the TARDIS. It was quite profound for me. I imagined what it would be like to be a small child again, thinking how wonderful the universe of the

Richard Hudolin was completely caught up in the *Doctor Who* mythos. This explains the creation of a 900-year diary for the Doctor, the appearance of a special Gallifreyan seal in the control room and the subtle evocation of the old TARDIS 'roundel' wall pattern on the interior door.

was comfortable enough to allow on to the set) and a couple of British tabloid people. They were, I believe, suitably impressed.

I was fortunate to have spent quite a while alone on that set. When it's all lit up and no one is around, you'd swear you could take that ship anywhere in the universe. Richard Hudolin and his crew really did a fine job. The true majesty of the TARDIS interior really couldn't be fully appreciated unless you were present.

The first thing that struck you was its immense size. As you walked through the main entrance to the set, you were actually walking through a beautifully panelled anteroom that led you into the main control room. It was finished in dark cherry and was

Doctor was. Each detail of that ship was lovingly crafted, and, as it came to life before my eyes, I felt a sense of fulfilment come over me. My only moment of sorrow was thinking how proud my grandfather would have been to see all this come alive.

Two days before we began the shoot, the BBC's publicity department arrived and began setting up interviews of their own. It seemed like every moment not spent in meetings was dedicated to interviews and press tours of the sets. For two minutes, the hottest ticket in town was an invitation to our sets. I remember walking some of the visitors on to the TARDIS interior set when it was complete, and being in awe of the whole thing myself.

There was a reporter, Alison Graham, from *Radio Times*, Gary Gillatt from Marvel's *Doctor Who Magazine* (the only genre magazine I

covered in similar roundels to those that graced the walls of the second TARDIS interior set seen in the Tom Baker era. I always loved that anteroom but unfortunately we never filmed in it because our director of photography, Glenn McPherson, had a hard time trying to light it. As you stepped through the double oak-panelled doors you stepped into the main control room. The walls on this part of the set were painted to look like faux marble. Two ornate figurines holding giant glass bowls of cut glass lit the way.

As you stepped down and to the left, you entered the library area. Books, antiques, giant over-stuffed chairs and several large pieces of artwork adorned the walls. Next to the library was a small study area with large file cabinets. This is where the Master pulled the bags of gold dust from. As a joke, we put the arm of a Dalek in one of the cabinets and filed it under 'D'. The gag was to see the Master rifle through the cabinets looking for the gold when he was courting Chang Lee, and come across the arm. The art department had a good time making the arm out of an old toilet plunger and painting it gold and silver. It also had bundles of wires protruding from the shaft end.

Next to the study was the music room, full of incredible old musical instruments. On the piano was a recorder, too, but alas it was never seen. The middle portion of the set away from the walls was layered with columns that got larger and larger as you looked towards the very back of set. This gave the illusion of size and it worked very effectively. Richard used hundreds of yards of muslin, hand-stencilled and draped behind the backs of the largest columns. The centrepiece of the whole set was the console, perched on a beautifully crafted wood-panel floor, all hand-painted.

Crows' feet adorned the base of the TARDIS console, all hand-carved with giant gargoyles. All the controls on the console itself were parts from old cars and radios. The switches and dials were wired to work, including the monitor that hung from a special scissor arm above the set. The monitor was in fact an antique black-and-white television set from the early '40s, while the handle used to pull it towards you was an old lavatory chain. I suppose that was the art department's way of having a little fun – and it worked for me.

The set dressing itself – the items that are placed in the set – is a separate task from that of the art department. The set dressers are responsible for the final appearance of the set, and, even though they work hand in hand with the production designer, they are allowed to add their own touches. Our set dressers did an outstanding job.

The Cloister Room set was no less impressive. Originally, we had planned for the Cloister Room to be over 100 feet long. Budget constraints reduced it to 60, but it made very little difference. This set was built out of plywood, and then giant blocks of foam were glued to it and shaped into oversized bricks. The Eye of Harmony was constructed out of fibreglass and its giant eye was opened and closed by a cleverly concealed pulley system under the stage. The giant balustrades were all hand-carved, as were the heads of the face of Rassilon. All the sconces that held the propane-fired torches were also constructed out of heavy aged iron, all hand-made in our prop department.

The work was endless and even I can't remember every detail. But, by illustrating

some of what I can recall being achieved, I hope I've given you an idea of how much passion and care went into the entire production. It was very difficult taking some of the criticisms that were levelled against us after we'd spent as many months as we all did putting this movie together. I truly hope reading this book will give some of you a newly found appreciation of the craft of film making in general, as well as an awareness of what went into our film in particular.

As the first several days of filming got under way, we all settled into the job and I for one took a huge breath and gave a great sigh of relief. The first week of filming was quite unremarkable, except for the fact that over the first four days or so we starting losing

The impressive console. A working prop, each button or switch activated lights or dials on the panels.

TARDIS CONTROL RM — CONCEPT SKETCH

TARDIS CONTROL CONCEPT SKETCH WONG

Michael Wong's conceptual designs for the TARDIS interior echoed Philip Segal's love of Victoriana and the stories of Jules Verne – but with an added dash of Heath Robinson.

ourselves regenerating another Doctor for the series.

After the first days of filming, Paul settled into his role quite nicely. We had ongoing chats about tweaking the character and from time to time I found Paul loosening up quite a lot. He started to enjoy his new-found persona. Daphne was also doing a good job – I liked her character more than most. I know she came under a lot fire from fans and industry types who didn't like Grace, but my view was a little different. Being a companion character in this franchise can be a very tough job and it's so easy to be upstaged by the Doctor's presence in a scene. Daphne was able to hold her own and brought a fair amount of humour to the story. For me she worked perfectly, and given the chance I would not have recast her.

By the beginning of the second week of filming, I had several problems to deal with. The first was that even more press had come to interview Paul about those private matters that had no place being discussed while he was working. Paul asked me to request that certain tabloid-type journalists not be allowed to come on to the set while he was working. Tactfully, I asked them to leave. They were not happy, but I had to choose between an unhappy actor and unhappy journalists who were going to write whatever they wanted anyway. I opted for a happy actor.

My second issue dealt with Yee Jee, the actor playing Chang Lee. It became apparent that he had not spent a lot of quality time on sets. His role was quite large and he was displaying some undisciplined behaviour. I pulled him aside and gave him a pep talk. It seemed to work. By the end of the second week, he seemed more settled.

I was very excited about working with Eric Roberts. Yes, there were all the industry rumours about how tough he could be, but I had no real problems with him. He conducted himself like a true professional, except for one small item that I'll share with you. He was never supposed to look like the Terminator. I wanted a very futuristic Victorian-gentlemen look with a costume that bore a resemblance to the Roger Delgado wardrobe from the Pertwee years, the sort of Nehru look. Certainly not leather and dark glasses.

Eric had different ideas. The leather jacket was the only thing he could wear because he felt that the Master wardrobe designed for him was uncomfortable and too tight-fitting. He was also supposed to wear contact lenses that would make his eyes look like a snake's. The lenses themselves were treated with a

time. The schedule was slipping. Geoff is an excellent director, but he's an artist too, and taking time with any craft will eventually catch up with you. This show had some heavy stunt work and special effects and I believe even Geoff had not worked on something this complicated.

We began the film shoot with some easy days, believing that it's always a good idea to get the crew and cast acclimatised before going into tougher scenes. I recall thinking Paul was a little stiff at first and had a hard time finding the fun of the character. Mind you, he did a remarkable job considering the fact he was plunged into this whole thing with very little rehearsal time.

Nerves were a bit on edge too – remember, none of us really knew just what sort of reaction the US audience, let alone the network, would have to this show. If it had been successful, we may have found phosphorescence that, when lit properly, would glow for us. We had an optician come and fit him for them and he approved them. However, they became uncomfortable and made his eyes water. We were stuck because he had shot several scenes with them in already. Hence the sunglasses – the only way to cover his eyes.

Eric was also fitted for prosthetic pieces that would be placed on his face as the movie progressed, to make him appear to be decaying. However, when we proposed making a life mask for him, we discovered it could not be done as it would cause a skin rash. So we were left with the look you see in the film.

I was very sad, and, if I have one regret, it is that I did not pay more attention to the details of Eric's wardrobe and insist on what I believed was right for the character. But I have only myself to blame.

The hard facts are that, when you're juggling as much as I was, you sometimes lose perspective and things move along at a pace that can be faster than you would like. Overall, I was very pleased with the look of the film and, even though Eric's wardrobe caused me some concern, it never upstaged the production to such an extent that you couldn't see past it.

After exterior shooting, we moved inside for the interior TARDIS sequences and then on to the Cloister Room set for the big final battle scenes. One morning I came on to the set and had my usual walk around to say good morning to the crew. I came upon Sylvester McCoy taking a quiet moment for himself on the TARDIS set. I approached him, we shook hands and had a chat. He seemed down or melancholy to me so I asked him if he was all right. He said that he was very appreciative of the chance to return as the Doctor one last time and I was very touched.

This moment made me realise just how important this project and property really was to a lot of people, including myself. I never thought about how profound something like this could really be, but it was a powerful moment. So many people's lives have been touched by this show, and having a chance to be a part of its history was one aspect of the production I had overlooked. I reflect back and now feel privileged to have shared that moment with a Doctor from the original series. It may not seem that important to some, but it will be a part of me for ever.

We shared a rather comic moment when Sylvester and I were joined by Paul. Paul wandered over and started pushing and playing with all the knobs and levers on the console. He looked at me, smiled and asked me how this thing worked. I laughed and said, 'Don't ask me, ask him,' pointing to Sylvester. We all got a giggle out of that. The funny thing is, I always believed that the Doctor never really knew what all the controls of the TARDIS did.

When you have a chance to bond with actors and share small moments like the one I just described, they seem to settle down and slide into the characters like feet into well-worn shoes. For Sylvester, this movie meant he had a chance to give closure to his reign as the Doctor and as the days went on he seemed to be at peace with the fact that the baton was truly passing.

Sylvester is a very gentle soul and someone I admire. He was what I refer to as the quiet professional – nothing was ever a problem. He was forced to lie on a cold hospital gurney during the hospital scenes. We were working in an old hospital wing that had been shut down and the heat was turned off. Sylvester was also asked to spend a long time on the ground in the alley during the TARDIS arrival sequence at the beginning of the movie. Remember, we were shooting in January and there was snow on the ground. Throughout, he never uttered one complaint or concern for himself.

Sylvester had told me he was never really satisfied with the growth of his character during his tenure as the Doctor. Given the chance, I believe he would have made his Doctor much darker and more mysterious. Sylvester's acting abilities far outweighed his

A later, more detailed sketch.

Three photos of the console room under construction. The doorway to the 'Green Room', containing the Doctor's collection of clocks, can be seen in the top picture.

The lower picture shows the room awaiting the addition of the semi-circular rows of stone-effect pillars.

opportunity to display them in the original series. I was one of those who were guilty of assuming he could not act.

I was wrong and so were the BBC – they fought against my having Sylvester appear in the opening sequence. Because we were attempting to link the original series to our film, I felt very strongly that the only Doctor to use was Sylvester. I did not consult the BBC on this at first: I simply had the script written that way. When Jo Wright read the script she phoned me to discuss the casting of the past Doctor, believing that the right thing to do was actually to offer the job to Tom Baker. I did not think that was a good idea and I resisted that notion from the beginning. I then explained to her that I must have Sylvester and that he was the only choice considering our tack – she, however, insisted that we not use Sylvester because some people at the BBC felt his reign as the Doctor, being the most recent, was the least relevant.

I have always been quite vocal about my own personal disdain for the McCoy years as an overall effort. However, it was still important to me to respect the continuity of the series and have the right Doctor appear. I explained to the Beeb that he was a very important part of the history of this series – I firmly believed that Sylvester was the link that would give Paul his official status as the Doctor. To some, the regeneration process meant very little. To me it was everything. If Sylvester regenerated into Paul, then the tradition started long ago would continue, and that's one legacy I wanted to maintain.

As time got closer to production and more important fights presented themselves (such as getting Paul McGann approved), the McCoy issue mysteriously went away. When I was discussing the McCoy situation, I also brought up the question of the possible inclusion of Ace. I was told that under no circumstances was that going to happen and it was not to be discussed further – the BBC simply would not approve that. I never asked again for fear that the whole conversation would continue to degenerate into an argument – and, sadly, I was not passionate enough about Ace to fight. I have nothing against Sophie Aldred as a person and an actor, but her character, as seen on screen, was rather cartoonish in nature and that was definitely one of the arguments that the BBC used to shut down any possible negotiations to bring Ace back.

The politics at the BBC make for interesting side notes. In my seven years of struggle to get a new *Doctor Who* launched, I watched three or four regimes pass through the halls of that hallowed institution. Each time a new

executive came into the ranks he or she had a differing opinion about the property. Some who grew up with the Doctor and were faithful to him considered that the notion of keeping the franchise alive was wonderful. Others whose childhood memories were not served by the good Doctor saw no place for what they labelled as 'tired' or 'old' in the BBC schedule, and so lobbied hard for my version of *Doctor Who* to simply go away. I felt that pressure all the way to the end of production.

The one thing that always angered me was the 'fair-weather fans' who popped up from every crack in the BBC when the film was finally going to be shot, all wanting a piece of it but not actually caring for anything except the kudos they might get for having 'been there'. It never ceases to amaze me how much of that behaviour goes on, not just in the UK but in the US as well.

When Sylvester arrived in Vancouver, he had very kindly brought with him as much of his original wardrobe as he had. The hat, jacket, question-mark sweater and umbrella. I must confess, I never liked the umbrella – and certainly not the sweater. I asked Sylvester not to wear them. He seemed relieved. Both he and I spent a long time talking about the old show and our likes and dislikes.

I was curious about one man, my direct predecessor as producer of *Doctor Who*, John Nathan-Turner, or JNT as he's known. I have never met the man, but subconsciously found myself thinking about him throughout the production. I suppose it was a simple matter of realising that, of all the producers associated with show, his tenure was the longest, and that gave me hope in some odd way. Sylv was always polite and respectful of the decisions Nathan-Turner had made during his era, even if he didn't agree with them. (Sylv! That's the first time I've called him that in these pages. All who know Sylvester call him Sylv, but to me, he will always be the Doctor!)

JNT and I will probably never see eye to eye on where *Doctor Who* went during his term as producer. But I want to say this: anyone who can endure what he endured deserves a medal in my book. In the seven years of peddling and selling and producing just one television film about this character, he produced as many series. Frankly, I don't know where he managed to find the stamina – I personally would have jumped off a building. So, to John Nathan-Turner and all the fellow producers who have worked on this property, a big thank-you. Thank you for

leaving a road map to follow, for without it, I might never have seen the light at the end of the tunnel.

But back to business. As production progressed, so did all the other aspects of the film. The digital effects rendered by Northwest Imaging were building. The main title sequence was being designed, and my dear friend John Debney was working on the music for me. We knew our air date prior to production and, once the gun went off, it was a race to the finish. Every day wasted brought us a day closer to the deadline and increased cost. Increased cost meant very unhappy studios and networks!

Twenty-one days into the picture, we called an emergency production meeting of Peter Ware, Alex Beaton, Geoff Sax, the first assistant director and me. The purpose of the meeting was to assess where we were in the schedule. At this point, we had lost four whole days. This happens when the unexpected occurs. Actors get sick, visual effects slow you down, scenes are more complicated to stage than they appear in script form. Lighting a scene can take hours and then, if you have to turn the camera around and shoot an opposing view, everything must be reset and relit.

We have a saying in the film business: 'Hurry up, and wait'. It seems that everything is rush, rush, rush and then you wait and wait and wait. When I worked for Spielberg, we had several office buildings that had names on the outside. The building that housed the feature film development team was called 'Movies while you wait and wait and wait'. Geoff, our director, was upset because he had originally been promised more time, as I mentioned earlier. It seemed from his perspective that he was on schedule. However, due to excessive cast costs and unexpected overpayments to Warner/ Chappel music for the rights to use the theme, we were rapidly running out of money. We had to find a compromise and get the film finished.

Our big problem was always the fight sequences at the end of the picture. They would be shot last and the script simply said, 'The Doctor and the Master fight'. We never had a detailed story plot for how they fought and how the Doctor would actually overcome the enemy. In the end, we decided the only way to be sure we could finish the film in a certain time period would be to thoroughly work out the fight sequence and block it with the actors and stuntmen. This scripting problem popped up quite a bit in this film.

Earlier on, when the Master appears out of nowhere in the TARDIS, everyone always asks the logical question: how did he get in? We

Michael Wong carefully sketched out each panel of the console.

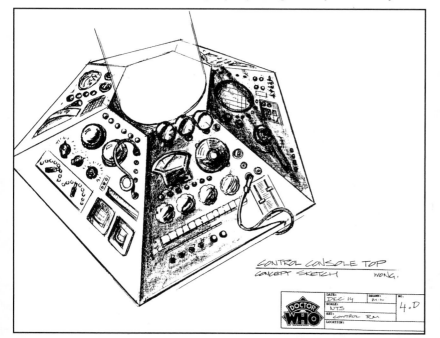

CONTROL CONSOLE TOP
CONCEPT SKETCH   WONG.

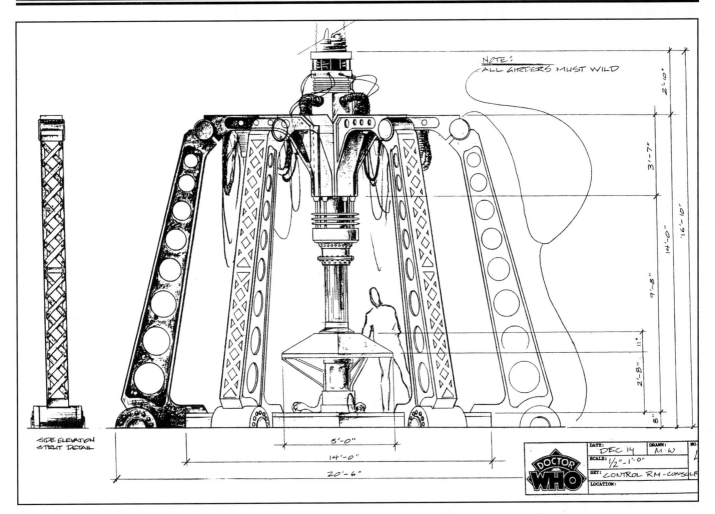

NOTE:
ALL GIRDERS MUST WILD

SIDE ELEVATION
STRUT DETAIL

5'-0"
14'-0"
20'-6"

2'-0"
3'-7"
14'-0"
16'-10"
9'-8"
11"
2'-8"
8"

DATE: DEC 14 DRAWN: M.W. NO.
SCALE: 1/2"-1'-0"
SET: CONTROL RM - CONSOLE
LOCATION:

DOCTOR WHO

struggled with that one for hours. We assumed, at script stage, that he simply found a way. You dismiss these things sometimes. But, when it comes time to shoot it or cut it together in the editing room, a different picture gets painted. All the little story holes and logic problems glare at you.

Once we had it blocked, the big question was how long it would take to finish the film. In the end, it took 29 days. One day less than Geoff had originally planned on and was originally given. Just another example of how studios ultimately hurt themselves. Instead of biting the bullet in the first place and reaching a goal in the true spirit of teamsmanship, they firmly believe the best results come from restriction and bullying. My obvious dislike for the studio system is apparent in these pages and I make no apologies for it.

The problem with spending more money to finish the film is that something always suffers because of it. The usual mistake made is cutting the funds for post-production: spending less time finishing the film, in other words shortening the amount of time you have to pull all the elements together (the dub or mix) and cutting corners, such as mixing all the sound effects and music in stereo instead of surround. These shortcuts

become apparent in the finished product. We were fortunate enough to have a very fast crew on the post-production team and they worked around the clock, at no extra charge, to get the movie finished. We were lucky.

Saying goodbye to the crew and cast was difficult for me. I had made new friends who quickly became an extended family. That's the way it is in film production. When you spend that much time with people, you really get to know them.

The film itself was finished and delivered to Fox on 2 May. Prior to its going to air we had a very memorable première party at the Directors' Guild Theater in Los Angeles. The press were very kind to us in most cases, as were the fans. Very special acknowledgment must go to one of the brightest and most special people I have ever met the fan world, Shaun Lyon, who is affiliated with the *Gallifrey One* convention held each year in Los Angeles. This man had been a good friend of the show and of our production from its inception.

At the première party, he was one of those responsible for organising getting the fans out to the event and publicising it. He was also my secret screener, who caught several

A drawing to give the production team an idea of scale within the control room.

Above: The cluttered TARDIS library and balcony. Again, very little of this detail was seen in the finished film.

Right: Action stations!

glaring problems with the rough cut of the film. The most obvious to him, but not to me at the time, was the fact that we had Paul explain that he had thirteen lives and not twelve. We replaced the word thirteen with twelve before the film was delivered, so no egg appeared on my face, thanks to Shaun.

Obviously we had our critics, and that's OK, too. Looking back on the entire experience I recall nothing but hard work and a lot of joy. Given the chance, I would gladly do it again.

After the movie went out, things ought to have died down somewhat. Although the ratings in the UK were nothing short of excellent, in the

Left: The Green Room and the Music Room.

Below: The vestibule where the Doctor places the Master's casket.

States they were disastrous. Up against a major-league ball game, *Roseanne's* husband's heart attack and a general apathy towards the Fox *Tuesday Night Movie* slot, *Doctor Who* really hadn't a hope in hell. The press reaction in the States leading up to transmission had, with the notable exception of *TV Guide*, been mostly favourable, with many urging viewers to give the Movie of the Week a try. *TV Guide's* preview had been less positive and, since it's the most widely read periodical in America, its effect on the potential viewers cannot be overlooked.

However, before it even went out, the various constituent parts of what had begun to look like an unholy alliance (BBC, BBC Worldwide, Fox and Universal, with Philip Segal trapped in the middle trying to keep all parties happy and out of reach of each other's throats) were beginning to express concern over the final product. In mid-February, as the Vancouver shooting wound down, Universal began questioning the amount of money spent and, via Jim Brock, claimed that the $170,000 overspend that ensued had been the BBC's fault. They claimed this was partly due to the late agreement to Geoffrey Sax's appointment, resulting in his having only nine days rather than a few weeks' 'prep' time. Universal pointed out that the parties were 'collectively unable to make a timely decision'. Universal also felt that Matthew Jacobs had not received enough help, meaning that Acts 6 and 7 were rushed and needed extra shooting days allotted, as the script had run so late. (Indeed, Philip Segal actually wrote a fair proportion of the dialogue from Matthew's extensive notes on and around the shooting days.)

Universal then pointed out that these

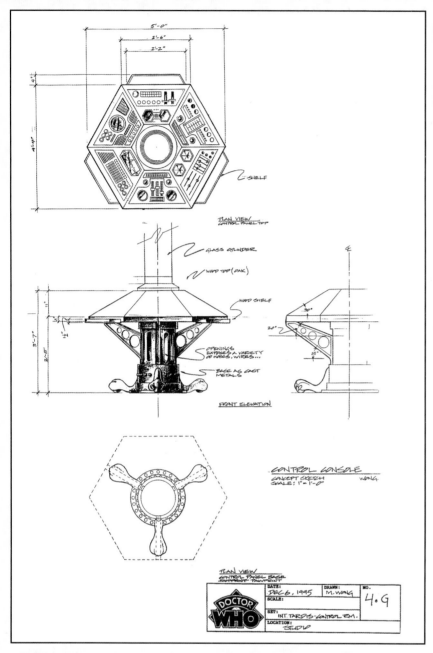

Various elevations of the console, demonstrating the attention to detail that was taken with every aspect of the prop.

representative.' Unsurprisingly, the BBC didn't take too kindly to this. They pointed out that they had no influence over Geoff Sax's appointment. Delighted as they were to have a British director, it was Fox who took that decision. They also responded that Jo Wright denied strongly any suggestion that she delayed the rewrites, necessitating extra scenes. Indeed, she pointed out that the final rewrites were done in Trevor Walton's office, with her, Matthew, Philip and Pat Wells from Universal in attendance.

The BBC also denied that they had entered into the co-production agreement 'without script approval'. The Harry Van Gorkum retaliation was more explicit. They cited the fact that it was Universal who had pressured them to cast the unknown so that they could spend more money on the Master – the BBC saw Harry's tapes and decided he was not strong enough to take such an important part. They thought that Eric Roberts was an 'unnecessary expense'. They then threw back the suggestion that they should have sent an accountant – 'if Universal had kept proper control over the production, then such a massive overspend would not have occurred' – and suggested that, as Universal had supplied the budget breakdowns in the first place, it was their responsibility to cough up the balance.

Two other ugly points reared their heads during this period as well – both concerning the emotive subject of credits on the finished productions. First, the UK casting agents John and Ros Hubbard were reminding everyone that, as the people who actually found Paul McGann, albeit some time previously, they still wanted their credit on this version of the movie. Although Fox and Universal objected, Philip Segal intervened, feeling that the credit was duly theirs – and they received one.

unanticipated overspends were due to the BBC's insistence on story points long after the $5 million budget had been agreed. The final twist of the knife came with a reminder that, contractually, the BBC were afforded only format approval for the movie, and the fact that Universal allowed them to query the script was a courtesy – and one they now clearly regretted. Brock went on to counter any potential arguments by saying the BBC had been advised that overspends were likely due to these delays and that it was the BBC who vetoed the casting of Harry Van Gorkum in favour of Paul McGann (who cost, Universal claimed, $25,000 more). If Jim Brock wanted to really rub salt in the wound, he could do no better than add an observation that 'the BBC would have been fully within its rights to send a production accountant … to monitor all production costs. It was the BBC's choice to send a creative representative such as Jo Wright rather than a more production-orientated

The second, and far more complicated, problem concerned John Leekley. He was claiming that, owing to his work on the bible and the early scripts, he should receive both his executive producer's credit and fee as well as one concerning the storyline. The fact that nothing in the eventual movie, bar the 'half-human' reference, bore any relation to Leekley's work caused friction among all concerned. It became Universal's responsibility to prove, via paperwork, that Leekley had no claim to such a credit, payments or recognition.

Luckily, Philip Segal, being the true Virgo that he is, had kept just about every memo and scrap of paper relating to *Doctor Who* since he first made contact with the BBC in 1989. The court case between Leekley and Universal was long and protracted and quite unpleasant, but ultimately found in Universal's favour, and Leekley received nothing by way of credit or monies from the finished production.

Later that month, the tabloids in the UK had a field day – suddenly deciding that Paul McGann had been guilty of 'having a high old time' and enjoyed the 'local recreational facilities' while making the movie, and was nearly sacked as a result. The piece, in the *Daily Mail*, went on to cast aspersions over McGann's behaviour on set, and dredged up an old story about how he had been replaced by Sean Bean in the *Sharpe* series after an alleged knee injury. McGann's lawyers were on to the *Mail* in an instant, claiming the article was defamatory, that it attempted to hint that McGann was using drugs, and suggesting that the tone of the remarks about the *Sharpe* incident implied there was more to it than just a knee injury.

Exactly what the financial award to McGann was from the *Mail* is unclear, but they rapidly printed an apology, acknowledging that there were no production difficulties, nor any circumstances or behaviour surrounding the filming that would reflect badly upon him. The *Daily Mail* then said it 'apologises unreservedly' to McGann and the matter was closed.

At BBC Worldwide, the marketing strategy was getting into its full stride. A ten-minute sales promo of the movie was made (which neatly condensed the first six acts without losing any of the salient plot points), and the company looked into ways of exploiting their reinvigorated franchise.

A blitz on products began – everything involving the past 30 years of *Doctor Who* was deleted, and many licences retracted or placed on hold. Only DAPOL, making action figures, and Marvel's *Doctor Who Magazine* were able to remain as they were. The biggest casualty was Virgin Publishing Limited, who had held the exclusive novels licence, as well as a licence to produce large-format factual books, since 1973 (under the various companies that eventually transmuted into Virgin Publishing in the late 1980s).

The publication by BBC Books of both a novelisation of the movie and a script book made them realise that there was a potential for them to make more money by doing original novels themselves, rather than just taking a percentage of Virgin's profits. So, by the middle of 1996, BBC Worldwide Publishing was able to announce that, within the year, 90 per cent of *Doctor Who* merchandise would either come directly from them, or be under tighter control via their licensing departments.

In America, while BBC Worldwide were gearing themselves up for this anticipated rush of new opportunities, post-production work was going ahead full steam, starting on Thursday, 22 February, the day after principal shooting ended. All parties had input into the editing, with copies at various stages of development

going back and forth among Universal, Fox and the BBC. All kinds of requests were made during this period: to make the Dalek voices more understandable, to ensure that the only bullet ricochets heard could be attributed to gunfire actually seen, and not to make Miranda's neck-breaking too grotesque.

Matthew Jacobs delivered the new opening voice-over to be supplied by Paul McGann on 2 April, which meant that neither the lengthy Dalek speech nor the Master's was required. It was also now that Matthew added the rewrite to cover an error when the Doctor referred to having only twelve, not thirteen, lives – 'something the fans will really jump on, especially in Britain apparently,' Matthew explained. There also followed some debate about whether the word 'millennium' or 'millennia' should be used as, strictly speaking, the new millennium isn't until 1 January 2001. On this point, Pat Wells at Universal found ways around all uses of the word 'millennium' bar one – when it was spoken by Professor

The destination panel of the Doctor's TARDIS with, below, the choices of other planets and times chosen for the unseen sides of the display. Long-term fans of the series will recognise many of the options!

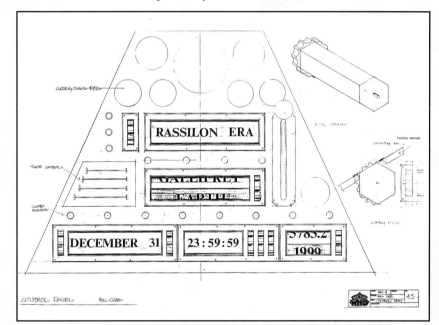

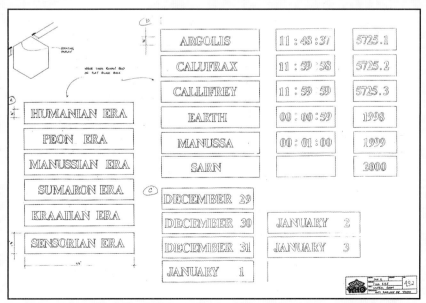

WORLDWIDE TRANSMISSION

In the US, 8 May 1996 saw the first official screening of the *Doctor Who* TV movie at a Los Angeles press event. The press received a 'world première' tin TARDIS containing a copy of the movie in a special box with Paul McGann on the front, some press notes, a couple of black-and-white photographs of the cast and a bag of jelly babies.

In the UK, BAFTA played host to two viewings on 13 May, one for the press, one for 200 fans who had won tickets through a competition run by BBC Worldwide and *Doctor Who Magazine*. Although the first broadcast took place on 12 May via a local station in Alberta, followed by two stations running it in Canada on the 13th, Fox transmitted *Doctor Who* at 8.00 p.m. Eastern Standard Time on 14 May. The BBC, however, were initially uncertain as to when they would broadcast it, with rumoured

suggestions of transmissions any time between May and Christmas. Ultimately, *Doctor Who* received its British première on the Bank Holiday Monday, 27 May, at 8.30 p.m. Prior to this ought to have been the video debut, on 15 May. Because BBC Worldwide had put so much money into the programme, the intention was to get a video release some months before its TV showing, thus generating a significant amount of revenue for Worldwide to get their money back. Not only did the May BBC TV transmission scupper that quite badly (and no: Worldwide were not very happy, as one could understand), the British Board of Film Classification demanded a swift re-edit in the light of the then recent Dunblane massacre. The BBFC demanded it be suitable for a 12 certificate, despite the original plan for a 15 certificate. The work necessary therefore delayed the video release by a week until 22 May.

Some cuts were made between the various versions shown. If we work on the assumption that the US-transmitted version (as broadcast on Fox) is the 'master' version, then we can note some of the changes. Incidentally, the BAFTA viewing in Britain was a fairly unique version. It contained the sound effect of Miranda's neck breaking, featured the full 'death' of Chang Lee and had three point-of-view shots of the seventh Doctor kicking the hospital's surgical implements off their table – the last one in slow motion. However, the gunfight at the start was as per the UK broadcast, having already been trimmed by the Dunblane-sensitive BBC. Therefore that version was different from the US version, the BBC-transmitted version and the BBC Video release. Confused? You should be …

The BBC-transmitted version – 84 minutes and 39 seconds – saw the caption, 'Based on the original series broadcast by the BBC' removed from the start, but did include a dedication to the late Jon Pertwee, who had died suddenly earlier that month. The request came directly from Philip Segal's office.

During the opening sequence, much of the gunfire action was edited. This includes Chang Lee's gang firing at the departing hoodlum's car and then Lee and his two friends trying to avoid being shot. This meant that UK viewers never saw Lee using a gun or his chums getting killed, and so Lee's apparent confusion at being alone seems a bit sudden, although one of their bodies is later seen before Lee checks on the Doctor.

Before all this, UK viewers were also denied the chance to see the gunmen aiming at Lee and then firing at the newly materialised TARDIS, although this particular shot is preceded by a reaction shot of the gunmen taken from a previously hacked-down shot.

Later, at the hospital, the operating-room scene has been chopped down somewhat, necessitating a rearrangement of the music score and sound effects. Grace's attempts to retrieve the probe and the efforts to revive the Doctor are trimmed – Grace's mentioning that the probe is still stuck in the body and the Doctor's final scream are gone

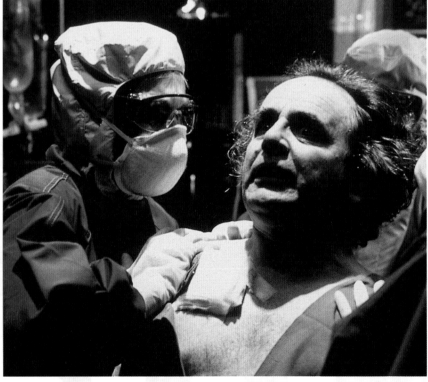

One of the scenes that concerned the BBFC.

completely and the aforementioned tray-kicking is reduced to just one shot.

As far as the involvement of the Master in actual physical killing is concerned, the sound of Miranda's of-screen neck being snapped is gone, and the twist to Chang Lee's head when the Master betrays him is also excised.

On 7 July, ABC in Australia transmitted *Doctor Who* as per the US broadcast, with the only cut being the sound effect of Bruce's wife's neck snapping. This was followed on 30 October by an identical broadcast on New Zealand's TVNZ (this is the version released on home video in both countries). The French broadcaster France2 aired the movie nearly a year later, on 18 March 1997 under the title *Le Seigneur Du Temps* (The Time Lord).

On 15 May, the preliminary ratings for *Doctor Who* on Fox were released. Philip Segal believed that a 15 per cent share of the available audience was necessary, and preferably a 17 or 18 per cent share to persuade Fox to commission further movies (remember, they already had an option on at least one more) or maybe even an ongoing series. Sadly, the movie got only 5.5 million viewers, a 9 per cent share, placing it joint 75th for the week. The 9 per cent share is a little below the average for the Fox's Tuesday night movie, which usually achieved an 11 per cent share.

Meanwhile, in the UK, *Doctor Who* found favour with 9.08 million viewers, placing it fifteenth overall in the BBC's Top Ten, trouncing ITV's big drama for the night, *Bramwell* – the show's highest figure since 1982 (*Time-Flight* Part One, for those interested to know). The video, meanwhile, did less well for BBC Worldwide. It entered the CIN sales charts at third place. The following week, it slipped to sixth and then disappeared off the Top 30 in its third week of sales. By the time this book is published, it will have sold just under 46,000 units. Even a DVD was released – but only in the Far East, and was deleted shortly afterwards.

Four years later, on Saturday 13 November 1999, BBC2 repeated the

The BBFC insisted that the gun attack on Lee be severely curtailed.

DWTVM, this time as per the US version – but again both Miranda and Lee's necks broke silently.

There is also a rough 'director's cut', about which much speculation has been offered, suggesting it could receive a video release someday. This seems unlikely, though. It's not a director's cut in the now accepted sense (an alternate – usually long – version with extra scenes and so on, popular in the home video and DVD market). This is merely a very rough edit, put together during editing on 7 March 1996, with stock sound effects and music (for instance Bing Crosby singing *Swinging on a Star* replaces *In a Dream* as the record the seventh Doctor is playing at the start of the programme) so that Geoff Sax and Philip Segal could monitor the progress being made. As the score had not been completed, a selection of tracks from Eric Serra's soundtrack to the film *Leon* were used. It does contain a few extra sequences which were lost, or just starts and ends to scenes clipped, all for timing reasons. Among these are brief extra sequences of the Master and Lee watching Grace and the Doctor in the park, a lengthier climax as the Master tries to

absorb the Doctor's life energies, and the sequence where the hapless ITAR (Institute of Technological Advancement and Research) guards confront the Master and Lee (although you never actually see them getting slimed, contrary to popular opinion).

At the start of the movie, there is no Paul McGann voice-over detailing the plot, and instead we hear the Gordon Tipple Master's voice asking the Doctor to take his remains back to Gallifrey, plus proper Dalek voices shouting 'Exterminate'. There's a nice humorous moment on the San Francisco bridge where a couple of drivers yell at the cop to 'give him the keys!', and in the hospital, there is an alternate take of the scene in the lift – the Doctor actually yells 'Puccini' at her rather than whisper it – and there is no talk of Grace being 'tired of life'.

Finally, when they reach her condo, the Doctor comments on how nice it is to see the city when it is still full of people. It is also worth noting that in this early cut there are no scenes featuring the security guard played by Dee Jay Jackson.

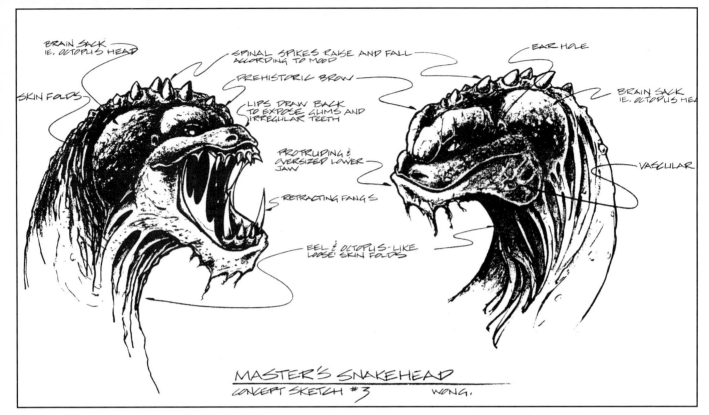

Labels on the concept sketch:

BRAIN SACK IE. OCTOPUS HEAD

SKIN FOLDS

SPINAL SPIKES RAISE AND FALL ACCORDING TO MOOD

PREHISTORIC BROW

LIPS DRAW BACK TO EXPOSE GUMS AND IRREGULAR TEETH

PROTRUDING & OVERSIZED LOWER JAW

RETRACTING FANGS

EEL & OCTOPUS-LIKE 'LOOSE' SKIN FOLDS

EAR HOLE

BRAIN SACK IE. OCTOPUS HEAD

VASCULAR

MASTER'S SNAKEHEAD
CONCEPT SKETCH #3   WONG.

Michael Wong's early concept designs for the morphant snake.

Wagg. Pat suggested 'this line remain as it is, as it could easily mean that we are entering a new millennium in telling time with the new clock. All nasty letters regarding the inaccuracy should be forwarded to [her boss] Tom Burke!'

The BBC, meanwhile, were far more concerned about the morphant snake, which, at this stage, they felt, wasn't scary enough. 'At times it is almost cartoon-like,' said Jo Wright. Understandably, in the light of the budgetary concerns of earlier, Jo was wary of just telling the FX people to do it again, but felt it did need looking at.

On 12 and 13 April, Eric Roberts, Paul McGann and Daphne Ashbrook were brought back to record their voice-overs in New Orleans, while the local Vancouver actors did theirs in their home town the following Thursday. With that completed, the movie was delivered to Fox and the BBC on 2 May 1996. Bar a few odd press events, the actors, the director, the crew and the studio executives were free of *Doctor Who*. Now it was just one more television programme to them.

Once the film had been delivered to Fox, we got nothing but praise and elation over the look and feel of it. Trevor Walton congratulated us on the effort and then dropped the biggest bomb of all. With great glee, he announced to us that Fox were so pleased with their new Movie of the Week that they would play it in the May sweeps period against John Goodman's having a heart attack on the *Roseanne* show. Needless to say, I was very concerned about *Doctor*

Who's ability to attract the right audience and enough of that audience on a sweep night.

Fox, it turned out, had nothing else to put there and gambled with our show. Fox lost. A 9 per cent share did not generate the kind of heat Fox was hoping for and, shortly after, everyone simply forgot about the movie. That is a rather bleak yet honest synopsis of my immediate reaction to what happened.

Peeling back the onion, one remembers that there were lots of conversations and events happening behind the scenes. To begin at the beginning, while the movie was be prepared for airing in the States, yet another regime change was happening back at the BBC. By this time almost everyone with whom I had dealt at the Beeb had either left or been forced out through restructuring. This is a rather overlooked yet critical factor about the development and production of the show. Whenever there is a personnel change, the rules of engagement change. Any project will lose momentum when its benefactor departs. Such was the case with *Doctor Who*.

Prior to going on the air, there were several conversations about the future of the project and the reality of its ever becoming a series on Fox. As the movie was never really commissioned as a pilot in the eyes of Fox, it was never scrutinised as a candidate to replace any other show on the network. Universal had no interest in *Doctor Who* as a series. In fact, they were pushing the reorder of more episodes of *Sliders*. They owned 100 per cent of that show and had only a 50 per cent stake in *Doctor Who*, so you can pretty much figure out which one they really intended to support. Needless to say, *Sliders* was renewed for another season and *Doctor Who* never even got discussed.

I do believe that my efforts to revive the series were not in vain. Even though we failed to attract a big enough audience in the US market, we did add another chapter to the *Doctor Who* saga and brought closure to the McCoy years. We bolted on some more story and mythology, like it or not, and ended the saga of the Master. All in all, it was a fun run. I do wish I had been surrounded by people who, like myself, wanted the Doctor to come back with a splash. But such is life – that did not happen.

If I have one regret, it was not seeing the film make it into series form. Our ratings were not strong enough, nor was the support of the studio. The Doctor was not really ready for a return to television. Someday, however, he will be. Since leaving Amblin and going independent, I have found the business to be far less exciting than it was when I first jumped in. We seem to have lost the art of entertaining people on a small scale. The prevailing winds are that if you can't spend hundreds of millions of dollars, you can't

seem to produce something wonderful. That certainly seems to be the view the BBC have now with regard to the Doctor.

I will personally never believe that notion, by the way. For that reason, I now have a company with great partners, people who care, the way I do, about controlling the costs of production, and have a burning desire to entertain. *Doctor Who* will be back and this time I believe he will come to the big screen in a spectacular vision. It may take a few years of development and there may be some false reports or bad information – after all, it would not be *Doctor Who* without all that, would it? *Doctor Who* is a very rare animal and to understand its influence on children and adults alike is to truly know only one thing: that deep within each of us burns the light of a child that is or was. When the flame burns low or goes out, we lose touch with that part of ourselves that understands and loves the world of *Doctor Who*.

As for the future of *Doctor Who* and my association with it, only time will tell. Have I seen the future? Well, let's just say this: when we wrapped production on the television movie, I secretly kept the key to the TARDIS. The only trouble is, I'm not quite sure how to use it yet …

Had a new series followed, would this have been the TARDIS crew?

The 'Seal of Rassilon' motif was used throughout the TARDIS interior – on doorways, wall panels, the Eye of Harmony and even on a tiny lever on the TARDIS console (opposite).

• 1996 •
DESIGNS FOR THE FUTURE

One of the most well-respected aspects of the production was the design work, ranging from the glorious TARDIS interiors that captured the spirit of the Jules Verne-inspired control room from the mid-Seventies through to the dashing and debonair outfit that the Eighth Doctor wore. Responsible for the impressive overall design of the movie, and responsible for coordinating all aspects of its look, was Canadian Richard Hudolin.

'I started in the November and filming started properly in January. That's very intense for that size of show – it's a huge scale show and it wasn't much time. It had a higher budget than most movies of the week, sure, but a bit less time. So the first thing I did was hire a great group of people to work with me – my job was to gather up the best people. They do the storyboards, the basic preliminary set designs, decals and all that. Then I develop it further, take it in a unified direction and ensure it all looks fluid and connected. Then there's the locations, where we can't actually design stuff, but we can design around it. When I came up with the initial designs they were much bigger, and far more intricate than Phil and the producers had imagined but amazingly they weren't put off by them. Credit where it's due, they let me know what they could do financially and I said what I

could do, what it could have been with more money and asked what they wanted me to do? And they said yes. At that point everybody's enthusiasm got really high because their contributions were being treated seriously, the great detail they'd put into everything was appreciated by everyone else.

'Next we got some old episodes in. This gave us an idea of what this was all about. I knew of *Doctor Who* but didn't know that much in depth about it. Phil Segal's been a fanatic for years and years and years and so had reference books, but he wanted to move beyond, create the next level of *Doctor Who* if you like, rather than just recreate it exactly – all the familiar icons but with a new slant. A step forward. We tried to retain the best elements such as the six-sided console but went for a more Victorian look and we used the Rassilon seal throughout all the sets. You will see it in six-inch form on the columns, you'll see it in various walls and even in tiny detail on crests and stamps all over the TARDIS. There's even one on a lever on the console. We kept the roundel theme from the original TARDIS interiors but sometimes reversed that, so we could actually shoot through them. By cutting through, say, the spider-like pylons, it gives the director greater shooting variety – he can use them to shoot through, just to give a more diverse viewpoint and a good focus onto the console. Because this is such a large room, it gives you a new

COSTUME DESIGN

Another Canadian, with vast TV and film experience, Jori Woodman was the costume designer for the movie. She, too, was not very familiar with the show's history, but quickly did her research via books, old videos and magazine articles.

'One of my main reasons for digging up the past was to see what Sylvester McCoy looked like as the previous Doctor. Philip didn't want him to wear the question-mark sweater so I needed to change that straight away. We gave him plaid pants, a velvet waistcoat, and a jacket to keep the same silhouette from the BBC show but a bit classier. He added the hat which I thought was great and he said he preferred our costume to his original, which was nice.

'Paul's costume came out of a silhouette. I wanted him to look like the previous Doctors – long coat, elegance and all that. But in bringing it to the States, the writer came up with going away from the British Edwardian look and originally came up with Abe Lincoln, the frock coat, waistcoat etc. I thought that was interesting but ultimately really boring. Black is so dull. So they then suggested Wild Bill Hickcock and I took that a bit further. For instance, the velvet frock coat isn't something Hickcock could have worn. We had a hat for the costume but decided never to feature it except when Paul discards it when he's in the locker room. I knew that lovely coat would look much richer on camera and I wanted to match the textures of the sets, very smooth, very elegant and sleek. Because Paul only has the one costume throughout, I wanted it to be memorable and something people can focus on. Everyone else changes at least one item of clothing during the movie, but once he's in his, the Doctor doesn't. And to be honest, on location you don't know if it's going to be warm or pissing down with rain, so its easier to give actors warmer clothes that can be taken off than thin things that they freeze to death in. We have three versions of the costume – one for the stuntman, two for Paul. I had a bit of time to do research, look for fabrics.

'When Daphne was cast, I had time

Black, orange, and 'snakeskin' fabrics were used for the Master.

Police officers seen in the film had costumes designed to look 'five minutes into the future'.

to do some research, look for interesting fabrics. So I sorted out a variety of things such as the ballgown and coat. San Franciscans dress to go out – here in Vancouver, people don't. Probably they don't in London any more. But if you go to the opera in San Francisco, people generally dress up, right up, for the night, so the ballgown was based on what today's San Franciscans are wearing to the opera. I wanted colour rather than black – it was set in the year 2000, and I needed her to be quite a contrast to everyone around her, so I went for this electric blue coat and dress. And for the hospital scenes, I tried to make it a bit futuristic: we put these biotec hoods on them, and the glasses and a new design of mask, just to give it that 'a few years away' look without risking it dating too quickly. It's a lot harder to design for four years away than two hundred years away. In knew that in four years we'd be wearing basically the same clothes but you can't predict the small changes to

style and taste that will happen in subtle ways. So I used colour as the main futuristic theme – I gave her a neon lilac blouse, and a textured coat that looks dark in the TARDIS but brighter outside. I gave all the police officers special riot forces helmets rather than traditional flat caps, again just to put it five minutes into the future. An inner city futurism.

'For Chang Lee I focused on silver and orange. The Master's tones are similar to Lee's – Lee wears a snake jacket, and the Master has flashes of Lee's orange in his final costume, although it's more a rust colour than the fluorescence of Lee's. but I wanted to keep those two thematically similar. I designed Bruce's paramedic jacket from scratch – it's heavier and darker than a real one, and I lined it with silver so you'd get these odd flashes of something not quite right. I enjoyed referencing back to the BBC show, Tom Baker episodes mainly, so that I could see the Time Lord stuff. I saw one on his home planet with

this woman dressed in jungle gear, Queen of the Woods or something, and these marvellous Time Lord costumes. I liked them and that's where the Master's cloak came from. Originally, he just wore this Nehru suit but when I saw the set I realised he'd get lost, because the set was amazing. It's dark and cathedral-like and I thought poor Eric Roberts would just be this thin figure in black, so I added this robe and they added the line about dressing for the occasion. He needed a bigger presence for that scene and I built his robe up bit by bit, adding more and more until I thought it really stood out. I looked at those marvellous Time Lord robes from the original show – they had these fantastically intricate high collars and skull caps, but I thought that would be too much, and it would hinder Eric's movements as he has to be quite active, so I went half way. I think it still has the wackiness of James Acheson's designs but not as large or overstated.'

Opposite: The TARDIS library and balcony.

Left: The Cloister Room had a belfry-like roof added via computer. An intricate model (below) was built for this 'extension'.

way of doing a close up. The whole set is like a sea shell, with everything at equal points from each other so that no matter where you are in it, everything is the same distance away.

'A lot of stuff was matted on later. The Cloister Room for instance was only half a set – we built a belfry model to be laid on later, but not full size. That gives the director and actors an idea of what the roof will look like so they don't look at the wrong thing. The sets had to be very textured, the walls very definite in their strength and depth because Glen McPherson is such a good director of photography he'll pick up on any flaws, so I made sure there weren't any. And the nice thing is that because he knew the sets were going to be good, he planned his shots easily, not having to worry that bits of wall might be loose or missing. Well, except the ceiling obviously. He trusted that no matter where he shot, it'd look like the TARDIS and not like a bit of wood erected in a studio. And Geoff Sax added so much to it as well; he understands how to really show off everyone else's work to great effect, give everyone their moment on screen.

'I talked very closely with Jori Woodman, so that her costumes and my sets didn't clash in terms of colour. Trying to make Vancouver look like San Francisco was fun – generally a colour scheme that implies water without actually seeing it. We used lots of reflective paints, Jori had lots of shiny fabrics and the Glen lit it very "watery". Little things like that just made the difference.

'The whole show had a great feel. I've had so

many people call me, tell me how lucky I was to do *Doctor Who*. Our construction co-ordinator grew up with the show, everyone knew it, talked about how important it was to their childhood. I'd never seen it – all I knew was that it was a British time travel show featuring a guy in a police box, but everyone else knew so much I picked a lot up. That enthusiasm for the production is rare and so it was really nice to find that everyone pulled together because they love it so much. If it had gone to a series, I doubt I'd have done it because I was booked for other things. But maybe they'd have asked me to act as a consultant for the series, keeping the design constant, but that'd be all.'

THE NOVEL OF THE FILM

HE'S BACK ... AND IT'S ABOUT TIME!

DOCTOR WHO

GARY RUSSELL

BBC

T he novelisation of *Doctor Who* was formally commissioned on 23 January 1996, although discussions began earlier in the month. On Friday, 12 January, two days after news about Paul McGann's casting had broken, I received a telephone message from Rona Selby at BBC Books. I called her back the following Monday, and she asked me if I knew they were doing a new *Doctor Who* television movie, and I told her in a rather understated tone that, yeah, I'd heard something about it.

'Well, do you want to do the novelisation for BBC Books?' Eleven simple words that opened up so many possibilities. It took me less than a second to say yes, we arranged a meeting for later in the week, and that was that. Sorted. Exactly why they chose me is one of those 'right place, right time' things. Since I'd left

editing *Doctor Who Magazine* at Marvel Comics seven months earlier, the various contacts I had made at BBC Worldwide tended to use me as an unofficial soothsayer in all things *Doctor Who*: checking copy for merchandise, writing press releases for BBC Video, telling them which writer created which monster, that sort of thing.

Through development work that had been going on while I was still at Marvel, I had got to know Andy Russell (no relation) at BBC Multimedia, who was in charge of the BBC's *Doctor Who* CD-ROM, which I was writing for them. At a meeting of all the department heads, which had taken place on the 9th, Andy had put my name forward to Rona as someone he knew and trusted in regard to the show. Apparently a nod of heads from Licensing, Home Video, Marketing etc. was all it took for Rona to decide on me. Andy had copies of my (then) two *Doctor Who* novels, so she and her assistant Nuala Buffini took one each and flicked through them over the weekend while they waited for me to return Rona's call.

Owing to problems in Vancouver over exactly which version of the script was being written at any one moment, it was over a week, on Monday the 22nd, before I actually met up with Rona and Nuala to be given a script to work from. They gave me a list of instructions – the novel was intended to act as an introduction to new viewers rather than long-term fans and, for that reason, continuity references to the old show were to be kept to a minimum. Also, they (mistakenly in my view) were determined to bring the age range of the book down below that at which Virgin – who held the novel rights to existing *Doctor Who* – were aiming their books. They wanted the novelisation to be aimed at thirteen-

year-olds rather than the seventeen-plus at whom Virgin aimed theirs. This was annoying but not difficult, although mentions of Chang Lee's gangland background, which I expanded on, were therefore trimmed to lose references to prostitution and other unsavoury aspects of street life.

Numerous small continuity mentions were lost – in the Cloister Room I had Chang Lee and the Master see all seven earlier incarnations of the Doctor in the Eye, and later had Grace quiz the Doctor on his past, being horrified (and a little confused) to discover he had a granddaughter somewhere. There were also a few back-references to the Master's past, a couple of nods to the Virgin range (one of which survived in the finished book) and an explanation as to Ace's whereabouts – tying into her eventual home as outlined in the Virgin novels.

I also opted to tell the whole story from either Grace's or Lee's point of view, which was a useful narrative tool to describe the alienness of the Doctor and the Master but a bit of a bugger, as both of them die two-thirds of the way through. Again, as the script was not entirely clear as to what happened, I chose to injure rather than kill them, which not only meant I could keep the story coming from their point of view but I could avoid the *deus ex machina* of the TARDIS bringing them back to life once it was in a temporal orbit, which, although probably quite dramatic on TV, didn't bear too much scrutiny on the printed page.

The biggest drawback to the whole thing was time – I had to deliver the book on Tuesday, 20 February (I actually gave it in on Friday the 23rd after promising it would be no later). However, one thing the BBC lacked was any illustrative materials. All I had to go on were one colour photocopy of Paul McGann from an upcoming edition of *Radio Times*, the fact that I knew what Daphne Ashbrook looked like as an alien in an episode of *Star Trek* and a ropy photo of Eric Roberts from ten years earlier. No other cast were known: I had no idea whether Eric Roberts played Bruce and the Master (the script sort of implied it could be someone different) and, worst of all, the script summed up Act 7 by saying 'The Master and the Doctor fight'. Not the most helpful of stage directions. Far less helpful was the stage direction that effectively read that Grace fits the medical apparatus to the Doctor. What medical apparatus? I wondered. What does this do? Unaware that the production team were having to make some of this up as they went along, Nuala did get Philip Segal to fax over to me the design sketch for the medical thingie (it struck me then, I must say, that this was not going to be a TV movie aimed at 13-year-olds, but there you go).

I delivered the manuscript on the Friday as promised, only to be shown about 300 colour photos by Nuala plus half an hour's worth of rushes (or dailies as the Americans call them). I saw the interior of the ambulance where the Master spits goo at Grace, a couple of hospital scenes and a lengthy panning shot of the inside of the ambulance, which neither of us understood until I suddenly realised the snake thing was going to be a CGI effect and this was probably some stuff it was going to be matted into. I remember that Nuala and I caught each other's eye when we saw the finished movie and gave each other a thumbs-up at this sequence – we were right!

Anyway, appalled at how far removed my guesswork had been in describing clothing, Grace's hair colour, the hospital interiors and Lee's clothes (I had him written as wearing really smart designer clothes and shades after the Master gave him the gold dust – it's what I'd have spent it on anyway!) I begged to be given the weekend to readjust the whole book. Understanding, Nuala said yes and I spent two days ferociously rewriting every description possible. Still neither of us knew what the interior of the TARDIS looked like, but luckily for me Gary Gillatt of *Doctor Who Magazine* was out there and he phoned through some descriptions, which was a life-saver. Also, a few people in Vancouver had watched the Rose Alley scenes being shot and could detail to me the make of car the gangsters used, the chain fence and so on (although no one mentioned the wonderfully ironic London tourism poster).

With the book finished, I thought that was it. I had no input into the script book the BBC were also doing and understood that a planned

The novelisation orignally offered an explanation as to Ace's whereabouts.

'Making Of …' book had been scrapped owing to lack of time. Then I had another call out of the blue from Sue Robinson at *Radio Times*, who asked me to go in for an informal but hush-hush meeting. Intrigued I did, and met her, Nick Brett (the then editor, famous for his red bow ties) and Anne Jowett, the features editor. Sue was keen to start up an SF page in the magazine, wanting to lead with a six-panelled comic strip featuring the eighth Doctor, and asked whether I wanted to write it. Again, I had no hesitation in saying yes, and we talked about artists, letterers and colourists (they believed that the artists did everything!).

Having therefore blown their planned budget out of the water by involving two extra people, I thought they'd drop it, especially as I really wanted to use Cybermen and have Lee Sullivan as the artist – unlike many artists working in comics, Lee understands the process of working in tandem with a writer rather than assuming the writer is a jerk and artists can tell stories so much better. They liked the samples Lee sent them and we were promised a minimum of a year's run with a likely extension to eighteen months because by then the BBC assumed a new series would be up and running.

The first strip was published the week

after the movie went out in Britain and ran for 40 weeks properly, during which time Lee and I upped the ante by making it an ongoing story, with subplots, ending one of them with the Doctor's companion, Stacy, being kidnapped by the alien Zygons and an evil duplicate placed aboard the TARDIS. Then Anne told us that Nick Brett had moved on, Sue Robinson was now editor and, as part of her changes, she wanted to expand the magazine's movie coverage, which meant losing four 'themed' pages, one of which was the SF one. We scrapped the next ten-parter and I wrote in an hour a two-part story, 'Coda', which resolved the Stacy situation most unsatisfactorily. The strip was over. There had been rough plans to issue the strips in a book along with at least one new one at some point, but the lack of a new TV series killed that idea quite quickly.

Ultimately however, all this did mean that when the *ManoptiCon* convention in Manchester came around in the April, the organisers very kindly realised that I probably knew the TV movie better than anyone else in the country. Since their main guest was Philip Segal, they asked if I'd do the onstage presentation and do the interview. Which is roughly how I come to be writing this book with him several years later!

• 1997 - 2000 •
A HOLIDAY FOR THE DOCTOR

In the aftermath of the TV movie, things seem to quieten down somewhat, almost as if everyone involved was suddenly very embarrassed. A lot of money had been spent on the movie and, although the results had been high as far as the UK audience was concerned, there was clearly a profound sense of disappointment that it had not led to a series Stateside.

Nevertheless, Universal still had a further option until the end of the year and, until then, the BBC could do nothing about finding a new co-partner, so they decided to wait and see what offers may be forthcoming. On 9 October, Will Wyatt, the chief executive of BBC Broadcasting, was attending a sponsored dinner for the Conservative Party, and presumably sat down to quaff copious amounts of whatever one quaffs at such parties when one is representing a nonaffiliated corporation.

Rather unexpectedly, one of the people attending the dinner suddenly asked him about the future of *Doctor Who*. Caught somewhat off-guard but surrounded by invited press likely to leap on his every word, Wyatt tried to be enthusiastic, but commented that the movie 'did not do well' and had not 'been right for the audience we hoped to attract'. Exactly what he thought was wrong with over 9 million viewers soundly trouncing the competition remains speculation, but, despite being 'impressed by

the very young, very enthusiastic' Philip Segal, whom he had met when visiting the *seaQuest DSV* set a couple of years earlier, he finished off by saying that there would not be more *Doctor Who* because 'we can't afford it'.

Now, maybe public figures are not exactly known for being able to think up good answers to questions they've not been primed for by press officers during the preceding 24 hours, but even Will Wyatt couldn't have failed to notice the irony in his comments nearly a month later, when the BBC, as part of their TV60 celebrations, held an awards dinner. The awards were given out to the favourite BBC programmes, as voted by the viewers via *Radio Times*, the fledgling BBC on-line service and a CEEFAX telephone poll. There, in front of the people who actually paid his salary, he had to watch as the results of 'all-time favourite drama' were read out. Was it *EastEnders*? Was it *All Creatures Great and Small*? Was it *I, Claudius*? No, it was *Doctor Who*.

Almost immediately, the BBC's publicity machine went into overdrive – the viewers had voted for the one programme that had been declared too expensive to continue making. The reaction from both the BBC and the press at large was rather disappointing, if not unexpected. Of course *Doctor Who* won, it was chorused. It was all a fix – everyone knows that die-hard fans are well organised and probably voted more than once. Trouble was that the awards had been announced so late in the day

unlikely that the BBC will be producing new *Doctor Who* stories in-house in the foreseeable future.'

Whether it was as a result of this award or not is unclear, but Universal applied to the BBC for an extension to its agreement, taking them up to the end of 1997 to find a new partner. Fox had clearly passed on any further involvement with the concept – as both Trevor Walton and Tom Burke had moved on from Fox, there was no one left in a position of authority who even knew what *Doctor Who* was, let alone who would support it as they had.

Sadly however, despite Universal's best efforts, no one else shared their enthusiasm and, as many of those within that company who had similarly been advocates of the Doctor moved onto pastures new, the whole idea faded away.

that no fan organisation, let alone any of the science-fiction magazines, would have had a chance to give them editorial space, let alone encourage a blanket vote. On top of that, the people compiling the votes pointed out that they had brought in systems specifically to avoid such multi-voting.

Grating as it was for the programme's detractors, it proved that the viewers loved *Doctor Who*. And, as the award's recipients, Peter Davison and Sylvester McCoy, so slyly pointed out on the night, this rather put the BBC in an embarrassing situation. The BBC responded by issuing a variation on the press releases of the last eight years – 'A great deal of careful thought has been given to the future of *Doctor Who*,' they claimed. 'We do appreciate the strength of affection of the programme's followers.'

Again, they were dismissing the 'casual' viewer, working on the proven-to-be-wrong assumption that only the die-hard fans wanted the show back, despite 9 million people showing them otherwise six months before.

'In the current financial climate,' they went on, 'we are severely restricted in our budgets for drama and we have to try and stretch the resources we have to meet the interests of as many viewers as possible. For this reason, it is

Philip Segal returned to the BBC for talks on the subject in February 1998. This time, not regarding the series, but he had been tipped off by Alan Yentob that the rights to remake the 1960s Dalek movies, starring Peter Cushing, had become available. These had originally been produced by Amicus films in the 1960s – indeed much of the Amicus back catalogue was up for grabs. Philip briefly looked into the viability of this but felt there was little point in remaking what were essentially remakes of William Hartnell TV episodes, and passed. Other companies subsequently showed interest but nothing more came of it.

As the millennial setting of the TV Movie drew closer, *Doctor Who* was the recipient of yet another viewers' award – this time they voted the first appearance of the Daleks to be the most exciting sequence in TV drama history. If nothing else, this proved again that the show's fans – both hardcore and more casual – could not forget a series that had inspired and delighted so many of them for over thirty-five years. They knew that the show's format was unique enough that one day, someone would appreciate it at sometime in the next century.

The fans knew that one day, the Doctor would come back.

Until then, thank you *Doctor Who* fans everywhere, you have kept the flame burning.

'We realise *Doctor Who* plays an important role in the BBC's history, but audience expectations for the effects in science fiction programmes are far higher than they once were. New technology and special effects to match people's expectations are expensive and we do not believe it is appropriate to continue with the programme as a low budget enterprise. This would serve neither *Doctor Who* itself or our reputation for quality programming. There are no plans by Fox TV to produce a series from the 1996 movie pilot starring Paul McGann. Paul McGann's option to play the Doctor for a period of five years expired at the end of 1996. Universal retained an option on making a series until the end of 1996, when the rights reverted back to the BBC. The series remains in the same position as it was in 1989 when production ceased. Nothing is cut and dried as far as this series is concerned. We appreciate that the 1996 movie was a long time coming but it may well be that there will be more of the Doctor in the future. What we cannot do is make any promises about the programme at present. If there is more to say our first action would be to issue a press release to that effect.

BBC statement – May 2000

THE MUSIC

The musical score for the TV Movie was overseen by John Debney, the composer Phil had worked closely with on *seaQuest DSV* a few years earlier. Debney in turn brought in two young musicians/composers to take on the bulk of the score. John Sponsier and Louis Febre worked alongside Debney, with Febre inparticular taking additional responsibility for finding additional pieces of music.

The breakdown of the writers' credits on the music is interesting, with each of the three receiving differing percentages of the copyright in each individual track. The music cues were as follows:

Skaro
(Sponsier – 40')

Doctor Who Theme
(Grainer, arranged Sponsier 70%, Debney 30% – 1"05')

That Should Do It
(Sponsier 70%, Debney 30% – 21')

In A Dream
(Barbara L Jordan, Pete Peterkin, Christopher Rhyne 33.3% each – 1" 44')
Performed by Pat Hodge Played by the Doctor in the TARDIS.

Break-Out
(Febre 12.5%, Sponsier 87.5% – 1" 35')

Sushi Tonight
(Carol Ann Wood – 32')
This is first heard when we see the elderly Chinese couple.

Wimps
(Sponsier – 1" 06')

Doctor Seven Shot
(Debney 30%, Sponsier 70% – 55')

Snake
(Debney 30%, Sponsier 70% – 53')

• Appendix •
FACTS AND FIGURES

No *Doctor Who* reference book can be considered complete without a good-old fashioned set of anally retentive lists, and so this is that bit. Flick over the next few pages if you hate such things; wallow happily like a hippo in a mud bath if you like them. After all, *Doctor Who* fans the world over make pilgrimages to various parts of the UK to go, 'Ah, so this is the tiny village that doubled as Devil's End in *The Daemons*,' or, 'Well, this pottery museum in Stoke certainly made for a good section of the Matrix on Gallifrey in T*he Trial of a Time Lord …*' and so on.

Of course Vancouver is somewhat further away than your average East Hagbourne, Hawkshurst or Shad Thames, but, with a bit of imagination on the part of the Vancouver Tourist Authority and, for the majority of the rest of us, an expensive airline ticket, this beautiful Canadian city could be a new Mecca. So what happened where exactly? And when? OK, here goes:

FILMING LOCATIONS

'Rose Alley'
Alley between East Georgia/Union Street, Vancouver

'Chinatown'
218 East Georgia/Venus Theatre (Puccini Building)/221 Union Street, Vancouver

'Chinatown Room'
222 Keefer Street, Vancouver

'Hospital'
BC Children's Hospital, 4480 Oak Street, Vancouver

'Hospital Car Park'
Golden Crown Center, 211 East Georgia Street, Impark Lot #420

'Grace's'
1998 Odgen Street, Vancouver

'ITAR' (Institute of Technological Advancement and Research)
Plaza of Nations, B100 – 750 Pacific Blvd, Vancouver

'Park/Pond'
Sun Yat Sen Garden, 578 Carrall Street, Vancouver

'Fountain'
John Livingston Park, Carrall Street/Keefer Street intersection near GM Place, Vancouver

'Vehicle exteriors'
Carrall Street/Keefer Street intersection, near GM Place

MAIN STUDIO

8651 Eastlake Drive, Burnaby, Vancouver

FILMING DIARY

Monday 15 January
to Wednesday 17 January 1996
Film Unit on location for Grace's condo interiors and exteriors/park

Thursday 18 January
to Friday 19 January
Film Unit on location for ITAR interiors and exteriors

Monday 22 January
to Tuesday 23 January
Film Unit on location for exterior ambulance and motorbike sequences
Second Unit on location for chase sequences

Wednesday 24 January
to Monday 29 January
(no shooting Saturday/Sunday)
Film Unit on location for hospital interiors

Tuesday 30 January
Film Unit on location for hospital interiors
Film Unit move to Burnaby studios for opera

Wednesday 31 January
Film Unit in studio for interiors of ambulance/TARDIS

Thursday 1 February
to Friday 2 February
Film Unit on location for Rose Alley/Chinatown/TARDIS exteriors

Monday 5 February
Film Unit on location for exterior hospital car park/interior Chinatown room

Tuesday 6 February
Film Unit on location for traffic jam

Wednesday 7 February
Film Unit on location for fountain exteriors/motorcycle chase close-ups

Thursday 8 February
Film Unit in studio for Bruce and Miranda's apartment/TARDIS interiors
Second Unit on location for continuation of chase sequences, including motorcycle cop going into TARDIS

Friday 9 February
Film Unit on location for ITAR interiors

Saturday 10 February
Film Unit in studio for TARDIS interiors
Second Unit in studio for Skaro/ambulance interiors, to have morphant snake added later

Monday 12 February
Film Unit on location for ITAR interiors
Film Unit in studio for ambulance interiors
Second Unit in studio for greenscreen shoot for debris etc. to be overlaid; TARDIS arrival/gunfight/shots of Doctor and Grace floating in Eye of Harmony; close-ups of Grace's TV screen
Second Unit on location for outstanding Chinatown/Rose Alley sequences

Tuesday 13 February
to Wednesday 21 February
(no shooting Saturday/Sunday)
Film Unit in studio for TARDIS interiors
Second Unit in studio for Greenscreen FX shots plus other backgrounds for FX to be laid over

Two Hearts
(Debney 30%, Sponsier 70% – 05')

In The Ambulance
(Febre – 28')

Un Bel Di
(Pucinni – 3" 17')
Heard at various points both during the performance of the opera and during the ER sequences

Open Eyes
(Sponsier 34')

No Double Exposure
(Sponsier 21')

Stop Him
(Debney 23%, Febre 24%, Sponsier 53% – 19')

City View
(Debney 23%, Febre 24%, Sponsier 53% – 15')

Snake
(Debney 23%, Febre 24%, Sponsier 53% – 37')

All Dressed Up
(Jim Latham – 54')
This is heard on the radio in the morgue scenes.

Slams the Door
(Debney 30%, Sponsier 70% – 16')

Snake
(Debney 30%, Sponsier 70% – 33')

Look Out
(Debney 30%, Sponsier 70% – 09')

He's Alive
(Debney 30%, Sponsier 70% – 23')

It's Alive
(Debney 30%, Sponsier 70% – 22')

In The Morgue
(Debney 30%, Sponsier 70% – 30')

No!
(Debney 30%, Sponsier 70% – 04')

Un Bel Di
(Puccini – 18')
Hummed by the Doctor

Walking
Debney 30%, Sponsier 70% – 1" 18')

Cityscape
(Debney 30%, Sponsier 70%
– 1" 37')

Pop Goes the Weasel
(Trad – arranged Sponsier –
04')

The Master
(Debney 30%, Febre 70% –
29')

Time
(Debney 30%, Febre 70% -
51')

I Quit
(Debney 30%, Febre 70% –
54')

Primitive Writing
(Febre 53')

The Asian Child
(Febre – 34')

Two Hearts
(Debney 30%, Febre 70% –
1" 02')

Un Bel Di
(Puccini – 19')
Hummed by the Doctor

The TARDIS
(Debney 30%, Febre 70% –
1" 02')

True Identity
(Debney 30%, Febre 70% –
57')

Night Walk
(Debney 30%, Febre 70% –
1" 27')

The Eye of Harmony
(Febre – 2" 39')

Half Human
(Febre – 1" 40')

Until Midnight
(Febre – 1" 05')

Atomic Clock
(Febre – 43')

Ambulance
(Sponsier – 11')

Green Eyes
(Sponsier – 46')

Chase
(Febre 5%, Debney 29%,
Sponsier 66% – 3" 36')

Forget Me Now
(Martin Wereski – 33')

CAST AND CREW

The Doctor Paul McGann
Doctor Grace Holloway Daphne Ashbrook
The Master/Bruce Eric Roberts
Chang Lee Yee Jee Tso
The Old Doctor Sylvester McCoy
Doctor Roger Swift Michael David Simms
Salinger John Novak
Curtis Delores Drake
Wheeler Catherine Lough
Pete William Sasso
Ted Joel Wirkkunen
Miranda Eliza Roberts
Professor Wagg Dave Hurtubise
Gareth Jeremy Badick

CHP Cop Bill Croft
Security Guard Dee Jay Jackson
Motorbike Cop Ron James
Anchor Mi-Jung Lee
Co-Anchor Joanna Piros
The Old Master Gordon Tipple
Drivers Ron James, Danny Groseclose
Lee's Friend 1 Dean Choe
Lee's Friend 2 Michael Ching
Gangster 1 Daryl Quan
Gangster 2 Byron Lawson
Gangster 3 Paul Wu
Gangster 4 Johnny Mah
Cop in Car at ITAR Ron James
Dalek Voices Geoffrey Sax

Doctor's Stunt Doubles
Charles Andre, Jamie Jones
Both Doctors' Stand-In Keith Provost
Old Doctor's Stunt Double
Mike Langlois
Grace's Stunt Double Dawn Stouffer
Grace's Stand-In Rita Whicker
Master's Stunt Double Fred Perron
Master's Stand-In Dale Reynolds
Lee's Stunt Double Michael Crestjo
Lee's Stand-In Ronin
Stunt Cop Bill Stewart
Car Chase Stunt Driver Lloyd Adams
Stunt Drivers Alex Green, Charles Andre,
Jacob Rupp, David Jacox

Executive Producers
Philip David Segal, Alex Beaton
Executive Producer for the BBC
Jo Wright
Producer Peter V Ware
Writer/Co-producer Matthew Jacobs
Director Geoffrey Sax
Production Designer Richard Hudolin
Set Designers Alexander Kameniczky,
Walter Ockley
Art Director Bridget McGuire
Art Assistant Ginny Sakamoto
Storyboard Artist Michael Wong
Draftsperson Ivana Vasak
Costume Designer Jori Woodman
Assistant Designer Terri Bardon
On-Set Costume Supervisor Debbie Douglas

On-Set Costume Assistant Tess Brummitt
Make-Up Joann Fowler
Make-Up Assistants Krista Young, Gitte Axen
Make-Up (Eric Roberts) James Ryder
Hairstylist Julie McHaffire
Hair Assistant Janet Sala
Script Supervisor Jessica Clothier
Music John Debney
Additional Music John Sponsler, Louis Febre
Director of Photography
Glen MacPherson CSC
Camera Operator Randal Platt
1st Assistant Camera Greg Fox
2nd Assistant Camera Nick Watson
Camera Trainee Rod Mawson
Gaffer Drew Davidson
Best Boy Steve Vincent
Rigging Gaffer John Adams
Lamp Operators Mike Bowen,
Saubrie Mohamed, Lee Miller, Ken Decker
Generator Operator Al McKinnon
Key Grip Dave Gordon
Lead Hand Set-Up Mike Bolan
Best Boy Brian Bouma
Dolly Grip Craig Munroe
Grip Timo Juonolainen, Mike Legree
Power Pod Operator Steve Lingard
Crane Operator Glen Forrieter
Video Playback Klaus Melchior
Sound Supervisor Jacqueline Cristianini
Sound Mixer Gordon W Anderson
Boom Operator Rob Hanchar
Cablesman Michel Hibberson
Editor Patrick Lussier
Additional Editing Daria Ellerman
Visual Effects Producer Tony Dow
Production Manager Fran Rosati
1st Assistant Director Patrice Leung
2nd Assistant Director David Klohn
3rd Assistant Director Kate Vanderbyl
Trainee Assistant Director Michelle Michals
Production Coordinator Sandra Palmer
Assistant Coordinator Catherine Howard
Production Assistants
Ruth Atkinson, Dom Webber
Property Master Dan Sissons
Props Mike Kruger, Terry Weaver
Head Set Decorator Cynthia Lewis
Assistant Set Decorator Faye Thorp
Buyer Della Johnston
Dressers Gordon Brunner, Brent Bennett
Set Decorators Cindy Lewis, Matt Reddy
Driver (Set Decorations) Drew Neville
Head Scenic Artist Barry Kootchin
Lead Hands John Hamilton Malcolm MacLean
Scenic Artists Lubor Cencak,
Lee Drummond-Hay, Gordon Hughes, Peter
Kennedy, Stewart Fairly
Scenic Painter Russell Mastine
Stand-By Painter Tom Robertson
Construction Coordinator Derick MacLeod
Construction Foreman Vance Conway
Construction Buyer Scott Mathers
Construction Ward Galvin, Ray Watts
Construction Driver Larry Hafachuk
Location Manager Ed Nesling

Location PA *Miriam Reid*
Location Assistants *Neil Robertson,*
Greg Rosati, Robin Smith, Sidney St Louis,
Nick Fairhead
Visual Effects *Northwest Imaging and FX*
Visual Effects Supervisor *Eric Alba*
Visual Effects Coordinator *Marush Kushniruk*
Special Effects Coordinator *Gary Paller*
Assistant SFX *James Paradis, Dave Paller*
Wrangler, Debra Coe
Stunt Coordinators *JJ Makara, Fred Perron*
Casting (UK) *John and Ros Hubbard*
Casting (LA) *Beth Hymson-Ayer CSA*
Casting Assistant (LA) *JB Annegan*
Casting (Vancouver) *Trish Robinson*
Casting Assistant (Vancouver)
Mary Montica-Poole
Extras Casting *James Forsyth*
UK Casting Consultants
John and Ros Hubbard
Still Photography *Joe Lederer, Doane Gregory*
Publicists (Universal) *Patty Triplett,*
Neil Schubert
Publicists (Fox) *Joe Earley, Kevin Fitzgerald*
Head Accountant *Beverly Wiens*
Accounts Assistant *Dana Perlman*
Accounts Clerk *Carol Urquhart*
Transportation Coordinator *Dennis Houser*
Driver Captain *John Oliver*
Cast Driver *Terry Newton*
Transport *Ed Dykstra, Ken Johnson,*
Rick Johnson, Bob Snyder, Mike Porohowski,
Bob Sinclair
First Aid/Craft Service *Jim Rankin, Alan Izsak*
Security *Mike Zosiuk, Shawn Labrie*
Catering *Mark Dibble*

Chef *Gordie Wise*
Assistant Chef *Diane Fatiaki*
Producer's Assistant *Ruth Atkinson*
Director's Assistant *Karina Sax*
Office PAs *Dominic Webber, Phil Katsikas,*
Jeff Farrington
Legal *David Karnes*

SECOND UNIT

Producer *Peter V Ware*
Production Manager *Fran Rosati*
1st Assistant Director *Kenna Marshall*
2nd Assistant Director *Mellanie Siteman*
3rd Assistant Director *Matthew Blecha*
Trainee Assistant Director *Chris Allen*
Director of Photography *Les Erskine*
Camera Operator *Robert Stecko*
Assistant Camera Operator *Scott MacDonald*
Craft Service *Susan Strubin*
Gaffer *Einar Hansen*
Best Boy *Guy Patterson*
Generator Operator *Kevin O'Leary*
Key Grip *John Zulinski*
Best Boy *John O'Neill*
Dolly Grip *Tim Spencer*
Power Pod Operator *Steve Lingard*
Location Manager *Michael Williams*
Location PAs *Liz Rumball, Lana Burton*
Script Supervisor *Nancy Eagles*
Script Assistant *Lana Krotenko*
Transportation Coordinator *Derek Rama*

BBC Production number
50/LDX071Y/01X
1996

Roger's Theme
(Martin Wereski – 1" 40')
Both at the Institute party

Beryllium Clock
(Debney 30%, Febre 70% –
11')

Slimed
(Debney 30%, Febre 70% –
1" 59')

Under the Influence
(Febre 40')

Crown of Nails
(Debney 30%, Febre 70% –
1" 07')

Ride Into the Moonlight
(Chuck Duran, Jess Harnell
– 13')
Heard at the hospital party

Lee's Last Chance
(Debney 30%, Febre 70% –
1" 07')

Open the Eye
(Febre 17.5%, Sponsier
82.5% – 2" 15')

Reroute Power
(Sponsier – 1" 51')

Temporal Orbit
(Debney 30%, Febre 70% –
4" 05')

To Hold Back Death
(Debney 30%, Febre 70% –
1" 42')

Contraption
Febre – 06')

Ride Into The Moonlight
(Duran, Harnell – 39')
Heard at the hospital party

Auld Lang Syne
(Trad – 22')
Heard at the hospital party

Farewell
(Debney 30%, Fbre 70% –
1" 18')

In A Dream
(Jordan, Peterkin, Rhyner
33.3% each – 41')
Performed by Pat Hodge
Played by the new Doctor
in the TARDIS

Doctor Who Theme
(Grainer, arranged Sponsier
70%, Debney 30% – 40')

Universal Logo!
(James Horner – 04')

AFTERWORD

• by Nicholas Courtney •

I t was with great pleasure that I accepted the invitation to contribute to this book. I was also rather surprised, since I had not been personally involved in the making of the movie, but I do remember one thing, however, that may explain my presence here.

A few years ago, I was at a *Doctor Who* convention in Manchester where I was somewhat gratified to hear from the stage my name being mentioned by Philip Segal, who was over in the UK promoting the then forthcoming movie. I was signing autographs at the time; he was answering questions from the attendees, one of whom wondered who his favourite character from *Doctor Who* might be. He opined that the Brigadier fitted that description perfectly.

I'm not sure exactly when I first met Gary Russell – we both seem to have been around forever. I mentioned in my autobiography – under the heading Acknowledgements – 'Nicholas Briggs and Gary Russell are two of the best interviewers in the business.' Gary knows how to 'fill in' when the poor interviewee has dried – that's a very special art.

My chief memories of the movie are Sylvester McCoy and Paul McGann. Sylv tends to play very mercurial characters and it was most rewarding to watch him as his closure approached. I thought Paul was very good casting, very handsome and an actor I greatly admire. And who wouldn't? Remember *The Monocled Mutineer* or *Withnail & I*? I can't wait for a chance for the Brig to bump into him.

'Nuff Said